WITHDRAWN

28
19

FACE IT

DEBBIE HARRY

In collaboration with
SYLVIE SIMMONS
and based on a series of recent exclusive interviews

Creative direction by
ROB ROTH

DEY ST.
An Imprint of WILLIAM MORROW

DEDICATED TO
THE GIRLS OF THE
UNDERWORLD

CONTENTS

INTRODUCTION

BY CHRIS STEIN

I don't know if I ever related this story to Debbie . . . or anyone for that matter. In 1969 after traveling around, driving twice cross-country, I was staying with my mom at her apartment in Brooklyn. This was a tumultuous year for me. Psychedelics—and my delayed reaction to my father's death—caused breaks and disassociations in my already fractured psyche.

In the midst of heightened states, I had a dream that stayed with me. The apartment was on Ocean Avenue, a very long urban boulevard. In the dream, in a scene that referenced *The Graduate,* I was chasing the Ocean Avenue bus as it pulled away from our big old building. I was pursuing the bus—yet inside it simultaneously. Standing in the bus was a blond girl who said, "I'll see you in the city." The bus pulled away and I was left alone on the street . . .

By 1977, Debbie and I were traveling extensively with Blondie. Far and away our most exotic stop was Bangkok, Thailand. The city then wasn't covered with cement and metal but was fairly bucolic, with parks all around and even dirt roads near our upscale hotel. Everything smelled of jasmine and decay.

Debbie developed a touch of "la tourista" and stayed behind one night in the hotel while the guys from the band and I went to the house of some British expatriate whom we'd met in some bar or other. His old Thai maid prepared a banana cake for us into which she had chopped fifty Thai sticks—the seven-ies equivalent of modern super-strong "kush" or other intense strains of weed. We'd also just come from a long stretch in Australia, where pot was strictly policed and forbidden at the time. We all got well stoned and somehow led each other back to the hotel.

Our room was also very exotic, with decorative rattan elements and two separate cotlike beds equipped with hard cylindrical pillows. Debbie had fallen into a fitful half sleep and eventually I drifted into a foggy blackness. Somewhere toward morning, my unconscious dream self became clearer and began an internal dialogue. "Where are we?" asked this internal voice—whereupon Debbie, still in a half sleep on her cot, said aloud, "We're in bed, right?" I sat up, suddenly wide awake.

Did I actually speak and produce a response from her even though we both were in semi-asleep states? To this day, all these years later, I am convinced that I only thought the question.

And another story that's even more subtle and weird and difficult to convey . . . Getting high was just a part of the music and band culture that we came up in. It didn't seem like anything extraordinary. *Everyone* at all the clubs drank or got stoned with almost no exception. I wasted a tremendous amount of time and energy dealing with substance abuse and self-medication. It's impossible to say if what I'd like to see as psychic events were merely induced delusions. Perhaps it's like any religious faith—you believe what you want to believe. Certainly, consciousness extends beyond oneself, one's body.

Anyway, Debbie and I were once again in some state of advanced intoxication at a very elaborate party downtown. Small events and views were sharply defined. I remember a spiral staircase and fancy chandeliers. Some fellow showed us his Salvador Dalí Cartier watch—and that fleeting glimpse has stayed with me forever. It was an amazing object, a standard tear-shaped Cartier design but with a bend that mimicked the melting watches in *The Persistence of Memory*. The crystal face was broken and the owner complained of having to spend thousands of dollars to replace it. To me, though, the cracked glass was a perfect Dadaist commentary on the original. I loved that.

The event—whatever it was—was very crowded. I remember being on a balcony when we were approached by an older man in a very fancy suit. He had a slight accent, maybe Creole. He introduced himself as Tiger. And that's it for my specific memories, except for the extravagant sense of connection that Debbie and I felt with this guy. It was as if we had known him forever—a person we'd known in past lives. Do I believe in that stuff? Maybe. I don't recall how much Debbie and I discussed this meeting afterward, but it was enough to compare notes and similar reactions.

Pretty early on—maybe 1975—Debbie found this person, Ethel Myers, who was a clairvoyant, a psychic. She'd likely come as a recommendation, but we might have simply found her through an ad in the *Village Voice* or *Soho News*. She worked out of an amazing ground-floor apartment that was on a side street uptown, right around the Beacon Theatre. Ethel's environment was beautiful. It probably looked the same as it had when her building was built near the turn of the century. Her sitting area was an atrium that was like a greenhouse taken up with furniture. Decorative plants and herbs hung all around. Yellowing books about ectoplasm and tarot lay on dusty end tables. The whole place was well worn and reminded me of the apartment in *Rosemary's Baby* when Mia Farrow and Cassavetes are first shown it.

We sat down with Ethel and she encouraged us to use a cassette machine we'd brought to record the session. She didn't have any idea of who we were but proceeded to do a great cold reading. She told Debbie that she saw her on a stage and that Debbie would be fulfilled and travel a great deal. At one point she said that a man, presumably my father, was watching and that this man sarcastically said of me, "I wouldn't touch him with a ten-foot pole." I derive a lot of my sense of humor from my father—and the "ten-foot pole" bit was something he actually said all the time. Was she just in touch with the vernacular of the fifties that the old man used or was it more?

Debbie still has the cassette in her archives but I remember us listening to it years after and Ethel's voice being very faint, as if it had somehow faded in the way of a ghost deteriorating over time.

Just now I called Debbie to ask what, if any, of this she remembered. She said, "You know, Chris, it was different back then, there was a lot more acid in the air."

We still have a connection.

CHRIS STEIN

New York City, June 2018

#1 STUD
PAL-THE TOWN STUD

1

LOVE CHILD

They must have met around 1930, in high school, I figure. Childhood sweethearts. She was a middle-class girl, Scots-Irish, and he was a farm boy, French, living somewhere around Neptune and Lakewood, New Jersey. Her family was musical. She and her sisters would play together, all day long. The sisters sang while she played on a battered old piano. His family was artistic too and musical as well. However, his mom was in a psych ward, for depression—or some kind of recurring nervous condition. Unseen, but a powerful presence. It sounds contrived to me but it is what I have been told by the adoption agency.

Her mom ruled that he was the wrong kind for her daughter. She nixed the relationship and their love was axed. To further kill any contact, they banished her to music school and from there, she supposedly began touring concert halls in Europe and North America.

Many years go by. He's married now, with lots of children. He works at a fuel company, repairing oil burners. One day, he heads out on a service call and boom, there she is. She's leaning against the door frame, hair down, and she's looking at him with that look. It's her heater that's broken . . . Well, that's quite a picture, isn't it, but I feel certain they were happy to see each other.

All those years, maybe they never stopped loving each other. Well, it must have been a wonderful reunion. She gets pregnant. He finally tells her that he's married with kids. She's pissed and heartbroken and she ends it, but she wants to keep the baby. She bears it all the way and at Miami-Dade hospital on Sunday, July 1, 1945, little Angela Trimble forced her way into the world.

She and the baby made their way back to New Jersey, where her mother was dying of breast cancer. She nursed them both. But her mom persuaded her to put Angela up for adoption. And so, she did. She gave her Angela away. Six months later, her mother was dead and her baby daughter was living with a childless couple also from New Jersey. Richard and Cathy Harry, from Paterson, had met socially after high school. Angela's new parents, also known as Caggie and Dick, gave her a new name: Deborah.

And that's it. I am a love child.

They claim it's unusual to have memories of your earliest moments, but I have tons. My first memory is at the three-month mark. Same day that my mother and father got me from the adoption agency. They decided on a little jaunt to celebrate at a small resort with a petting zoo. I remember being carried around and I have a very strong visual memory of gigantic creatures looming at me out of the pasture. I told my mother the recollection once and she was shocked. "My God, that was the day we got you, you can't remember that." It was just ducks and geese and a goat, she said, maybe a pony. But at three months, I didn't have much to filter with. Well, I'd already lived with two different mothers, in two different houses, under two different names. Thinking about it now, I was probably in an extreme state of panic. The world was not a safe place and I should keep my eyes wide open.

For the first five years of my life we lived in a little house on Cedar Avenue in Hawthorne, New Jersey, by Goffle Brook Park. The park ran the whole length of the little town. When they'd cleared the land to build the park they built these temporary migrant worker houses—think two little railroad flats with no heating except for a potbelly stove. We had the migrant workers' boss's house, which by then had its own heating system and sat on the edge of the park's big wooded area.

These days, kids are organized into activities. But I would be told, "Go out and play," and I would go. I really didn't have many playmates there, so some days I would play with my mind. I

Oak place.

was a dreamy kind of kid. But I was also a tomboy. Dad hung a swing and a trapeze on the big maple tree in the yard and I'd play on them, pretending to be in the circus. Or I'd play with a few sticks, dig a hole, poke at an anthill, make something, or roller-skate.

What I really liked most was to fool around in the woods. To me it was magical, a real-life enchanted forest. My parents were always warning, "Don't go in the woods, you don't know who's in there or what might happen," like they do in fairy tales. And fairy tales—all the great, terrifying stories by the Brothers Grimm—were a big part of my growing up.

I have to admit, there were some scary folk skulking around in those bushes, probably migrants. They were genuine hobos who rode through on the train and would hunker down in the woods. They'd maybe get some work from the parks department cutting grass or something, then jump back on the train and keep on going. There were foxes and raccoons, sometimes snakes, and a little stream with tributaries and frogs and toads.

Along the brooks where nobody went, the abandoned shacks had crumbled to their foundations. I used to clomp around there, in the swampy, old, overgrown, moldy piles of brick that stuck up out of the ground. I would sit there forever and daydream. I'd get that real creepy kid feeling that you get. Squatting on my haunches in the underbrush, I would have fantasies about running away with a wild Indian and eating sumac berries. My dad would wag his finger at me and say, "Stay out of the sumac, it's poison," and I would chew that incredibly bitter-sour sumac right up, thinking, dramatically, *I'm going to die!* I was so lucky to have all that kind of creepy kid stuff—a huge fantasy life that has led me to be a creative thinker—along with TV and sex offenders.

I had a dog named Pal. Some kind of terrier, brownish red, completely scruffy, with wiry hair, floppy ears, whiskers and a beard, and the most disgusting body. He was my dad's dog really, but he was very independent. And wild—a real male dog that hadn't been fixed. Pal was a stud. He would wander off and slink back after being gone for a week, completely exhausted from all these flings he'd had.

There were also hundreds of rats infesting the woods. As the town became less rural and more populated, the rats started swarming into the yards and gnawing through the garbage. So, the local powers put poison in areas of the park. Such a suburban-mentality thing—and let's face it, they were poisoning everything back then. Well, Pal ate the poison. He was so sick that my dad had to put him down. That was just awful.

But really, it was the sweetest place to grow up: real American small-town living. It was back before they had strip malls, thank God. All it had was a little main street and a cinema where it cost a quarter to go to the Saturday matinee. All the kids would go. I loved the movies. There was still a lot of farmland then—rolling hills for grazing, small farms that grew produce, everything fresh and cheap. But finally the small farms faded away. And in their place housing developments sprang up.

The town was in transition, but I was too young to know what "transition" meant or have an overview or even care. We were part of the bedroom community, because my father didn't work in the town; he commuted to New York. Which wasn't that far away, but God, at the time it seemed so far away. It was magical. It was another kind of enchanted forest, teeming with people and noise and tall buildings instead of trees. Very different.

My dad went there to work, but I went there for fun. Once a year, my maternal grandmother would take me to the city to buy me a winter coat at Best & Co., a famous, conservative, old-style department store. Afterward we'd go to Schrafft's on Fifty-Third Street and Fifth Avenue. This old-fashioned restaurant was almost like a British tearoom, where well-dressed old ladies sat primly sipping from china cups. Very proper—and a refuge from the city bustle.

At Christmastime my family would go to see the tree in Rockefeller Center. We'd watch the skaters at the skating rink and look at the department store windows. We weren't sophisticated city-goers, coming to see a show on Broadway; we were suburbanites. If we did go to a show it would be at Radio City Music Hall, although we did go to the ballet a couple of times. That's probably what fostered my dream of being a ballerina—which didn't last. But what did last was how excited and intrigued I was about performance and the whole thing of being onstage. Though I loved the movies, my reaction to those live shows was physical—very sensual. I had the same reaction to New York City and its smells and sights and sounds.

One of my favorite things as a kid was heading down to Paterson, where both my grandmothers lived. My father liked to take the back roads, winding through all the little streets in the slum areas. And much of Paterson was very old and neglected at that time, pre-gentrification, full of migrant workers who'd come to find jobs in the factories and the silk-weaving mills. Paterson had earned the title "Silk City." The Great Falls of the Passaic River drove the turbines that drove the looms. Those falls had stared me in the face throughout my childhood, thanks to the Paterson *Morning Call*. On its masthead at the top of its front page sat a pen-and-ink drawing of the billowing waters.

Dad would always drive real slow down River Street, because it teemed with people and activity. There were gypsies who lived in the storefronts; there were black people who'd come up from the South. They dressed in brilliant clothing and wrapped their hair in do-rags. For a little girl from a white-on-white, middle-to-lower-middle-class burb, this was an eyeful. Wonderful. I would be hanging out the window, crazed with curiosity, and my mother would be snapping, "Get back in the car! You're going to get your head chopped off!" She'd have rather not driven down River Street, but my dad was one of those people who like to have their secret way. Yay for Dad!

I find it mysterious now, how little was ever revealed, within our family, about my father's side. Nobody talked about them, what they did, or how they came to be in Paterson. I remember, when I was much older, quizzing my dad about what his grandfather did for a living. He said he was a shoemaker or maybe a shoe repairman from Morristown, New Jersey. I guess he was too low-class for anyone in the family, my father included, to want to be associated with him. Which was kind of tragic, I thought. But my father would remark on how very fortunate his father had been to keep his job all through the Great Depression, selling shoes on Broadway in Paterson. They'd had money coming in when so many, many people were unemployed.

My mother's family's Silk City was far more elitist. Her father had had his own seat on the stock exchange before the crash and owned a bank in Ridgewood, New Jersey. So they must have been quite wealthy at some point. When my mother was a child, they would sail to Europe and visit all the capitals on a grand tour, as they used to call it. And she and her siblings all had college educations.

Granny was a Victorian lady, elegant, with aspirations of being a grande dame. My mother was her youngest child. She'd had her rather late in life, which was a cause for arched eyebrows and whispered innuendo within her politely scandalized circle. So when I knew her, she was already quite old. She had long white hair that reached to her waist. Every day Tilly, her Dutch maid, laced her into a pink, full-length corset. I loved Tilly. She had worked for Granny from the time she emigrated to America—first as my mother's nanny and then as Granny's cleaner, cook, and gardener. She lived in the house on Carol

Street in a beautiful little attic room whose windows opened to the sky. Across the hall, in the storage part of the attic, there were dusty trunks full of curious stuff. I spent many a wonderful hour poking and rummaging through the frayed gowns and yellowed paper and torn photos and dusty books and strange spoons and faded lace and dried flowers and empty perfume bottles and old dolls with china heads. Then finally, breaking into my reverie, a worried call from below. I would close the door softly and slip away. Until next time.

My dad's first real job after graduating high school was with Wright Aeronautical, the airplane manufacturer, during World War II. His next was with Alkan Silk Woven Labels, who had a mill in Paterson. When I was a little girl and he had to visit the plant, he would take me along with him. I took the tour of the mill many times, but I never once heard what the tour guide said because the looms were so fierce and loud.

The looms really did loom. They were the size of our house, holding thousands and thousands of colored threads in suspension while the shuttles at the bottom zoomed back and forth. At the confluence of all the threads, ribbons would appear and curl out, yard upon yard of silk clothing labels. My father would take these to New York and, like his father before him, play his own small part on the furthest peripheries of the fashion world.

As for me, I loved fashion for as long as I can remember. We didn't have much money when I was growing up and a lot of my clothes were hand-me-downs. On rainy days when I couldn't go out I would open up my mother's wooden blanket chest. The chest was stuffed with clothes she'd picked up from friends or that had been discarded. I would dress up and trot around in shoes and gowns and whatever else I could lay my grubby little hands on.

Television, oh, television. Glowing, ghostly seven-inch screen, round as a fishbowl. Set in a massive box of a thing that would've dwarfed a doghouse. Maddening electronic hum. Reception through this bent antenna. Some days good, some days rotten—when the signal flickered and skipped and scratched and rolled.

There wasn't a whole lot to watch, but I watched it. On Saturday mornings at five A.M. I would be sitting on the floor, eyes glued to the test pattern, black and white and gray, mesmerized, waiting for the cartoons to start. Then came wrestling and I watched that too, thumping the floor and groaning, my anxiety levels soaring at this biblical battle of good vs. evil. My mom would holler and threaten to throw the goddamned thing out if I was going to get that worked up. But wasn't that the point of it, getting all goddamned worked up?

I was an early and true devotee of the magic box. I even loved watching the picture reduce to a small white dot, then vanish, when you turned the set off.

When baseball season started, Mom would lock me out of the house. My mother, oddly, was a rabid baseball fan, and I mean rabid. She adored the Brooklyn Dodgers. They used to go to Ebbets Field in Brooklyn and watch the games when I was small. So I was always frustrated that I'd be locked outside for a baseball game. But I was a pest, I suppose—with a big mouth to boot.

My mother also liked opera, which she listened to on the radio when it wasn't baseball season. As far as listening to music, we didn't have much of a record collection though—a couple of comedy albums and Bing Crosby singing Christmas carols. My favorite was the compilation album *I Like Jazz!*, with Billie Holiday and Fats Waller and all these different bands. When Judy Garland launched into "Swanee," I would burst into sobs every time . . .

I had a little radio too, a cute brown Bakelite Emerson that you had to plug in, with a light on the top and a funny old dial with art deco numbers like a sunburst behind it. I would glue my ear to the tiny speaker, listening to crooners and the big band singers and whatever music was popular at the time. Blues and jazz and rock were yet to come . . .

On summer evenings, a drum-and-bugle corps would practice in the parade ground just beyond the woods. These men, the Caballeros, would gather after work. They were just starting out and couldn't afford uniforms, so they wore big navy-surplus bell-bottoms, white shirts, and Spanish bolero hats. They only knew how to play one song, which was "Valencia." They would march back and forth all evening and sometimes they would dance, and you could hear the music drifting up from out of the woods. My room was up in the eaves of the house with little dormer windows, and I would sit on the floor with the windows open and listen. My mother would say, "If I hear that song one more time, I'm gonna scream!" But it was brass and snare and loud and I loved it.

There were so few distractions then, before I started school, and I had so much time for daydreaming. I remember having psychic experiences as a little girl too. I heard a voice from the fireplace talking to me, telling me some kind of mathematical information, I think, but I have no idea what it meant. I would have all sorts of fantasies. I fantasized about being captured and tied up and then rescued by—no, I didn't want to be saved by the hero, I wanted to be tied up and I wanted the bad guy to fall madly in love with me.

And I would fantasize about being a star. One sun-drenched afternoon in the kitchen, I sat with my aunt Helen as she sipped at her coffee. I could feel the warm light playing on my hair. She paused with the cup at her lips and gave me an appraising stare. "Hon, you look like a movie star!" I was thrilled. Movie star. Oh, yes!

When I was four years old, my mom and dad came to my room and told me a bedtime story. It was about a family who chose their child, just like, they said, they had chosen me.

Sometimes I'll catch my face in a mirror and think, that's the exact same expression my mother or father used to have. Even though we looked nothing like each other and came from different gene pools. I guess it's imprinted somehow, through intimacy, through shared experience over time—which I never had with my birth parents. I've no idea what my birth parents look like. I tried, many years later, when I was an adult, to track them down. I found out a few things, but we never met.

The story my parents told me about how I was adopted made it sound like I was someone special. Still, I think that being separated from my birth mother after three months and put into another home environment put a real inexplicable core of fear in me.

Fortunately, I wasn't tossed into God knows what—I've had a very, very lucky life. But it was a chemical response, I think, that I can rationalize now and deal with: everybody was trying to do the best they could for me. But I don't think I was ever truly comfortable. I felt different; I was always trying to fit in.

And there was a time, there was a time when I was always, always afraid.

2

PRETTY BABY, YOU LOOK SO HEAVENLY

One visit, when I was a baby, my doctor gave me a lingering look. And then he turned in his white coat, grinned at my parents, and said, "Watch out for that one, she has bedroom eyes."

My mother's friends kept urging her to send my photo to Gerber, the baby food company, because I was a shoo-in, with my "bedroom eyes," to be picked as a Gerber baby. My mother said no, she wasn't going to exploit her little girl. She wanted to protect me, I suppose. But even as a little girl, I always attracted sexual attention.

Jump-cut to 1978 and the release of Louis Malle's *Pretty Baby*. After seeing the movie, I wrote "Pretty Baby" for the Blondie album *Parallel Lines*. Malle's star was the twelve-year-old Brooke Shields, who played a kid living in a whorehouse. Nudes scenes abounded. The movie created a firestorm of controversy regarding child pornography at the time. I met Brooke that year. She had been in front of the camera since she was eleven months old, when her mother got her a commercial for Ivory Soap. At age ten, with her mother's consent, she posed naked and oiled up in a bathtub for the Playboy Press publication *Sugar and Spice.*

One time, when I was around eight years old, I was put in charge of Nancy, a little girl of four or five, whom my mother was watching for the afternoon for her friend Lucille. I was to walk Nancy over to the municipal pool, which was about two blocks from my house, and my mother was going to join us there. I guided Nancy down the busy thoroughfare that bordered the end of the town, holding her little hand for safety. It was a seriously hot day, the bright hard sun bouncing up off the sidewalk at us. We turned a corner and were about to pass this parked car, with its passenger window rolled all the way down. From inside came this voice: "Hey, little girl, do you know where such-and-such is?" A messy-looking, rather nondescript older man, with washed-out and faded hair . . . He had a map over his lap, or maybe it was a newspaper. He was asking all kinds of questions and directions, and his one hand was moving around underneath the paper. Then the paper slid off and out popped his penis. He had been playing with it. I felt like a fly on the edge of a spiderweb. This wave of panic flushed through my body . . .

I freaked and fled to the pool, dragging Nancy along, her tiny feet trying to keep up. I rushed up to my teacher, Miss Fahey, who was at the entrance, making sure that everyone had their pool pass. I was really upset, but I just couldn't tell her about this creep showing me his penis. I said, "Miss Fahey, please watch Nancy, I have to go home," and I ran back. My mother was beside herself. She called the police. They came screeching up to the house and my mother and I rode around town in the back of the squad car, trying to spot the pervert. I was so small, I couldn't see over the back of the seat. I just sat there as we rode around and around, peering over the seat as best I could, my heart pounding and pounding.

Well, that was an awakening. My first indecent exposer, although my mother said there were others. Once, we were stalked at the Central Park Zoo by a man in a trench coat who kept flapping it open. Because of their frequency, over time, these kinds of incidents started to feel almost normal.

For as long as I can remember I always had boyfriends. My first kiss was given to me by Billy Hart. How sweet to be initiated by a boy with such a name. I was stunned, alarmed, angry, pleased, excited, and enlightened. Maybe I didn't realize all of this at the time and I probably couldn't have put it into words; nevertheless, I was confused and conflicted. I ran home to tell my mother what had happened. She gave me a mysterious smile and said it was because he liked me. Well, up to that point I had liked Billy too, but now I was embarrassed and got all shy around him. We were very young, maybe five or six years old.

And then there was Blair. Blair lived up the street and our mothers were friends, so he and I sometimes played together. This one time, we went up to my room and we ended up sitting cross-legged on the floor, Indian style, facing each other and taking a good look at each other's "things." This was innocent too. I was about seven and he was maybe eight and we were curious. I've always been curious. Well, Blair and I must have been quiet for too long because our mothers came in and we got caught. They were more embarrassed than angry, being longtime friends, but Blair and I were never encouraged to play with each other again.

My parents held to traditional family values. They stayed married for sixty years, holding on through all the ups and downs, and they ran a tight ship at home. We went to the Episcopalian church every Sunday and my family was very much involved in all the church activities and its social life. Which may have been why I was in the Girl Scouts and was definitely why I was in the church choir. Fortunately, I really enjoyed singing, so much so that I won a silver cross when I was eight for "perfect attendance."

I guess it's not really until you approach your teens that you get all these doubts and questions about religion. I must have been twelve when we stopped going to church. My father had had a big falling-out with the rector or the minister. Anyway, by that time I was in high school and probably much too busy to go to choir practice.

I hated the whole process of arriving at a new school. It wasn't the school itself. It was just a little local school, fifteen or twenty kids in each grade, and I wasn't afraid of studying; I'd learned the alphabet before kindergarten. First, for some reason, I would get incredibly anxious about being late. Maybe I needed approval that badly. However, my bigger problem was separation—being separated from my parents. Abandonment. It was traumatic. I would be a nervous wreck. My legs would turn to jelly and I struggled to climb the stairs. I guess somewhere in my subconscious, a scene was playing on a loop of a parent leaving me somewhere and never coming back. That feeling never really went away. To this day, when the band separates at the airport and we all go our different ways, I still get that gut reaction. Separation. I hate parting with people and I hate goodbyes.

Things were changing at home. At the age of six and a half, I had a baby sister. Martha was not adopted; my mother gave birth to her after a really rough pregnancy. Around five years before she adopted me, my mom had had another baby girl, Carolyn, premature I think, who died of pneumonia. There was a boy too, whom she miscarried. Then a drug came along that helped her go to term. Martha was premature, but she survived. My father said her head was smaller than the palm of his hand.

You might have thought that the arrival of another pretty baby in my house—and one that actually came from my mom—

ZAP!

might have triggered my insecurity and abandonment fears. Well, at first I was probably a little disturbed by not being the complete focus of all my mother's attention, but more than anything else I loved my sister. I was always very protective of her because she was so much younger than me. My father called me his beauty and my sister his good luck, because when she was born his fortunes changed.

I scared my parents one morning. It was probably the weekend and they were sleeping in a little bit. Martha had woken up and was crying for her bottle. So, I slipped down to the kitchen and heated up the bottle, which I had watched my mother do so many times, and I brought it upstairs and gave it to her. My parents freaked when they discovered what I was up to, convinced that I was scalding her. But there Martha was, happily chomping down on that nipple . . . So, I found myself with a new job, which became my morning contribution to all the many routines in our Hawthorne home.

Hawthorne was the center of my universe then. We never left. I didn't understand about finances as a young child and I didn't grasp that there wasn't much money and my parents were trying to save up to buy a house. All I knew was that I had a powerful yearning to travel. I was so curious and restless all the time. I loved it when we would all pile into the car and drive to the beach on our vacations, which almost always meant visiting family.

One year—I must have been eleven or twelve—we went on vacation to Cape Cod. We were staying in a rooming house with my aunt Alma and uncle Tom, my dad's brother. My cousin Jane was a year older than me and we had lots of laughs, giggling and playing together. One particular day, while our parents were downstairs, we sat in front of the mirror fixing our hair, as we loved to do. But this time, we called down and said we were going for a walk. As soon as we were far enough away, we took out our stolen pile of lipstick and eye makeup and carefully transformed ourselves into these hot-looking babes. We probably looked like two nubile characters from *The Rocky Horror Picture Show.* We stopped at a stand to buy some lobster rolls, then strolled on down the street, admiring our reflections in the shop windows. But we weren't the only ones admiring ourselves: these two men approached us and started to come on to us. They were way, way older than us. Both in their late thirties, we would discover. Pretending to have no idea that we were actually preteens, they invited us out that night and said they'd meet us at our place. Of course, we were not going to tell them our address, but we played along and said we'd come back and meet them somewhere else.

That night, our faces scrubbed clean, we were in bed playing cards and wearing our baby-doll pajamas when there was a knock on the door. It must have been eleven o'clock. Without our noticing, the two guys had followed us home and they were there to pick us up. I think by then our parents had enjoyed a few cocktails and they just thought it was hilarious. So, they threw open the bedroom door and there we were, children. It turned out that we didn't get into too much trouble. It also turned out that one of our suitors was a very famous drummer, Buddy Rich. I later discovered that, besides being a close friend of Sinatra's, Buddy had been married at the time to a showgirl named Marie Allison. They remained together until his death from a brain tumor at age sixty-nine, in 1987. Shortly after his visit, a large envelope arrived in the family mailbox. Inside was an autographed, eight-by-ten black-and-white glossy of my Buddy, who was once hailed as "the greatest drummer who ever drew breath."

Interestingly, Buddy Rich returned as a presence in my life decades later, when some of my close colleagues in the British rock scene—like Phil Collins, John Bonham, Roger Taylor, and

Bill Ward—would count Buddy as their greatest influence . . . My life has so often circled back on itself in these intricately obscure ways.

There was a whole lot going on that year, now that I look back on it. It was the year I made my stage debut. It was a sixth-grade school production of *Cinderella's Wedding*. They didn't give me the part of Cinderella, but I was the soloist who sang at her wedding to the prince. The song I sang was "I Love You Truly," a big ballad featured in the movie *It's a Wonderful Life*. When I came onstage I had the worst stage fright—all those eyes staring at me, kids, teachers, parents; my mom and dad were there with my sister, Martha. But I pulled it together. I just wasn't a natural performer or a big personality. I think I had a big personality inside, but I didn't have one on the outside; I was very shy. Whenever the teacher would come up to me and say, "You were so good!" my misfit mind added an unspoken, "Not really, have you lost your mind?"

My experience with ballet wasn't really much better. Like a lot of little girls, I wanted to be a ballerina. I'd been exposed to Margot Fonteyn and other wonderful dancers by my mother, who'd had a cultured childhood and wanted me to have some of that experience. But in ballet class I always felt very self-conscious because I was convinced I was too fat, which I wasn't at all. I had an athletic body. But I wasn't birdlike and delicate like all the little girls who looked so cute and perfect and like each other in their little tutus. I felt that I fucked the whole thing up by being so chubby and standing out.

The biggest thing that happened that year was that my family finally bought that little house and we moved. Our new neighborhood was not much different from our old one and it was not very far away. But it was in another school district, which meant that I had to switch schools. It was not easy being the new kid in sixth grade. I didn't know anybody there, apart

Martha and me.

from two girls I knew from Girl Scouts. I had no friends. Even more startling, Lincoln School had a whole different curriculum, which was much more focused on academics than my old school, so I had a lot of work to do to catch up. But there was a silver lining to this very dark cloud, I told myself. Which was: no more Robert.

Robert was a new boy at my old school and he was a different kind of kid, kind of wild and dressed in clothes that were usually too big for him. His clothes were very messy. His hair was messy too. Even the features on his face were messy. He also had a problem with wetting his pants. His sister Jean, on the other hand, was a model of perfection with pretty, curly hair; she was nicely dressed and brainy, maybe top of her class. Robert's grades were so low they couldn't be measured. He was the class freak. Mostly he was avoided or made fun of.

Perhaps because I was less cruel to him than the other kids, Robert became fixated on me. He started following me home. Sometimes he would leave me little presents. This went on and on. But since we were in a different house and I didn't go to that school anymore, I thought I would be free from his hauntings. I wasn't. We had been in the new house for just a few days and I was standing at the front door. My sister, Martha, asked me a question about Robert and I just let rip. I said exactly what I felt about his unwanted attentions. I did not know that Robert was outside, hiding behind a tree. He heard everything. I will never forget the look of astonishment and pain on that boy's face as he slipped away. I felt awful. I never saw him again, but from what I heard he remained a social catastrophe and in high school he hung out with another outcast. They would go hunting. A few years later, when they were fooling around with guns in Robert's basement, his friend shot him dead and this was ruled an accidental shooting, kids playing with guns.

Summers were for wandering in the sun, my mind running free. The days so muggy it felt like being swaddled in a hot compress. I swam and did all those summer things and I read a lot—everything I could get my greedy little hands on. Literature was my great escape and my expedition into other worlds. I hungered to learn about everything and everywhere that was beyond Hawthorne. And there were family outings to see my grandparents and aunts and uncles. Just the usual kid stuff, all of it a blur now, except for that deep, sinking sensation of dread in my stomach at the thought of going back to school.

Hawthorne High was my third school. I can't say I liked it any better than the others. It made me nervous, but I did like the sense of freedom and independence that came along with going to high school, where you're treated a little more like an adult. My parents made it pretty clear that they wanted me to be an achiever. And if they hadn't pushed me in this way, I think I might have just wandered off into dreamland. I was still trying to discover who I was, but I knew even then that I wanted to be some kind of artist or bohemian.

My mother used to make fun of artists. She would put on a WASP-y accent, make one wrist go limp, and exclaim, "Oh, you are such an *artiste*." That made me even more nervous and annoyed, and there's nothing worse than an angry and pissed-off teenager. Now, my life was not awful; it was blessed. My parents heaped so much love on me. But I felt like I had a split personality with half of the split missing, submerged, unexpressed, unreachable, and hidden.

I didn't make trouble at high school and my grades, although not straight A's, were good. I actually liked the classes where we were given literature to read, and I got good at geometry, because it was like figuring out a puzzle. One of the first things I noticed about high school was how much more grown-up the girls were, particularly their clothes. I immediately became extremely conscious of my clothes, which were either too dull, too constricting, or both. My mother dressed me like a little preppy girl, clean-cut American, with clunky shoes. What I wanted to wear was tight black pants and a big loose shirt or a back-to-front sweater, like the beatniks, or something tough looking and ballsy. Or at least something jazzier, with bright colors or a fringe. But when my mom took me shopping she would go straight for a white blouse with a round collar and a navy-blue skirt. Basically, when it came to clothing choices, my mother and I were always poles apart.

As I got older, life looked up. I started making my own clothes. I would fool with things, some of them hand-me-downs, tearing the sleeves off of one piece and sewing them onto another. I remember showing this one concoction to perhaps my first friend, Melanie, who remarked, "It looks like a dead dog." I have no idea where that dead dog went.

But for the longest time, I held on to one of those dresses I inherited from my mother's friends' daughters. I see it clearly now: this pink cotton summer dress with its full skirt and its great movement. Later, my father would take me to Tudor Square, one of his clients in the garment industry. And I remember getting a couple of brightly colored, really cool tweedy plaid outfits that I kept for a long time.

By the time I was fourteen, I was dyeing my hair. I wanted to be platinum blond. On our old black-and-white television and at the theater where they screened Technicolor movies, there was something about platinum hair that was so luminescent and exciting. In my time, Marilyn Monroe was the biggest platinum blonde on the silver screen. She was so charismatic and the aura she cast was enormous. I identified with her strongly in ways I couldn't easily articulate. As I grew up, the more I stood out physically in my family, the more I was drawn to people that I felt I related to in some significant way. With Marilyn, I sensed a vulnerability and a particular kind of femaleness that

I felt we shared. Marilyn struck me as someone who needed so much love. That was long before I discovered that Marilyn had been a foster child.

My mother colored her hair, so there was always peroxide in the bathroom. On my first attempt I didn't get the mix right, so I ended up bright orange. I must have had at least a dozen different colors after that. I was also experimenting with makeup. I went through a beauty mark phase; I'd show up at school, my face looking like one of those connect-the-dots puzzles. My skills improved, but I still enjoyed experimenting.

At fourteen I was a majorette. I'd dress up in the tasseled boots, the tall hat, and the skirt that didn't cover much at all, and I would march and twirl a baton. I was better at marching than baton twirling. I would always drop the baton, which meant I had to bend and pick it up, and which obviously added something extra to the performance.

I also joined a sorority, because that was what you were supposed to do, and it was the cool thing to do. These high school sororities and fraternities were curious groups—a sociologist or anthropologist would have a field day with them, I am sure. Each group had a strong identity and each was very competitive. But there were plenty of pluses too. When you're a high school girl looking for an identity, a sorority gives you somewhere to belong. The girls ranged in age from freshmen to seniors and all called each other sister, so there was a lot of affection and camaraderie. The younger ones just needed to survive being pushed around on initiation night by their "sisters."

Later on I quit. I don't remember exactly how it went down, but I had some friends that they didn't think were appropriate. I was offended by their telling me who I could and couldn't have as friends and I left.

Though I wasn't a troublemaker, I sometimes got detention—not for anything really bad, just cutting school.

I'd go to Stewart's Drive-In for a root beer and never come back. The worst thing about detention was having to sit there and write one stupid sentence over and over, thousands of times. I noticed that this one girl, K, would initial every page at the top with "JMJ." When I asked why she did that, a little surprised at my ignorance, she let me know in no uncertain terms that the letters stood for "Jesus, Mary, and Joseph."

K had been kicked out of Catholic school. So sitting next to her was the best thing about detention. She was a big, tough, gum-chewing Irish girl with sandy red hair and pimply teenage skin. She was always in detention for fighting. She had been labeled the town pump, the blow job queen, whether she deserved it or not. In small towns like ours, you could end up being caught forever in cruel traps. Small towns' stigmata. However, K and I became friends. I was always interested in anyone who was so out front like that. I was fascinated by their danger. I wanted to be dangerous too but still wanted to protect myself. So I wasn't dangerous—yet.

There was another friend whose mother was a nurse. One day she said she was going to Florida for a vacation. I said, "Gee, you're so lucky!" I was dying to get out of this town and the idea of going to Florida for a vacation was very exotic—especially since I was born in Florida and had never been there since. But she actually went to Puerto Rico for an abortion. When she came back I looked at her and said, "My God, you don't have a tan." She just glared at me. I didn't know that she had gotten knocked up. No one said anything.

I had a lot of boyfriends, usually one at a time, because that was the way it was done in this kind of small, uptight little town where reputations were made and lost in seconds. I would see one boy for a month or two and then I would see someone else. I really loved sex. I think I might have been oversexed, but I didn't have a problem with that; I felt it was totally natural. But in my town in those days, sexual energy was very repressed, or at least clandestine. The expectation for a girl was that you would date, get engaged, remain a virgin, marry, and have children. The idea of being tied to that kind of traditional suburban life terrified me.

Some nights I would get a ride with a girlfriend and we would go to Totowa borough next to Paterson where my grandparents lived. Totowa had a notorious reputation back then and its main street was sometimes referred to as "Cunt Mile." It was the thoroughfare where a lot of kids hung out. All the girls would walk around looking as hot and trashy as possible and the guys cruised the street looking at the girls. I would find a guy I liked and make out with him. They had great dances up there too. The town I came from was all white kids, but at these dances there was a really integrated crowd. And the music was just great because they played a lot of hot black music and everyone danced their ass off. I loved dancing. Still do.

For a while now, I had taken to going to New York; the bus fare was less than a dollar then. My favorite place to wander was Greenwich Village. I'd get in around ten in the morning, when all the bohemians and beatniks were still sleeping and everything was closed. I would just walk around, not looking for anything in particular, looking for everything really, and ingesting and digesting it all. Art, music, theater, poetry, and the sense that everything was up for grabs, you just had to see what fit. I was desperate to live in New York and be an artist. I could not wait for high school to end.

Well, finally it did end, in the summer of '63. They held the graduation ceremony outside on the football field in the back of the high school. It was boiling hot that day, ridiculously hot, and I was melting in my cap and gown. I guess I felt off balance all through high school, so it seemed appropriate for the graduation ceremony to end this way.

Family. Christmas.

So, this is where I pack my suitcase, wave goodbye to the folks, get on the bus, and watch through the window as New Jersey fades into the distance and the New York City skyscape looms? Well, actually no. I went to a junior college.

Centenary College in Hackettstown, New Jersey, was a women's Methodist school run by some very old Southern ladies. Essentially, it was a finishing program to groom you for a respectable married life. I once referred to it as a "reform school for debutantes" and that's really what it was to me—only I was no debutante and I did not want reforming. My reformation would be much, much different.

It was always planned that I would go to school. I told my parents that I wanted to go to an art school, preferably the Rhode Island School of Design—but it was a four-year program and it was beyond the budget. So, going to a two-year college was a compromise with my family, and that meant Centenary.

I wasn't sure at all that I wanted to go to college. I just wanted to get out in the world and be an artist. I think my mother wanted me to go there because she felt that, since I was so shy, I wouldn't do well anywhere else, and if I got homesick, it was only an hour and a half from home. So, in the fall I left for Hackettstown. I moved into a dorm, where I shared a room the first year with a girl named Jan and later with Karen—when they switched with each other. The second year, I roomed with a very smart, sweet girl named Carol Boblitz.

Now, the college did have a few good professors. Dr. Terry Smith taught American literature, which I absolutely loved—I loved Mark Twain and Emily Dickinson. And I liked the art teachers, Nicholas Orsini and his wife, Claudia. I was doing some painting and drawing while I was there. It wasn't the kind of school where you had to work too hard. You could take very easy courses if you wanted and you would still be going to all the social events at other colleges, which was basically a dating service.

In my second year I went out with a guy called Kenny Winarick. His grandfather built the enormous Concord Resort Hotel in the Borscht Belt in the Catskills. They had first-rate entertainment—Judy Garland, Barbra Streisand—and lots of Jewish families would go. One day Kenny asked me, "Do you want to go to the mountains?" which is what they called the Catskills, but I was so naive I thought we were going hiking. He took me to this magnificent hotel, where everyone was dressed to the nines and I was in funky jeans and trying to be cool.

After we had gone out for a while, Kenny brought me to visit his mother at her place in New York. As I stood gazing out from the terrace of her wonderful apartment, my dreams of big-city living took further flight. It was just right. Just perfectly right. The spacious rooms weren't overdecorated or too, too proper. A real environment where real people lived. People who loved being New Yorkers. Her prewar apartment building was named the Eldorado, at 300 Central Park West.

At the time, this mythological reference meant practically nothing to me, except that it was beautiful and exciting and something out of my wildest dreams. It was too soon for me to be drawing parallels between my own quest for an identity and the conquistadors' quest for their fabled city of gold. But looking back, it was an ideal parallel to my entering the allure of New York through the gilded portals of the Eldorado. It was my personal sixties happening, as I joined the growing band of latter-day conquistadors searching for special treasure in the new city of beckoning promise.

All this sounds quite serious. And in a way it was. I was intense and determined but also floating in an often-turbulent sea of mixed emotions. I don't think I was bipolar or depressed or schizophrenic or any such thing. I think I was normal enough, but in a time of expanded consciousness we were looking at the world in new and different ways.

Then there was also the psychedelic experience. Kenny's mother, Gladys, was a psychoanalyst. She had a strength and curiosity and vitality that I absolutely loved. Her kids had an assurance and sense of humor about themselves that was way ahead of most of the people back home. Simply put, it was sophistication. As an analyst, Gladys was in on the latest lectures and symposiums and talks related to her field. So, she got an invitation for a session with Timothy Leary. She couldn't go to this one, so Kenny and I went in her place. I think Leary may still have been teaching at Harvard or was about to be fired—and Alan Watts was there too. Leary's book *The Psychedelic Experience: A Manual Based on the Tibetan Book of the Dead* had recently been published and I guess the idea behind these simulated "experiences" was to further legitimize their passion for LSD and its therapeutic potential.

The day came for our "trip" and we went to one of the most beautiful town houses I'd ever seen. It was on the Upper East Side of Manhattan, between Madison and Fifth Avenues. A truly elegant building with a carved entry and wrought iron railings with a barred doorway. We were led to a ground-floor room, where a small circle of people were sitting on the carpet. Leary was explaining the chakras and the stages of the experiment and encouraged us to relax and go with it. There were no drugs, no drinks, no food, only suggestions and directions about what this LSD trip could be like. In fact, it was based on a spiritual journey through different states of consciousness, known as the bardo.

At this time, Leary's ideas were breathtakingly new and he had gotten some really dicey press about his teachings and drug use. We sat in the circle with the others and listened to Timothy chanting and speaking, guiding us through what might have been a mind expansion—if we could let ourselves go with it. Well, Kenny and I both were curious and wanted to learn something, so we hung in with the lecture. It went on forever and I was hoping there would be a snack at some point, but no such luck. We sat there for hours while Professor Leary and Alan Watts spoke about these levels of the mind. Finally we were all asked to interview each other.

There were all kinds of people there that day, not just hipsters or students. All kinds of businessmen and women; doctors, local and foreign; some nicely dressed uptown types; a few art-world people from the neighborhood; and analysts, of course. There was one man who made me nervous because he just radiated resistance. He held himself apart as if simply observing. He wore a white business shirt and dark gray trousers. He was balding and clean-cut. Of course, I was put opposite him for the interviews—the "getting to know you" part of the afternoon. I was uptight, not nice at all, and starving by then. So, I had it in for this poor man from the get-go and quizzed him in a way that he wasn't expecting. It turned out he was there in some official capacity from either the CIA or the FBI. Which came as a jolt to Leary . . .

Kenny's father was interesting too. He had a company called Dura-Gloss that made nail polish. A brand that my mother used. I used to love the little bottles it came in. It seemed a bit synchronistic that I should be seeing this guy. My mother must have thought so too, because she was putting the screws on Kenny to get serious. I thought he was great, but I wanted to experience what the world was and find out who I was before settling down. I think he did too. He went on to get his master's degree and in a way I did too, eventually.

Me, I graduated with an associate of arts degree. I found a job in New York, but I couldn't live there, I had no money, so I commuted back and forth, which I hated. I spent hours looking for an apartment in the city, but I couldn't find anything remotely affordable. I guess I was moaning about it to my boss Maria Keffore at work. Maria, who was a very pretty Ukrainian woman, said, "Oh, you don't have to worry. Come see my apartment. The rent is only seventy dollars a month." *OH MY GOD, how can it be so cheap,* I thought, *what must it be like?* Well, it was fantastic. It was on the Lower East Side, which was a Ukrainian and Italian neighborhood at that time, and under rent control.

With Maria's help I found an apartment with four rooms for just $67 on St. Mark's Place. That first night in my new home, lying on the bed listening to the sounds of the street floating through my window, I felt like I was finally, twenty years into my life, in the place where my next life would begin.

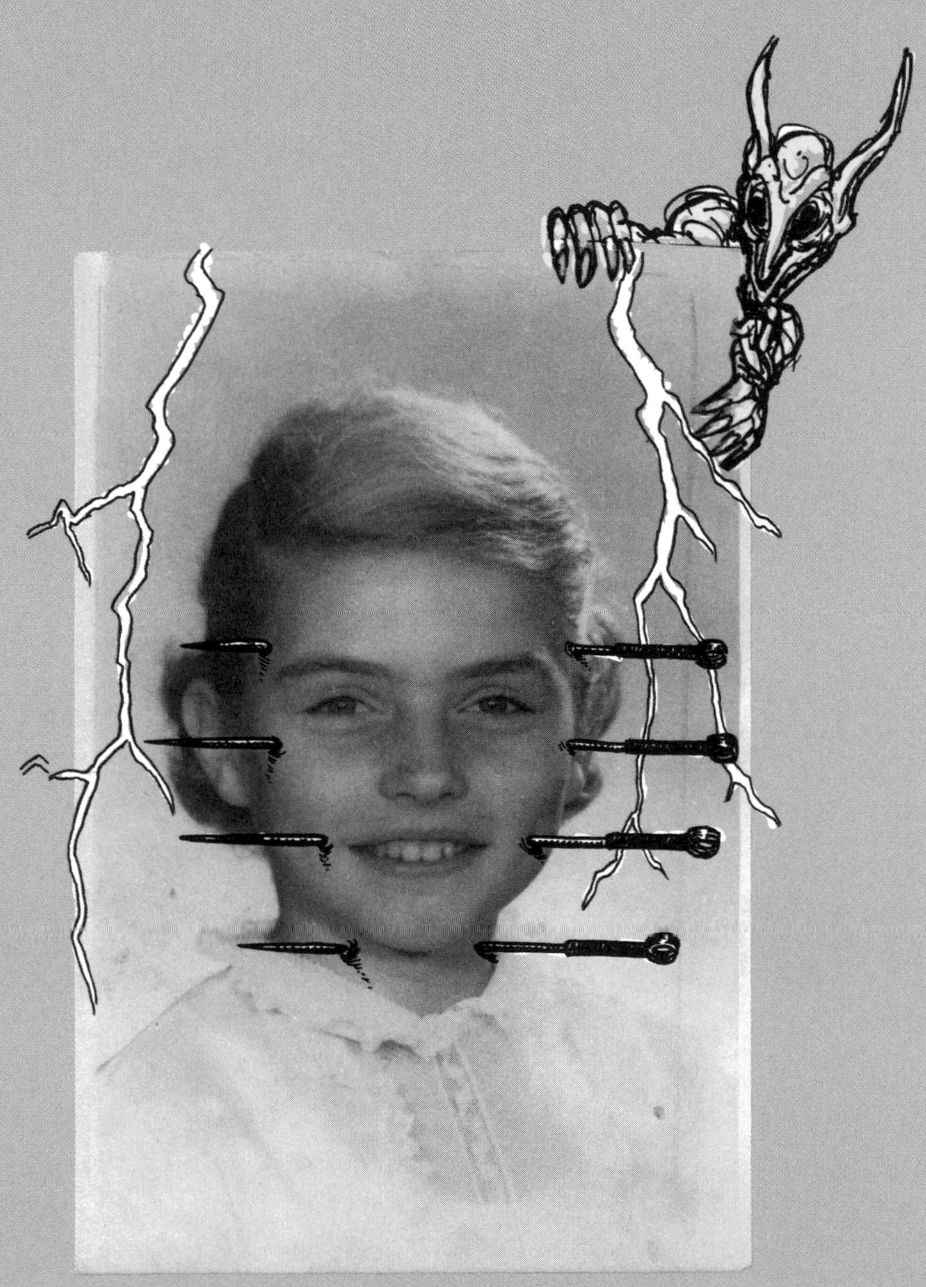

They used to say I looked European.

3

CLICK CLICK

I hated my looks as a kid but couldn't stop staring. Maybe there were one or two pictures that I liked, but that's all. For me, capturing those looks on film was a horrible experience. Eventually the peeping, secretive, naughty aspect of it made being photographed all right, but voyeurism was not part of my vocabulary as yet. How could I know then that this face would help make Blondie into a highly recognizable rock band?

Does a photograph steal your soul? Were the aboriginal people right? Are photographs part of some mystical image bank, a type of visual Akashic record? A source of forensic evidence to examine the hidden, darker secrets of our souls, perhaps? Now, I can tell you that I've had my picture taken thousands of times. That's a lot of theft and a lot of forensics. Sometimes I read things into those pictures that no one else seems to see. Just a tiny glimpse of my soul maybe, a passing reflection on a piece of glass . . . If you were me, by now you might be wondering if you had any soul left at all. Well, I had one of those Kirlian photographs taken once at a new age fair—

and there supposedly was my soul, my aura, staring back at me. Yes, maybe there is still some of my soul to go around.

I was working in an almost soulless place: a wholesale housewares market at 225 Fifth Avenue, a huge building full of everything you can think of that had to do with housewares. My job was selling candles and mugs to buyers from the boutiques and department stores. This had not been part of the dream. I started thinking that since I was pretty—well, my high school yearbook had named me Best-Looking Girl—maybe I could get some modeling work. I'd met two photographers, Paul Weller and Steve Schlesinger, who did catalog work and paperback book covers, and I decided I would make a portfolio. My modeling book had shots running from hairstyles to yogic poses in a black leotard. What was I thinking? What kind of jobs could I possibly get with these weird photographs? Answer: one and done.

Then I saw a blind ad in the *New York Times* looking for a secretary. It turned out to be for the British Broadcasting Corporation. This was my first link to what would become a long, lovely relationship with Great Britain. They gave me the job on the strength of the sensational letter that my uncle helped me write. Once they had me, they realized that I wasn't very good at what I was supposed to do, but they kept me anyway and I grew into the job. I learned to operate a telex machine. I also met some interesting people—Alistair Cooke, Malcolm Muggeridge, Susannah York—who came into the office/studio for radio interviews.

Plus, I met Muhammad Ali. Well, not exactly met him. "Cassius Clay is coming in to do a TV interview," they said, so I snuck around the corner and *wow*, I saw this big, beautiful man walk into the TV studio and close the door. It was a soundproofed room with a small window way up high, so I decided, being athletic, that I was going to grab the windowsill and pull myself up and watch the taping. But, as I pulled myself up, my feet kicked the wall with a thud. In a flash, Ali's head whipped round and he stared right at me. He nailed me and I was transfixed. He'd responded with the animal instinct and lightning reflexes of the supreme champion he was . . . I quickly dropped down to the floor, shocked and excited by the primal exchange. I could have gotten into trouble, particularly if they had already started to record, but fortunately no one else in the room had even noticed.

The offices for the BBC New York were in the International Building at Rockefeller Center, directly across from the monumental St. Patrick's Cathedral. When I was working at the BBC, I believe Fifth Avenue was a two-way street, and the traffic was immense. A block south of the cathedral was Saks Fifth Avenue. In front of the International Building was and still is the enormous bronze statue of Atlas holding up the world. Behind it is Rockefeller Plaza, where the skating rink and the big Christmas tree are located during the holidays. During the summer the rink becomes an outdoor café. Directly behind the rink is the NBC building, with the Warner Bros. offices nearby too.

Strolling past the store windows and through the canyons of buildings was always interesting, and I made it a point to go over to visit one of my favorite characters, "Moondog." This tall, bearded old man with his horned Viking helmet was a vision. He stood on the corner of Sixth Avenue and Fifty-Third in his long reddish cape holding his spearlike pole, selling booklets of his poetry. Moondog now has his own Wikipedia page, but back then few people who walked past him knew who the fuck he was. Most people steered clear of or didn't even notice him—just another crazy "weirdo" to avoid or blank out.

Some thought he was an eccentric, blind, homeless man, but he was much more. Moondog was also a musician. He had an apartment uptown but kept his image and his privacy closely guarded. He designed instruments and also recorded, and he became adored by most New Yorkers. A beloved fixture, a true New York character who sometimes recited his poems to the businessmen and tourists hurrying past him. He was freaky but he was fondly called the Viking guy—even if no one knew about all his artistic achievements.

And then there were the more sinister types: the silent men in black selling small newspapers or booklets. They were serious, intense, kind of scary, which made them all the more intriguing, of course. They called themselves "the Process"—short for the Process Church of the Final Judgment—and were scary but compelling in their intensity. Never alone, they stood in groups on the midtown corners in their quasimilitary black uniforms.

Scientology wasn't so well-known at the time, but cults, communes, and radical religious movements would come and go all the time. I wasn't aware completely of Scientology or the Process Church, but I respected the commitment it took for these guys to stand and deliver in midtown to a straight bunch of bros. They roamed around downtown as well, among much more sympathetic audiences in the West and East Village.

It was a business, it was a religion, it was a cult; maybe it still is but I don't think they call it the Process anymore.

I had come to the city to be an artist, but I wasn't painting much, if at all. In many ways I was really still a tourist, just experiencing the place, having adventures, and meeting people. I experimented with everything imaginable, attempting to figure out who I was as an artist—or if I even was one. I sought out everything New York had to offer, everything underground and forbidden and everything aboveground, and threw myself into it. I wasn't always smart about it, admittedly, but I learned a lot and came out the other side and kept on trying.

Drawn to music more and more, I didn't have to go far to hear it. The Balloon Farm, later called the Electric Circus, was

Trying to keep time at the Mudd Club.

on my street, St. Mark's Place, between Second and Third. The old building the shows were held in had some serious history: from mob hangout, to Ukrainian nursing home, to Polish community hall, to the Dom restaurant. The whole neighborhood was Italian, Polish, and Ukrainian. Every morning, on my way to work, I would see the women in babushkas with their buckets of water and brooms, washing the sidewalks clean of whatever went on the night before. A ritual carryover from the old country.

One evening, as I walked past the Balloon Farm, the Velvet Underground was playing, so I went inside and into this brilliant explosion of color and light. It was so wild and beautiful, with a set designed by Andy Warhol, who was also doing the lights. The Velvets were fantastic. John Cale brilliant, with his droning, screeching electric viola; proto-punk Lou Reed with his hyper-cool, drawling delivery and sneering sexuality; Gerard Malanga, gyrating around with his whip and leathers; and the deep-voiced Nico, this haunting, mysterious Nordic goddess . . .

Another time, I saw Janis Joplin play at the Anderson Theater. I loved the physicality and the sensuality of her performance—how her whole body was in the song, how she would grab the bottle of Southern Comfort on the piano and take a huge slug and belt out her lines with crazed Texan soul. I'd never seen anything like her onstage. Nico had a very different approach to performing; she just stood there, still as a statue, as she sang her somber songs—much like the famed jazz singer Keely Smith, with the same stillness but a different kind of music.

I would go see musicals and underground theater. I bought *Backstage* magazine and I'd take notes on all the auditions and then join the endless lines of hopefuls who, along with me, never got past first base. There was also a strong jazz scene on the Lower East Side with haunts like the Dom, the renowned Five Spot Cafe, and Slugs'. At Slugs', in particular, you'd get to hear luminaries like Sun Ra, Sonny Rollins, Albert Ayler, and

Ornette Coleman—and find yourself at a table next to Salvador Dalí. I met a few of the musicians. I remember showing up and sitting in on a couple of loose, "happening"-like gatherings, the Uni Trio and the Tri-Angels—free, abstract music where I sang a bit or chanted and banged some percussion instrument or other. That was the same thing we did in the First National Uniphrenic Church and Bank. The leader was a guy from New Jersey named Charlie Simon who later christened himself Charlie Nothing. He made sculptures out of cars that he called "dingulators" that you could play like guitars. He also wrote a book called *The Adventures of Dickless Traci,* a detective novel with a weird sense of humor, but that was later. He was multidimensional in music, art, and literature—a free spirit who was more beat than hippie. And he made me curious. I liked the curiosity because I was curious myself. If any other guy had come along and played me a track from a Tibetan temple with men giggling and growling in the background, I would have liked him too.

The sixties were the age of happenings. It was also the time of a great New York loft scene where so many of these wonderful parties and happenings took place. The lofts down below Canal Street and in Soho were former manufacturing spaces and most were illegal living, but they were very cheap, $75 or $100 a month, so all the artists rented these enormous two-thousand-square-foot spaces. That's where we played our anti-music music. Charlie played saxophone. Sujan Souri, a jolly, Buddha-bellied Indian man who was a philosophy student, tapped away on the tablas, and Fusai, a countrywoman to Yoko Ono, sort of sang in a very high voice. I don't know if I banged sticks together or screamed; probably both. Our drummer, Tox Drohar, was wanted for something somewhere—and I surmised he was hiding out, which forced him to change his name and disappear. And then he left to go live with his girlfriend in a little shack in the Smoky Mountains on the great Cherokee reservation.

My boss at the BBC told me I had two weeks' vacation. I wasn't allowed to choose the dates and they gave me two weeks in August. It was the hottest, most awful time of summer. Phil Orenstein was an artist working in plastic who made inflatable pillows, furniture, and bags with silk-screened paintings on them. He needed help assembling the straps on some of the bags. So, there I was, in this little plastics factory, tying knots and cutting the ends off with a hot knife. But the fumes from the plastic in that heat were unbelievable. I was seeing spots. I think I lost a piece of my mind from doing it.

But I had those two weeks off, so Charlie Nothing and I decided to take my saved-up $300 and go visit Tox and his very, very pregnant girlfriend, Doris, in Cherokee, North Carolina. We drove down and stayed there for a week and managed to spend my $300. I went back to the BBC covered in mosquito bites, still seeing spots from the plastic fumes and too much pot. But it was a fair exchange: the Smoky Mountains were magnificent and I would have never gone to Cherokee on my own and sat around in rocking chairs with old-timer Indians as they chewed tobacco and spat juice into paint cans.

In 1967, the First National Uniphrenic Church and Bank released an album, *The Psychedelic Saxophone of Charlie Nothing*, on John Fahey's record label Takoma. But I had left by then. I also quit the BBC, which I felt was too time consuming. I got a job at Jeff Glick and Ben Schawinski's Head Shop on East Ninth Street—the first-ever head shop in New York City. Pipes, posters, bongs, black-light bulbs, tie-dyed T-shirts, incense, the usual stuff, only then it was unusual. Right next door was a peculiar storefront with filthy windows plastered with button cards yellowed from age. The crone who had the store lived in the back. Wrapped in her shawl, she looked like an image from a fairy tale. Veselka, which translates to "rainbow," is a no-frills, twenty-four-hour-a-day Ukrainian eatery next door. When the old woman eventually died they incorporated her store, enlarging their restaurant. The Head Shop was just around the corner from my apartment on St. Mark's place, so no commute, and it was fun. All the downtown people, the uptown people—in fact, everyone—came in there and it was a really good scene. The Head Shop was an ideal place to meet people who were looking to break some rules.

Ben's father was a Bauhaus painter and Ben was a sculptor, furniture designer, and builder, easygoing, very cute, and a ladies' man. We had started going out and we were pretty interested in each other. Eventually he met these guys from California who had a commune, in Laguna Beach I think. He made all these plans to move out there and be with these people and he wanted me to go with him. I really liked him, but I couldn't drop everything and blindly follow him. I was still working on music and I was really upset that he wanted me to just throw everything away and go with him. For a while I didn't know if I had made a mistake or not. Well, a few years later he ended up coming back. He'd had this very fancy Volkswagen bus that he had fitted out beautifully—but as soon as he got out there the van sadly got lost in a mudslide.

One day two handsome, long-haired leather boys strode into my domain—two rebels without a cause. These pierced puppies pressed up against the counter, asking to buy rolling papers and flirting like crazy. I liked the older one, whose name I can't remember now because he was sweet natured, on the shy side, easy to talk to. The other one, the intense one, just stood staring at me, adding the occasional quip, trying to be funny. That one's name was Joey Skaggs. Joey came back to the shop a few days later without his friend. It was Valentine's Day and he had come to see the girl with the heart-shaped lips.

He invited me over to his big funky loft on Forsyth Street below Houston. Joey was truly a man for all seasons. He had three bikes that he kept upstairs, real heavy-duty motorcycles, one of them a Moto Guzzi, one of them British; how he got them up those stairs I don't know. He was also a performance art hustler. One of his more famous shows was on Easter Sunday in Central Park's Sheep Meadow, when he carried a gigantic cross on his back and dragged it around the park during a peace rally. He had that Christlike look with his long hair and thin body, though the leather pants and biker boots were a bit of a stretch. He made the papers posing atop a large boulder at the edge of the field, draped with his cross, à la Christ on the way to Golgotha.

Joey had a friend who was a filmmaker. I can't remember his name either, but he was very handsome. One day Joey invited me over and when I walked in, Joey grabbed me and started tearing off my clothes, kissing me, fondling my breasts, playing with my pussy. Then he threw me down on his bed. He got me really hot and I reached to yank off his pants. But he wouldn't let me. He backed off, stood up, and out from the shadows slunk this dude with a movie camera. There I was, naked, spread, and very wet—and suddenly this thing, this all-seeing eye, is wiggling toward me, voyeur attached. Well, that was a rush. I felt shocked, furious, betrayed, and disrespected, but I was also very turned on. I wanted to knock his teeth in and fuck him at the same time. Scream, cry, get dressed, or go for it? I tried to be cool, silly me. I finally climbed onto a small pedestal and posed like a statue. All of this is on film somewhere. Don't ask me what happened to the footage. Absorbed into the cosmic ether of the sixties, I suppose.

This was all pretty typical for Joey, actually, who's maintained himself as a professional media prankster ever since. I've had a few laughs at his antics over the years: his fake ad for a dog brothel, which got covered by ABC and won them an Emmy; his Hair Today company, which marketed a new kind of hair implant—using whole scalps from the dead; his fake SEX-ONIC sex machine, which he claimed had been impounded at the Canadian border; his Bullshit Detector Watch (which flashed, mooed, and shat). And so much more . . .

I can still remember Joey's loft. That part of the Lower East Side wasn't gentrified at all in the sixties; it was Alphabet City, gangland, dangerous. So, whenever I went there, after turning the corner off of well-lit Houston onto dark and narrow Forsyth, I'd run down the street and into the building and up those wooden stairs, the darkest, scariest staircase of them all, and I'd arrive at Joey's breathless from running and climbing. He probably thought I was just hot for him and couldn't wait. Which was also true.

Then Paul Klein, the husband of a very close friend of mine from high school, Wendy Weiner, invited me to join them in making some music. We would sit around and sing songs together and I would harmonize. It began casually but eventually evolved into a band, the Wind in the Willows, named after the classic children's book by Kenneth Grahame. I got the job, for what it was worth, as backup singer. Wendy and Paul were Freedom Riders who went to Mississippi to register black people to vote. Stokely Carmichael, who was the organizer of the Student Nonviolent Coordinating Committee, told them, "You can't share a room in Mississippi without being married and expect not to be arrested," and so they got married. When they came back they moved to the Lower East Side and we resumed our friendship. I knew I wanted to be a performer—I was still vague on what kind, but at least I knew that.

Paul was a bearded, folky, big bear of a man. He sang and played a little guitar and he was another likeable hustler. It was the age of everyone looking for the golden opportunity and in

Painting by Robert Williams
The Purposed Mysteries, Fears and Terrifying Experiences of Debbie Harry
Remedial title: The Jersey Towhead Who Traffics in Saccharine Details

THEO. BUNDY
ROBT. WMS.

the midsixties, record companies were working their own major game: so loaded with cash, they'd put bands up in houses and give them money to live on and to record. A kind of patronage system. And if the music didn't sell, then fine, they had an excuse for a write-off.

Eventually there were eight or nine people in the Willows after Paul kept adding and adding. Peter Brittain, who also played guitar and sang, was married to another of my closest friends since childhood, Melanie. There was a double bass player, Wayne Kirby, who was from Paterson, where both my grandmothers lived, and had left to study at Juilliard. There was a woman named Ida Andrews, also from Juilliard, who was a real pistol and played oboe, flute, and bassoon. We had keyboards and a vibraphone and strings. It was sort of like a small orchestra. A kind of baroque folk music but with these percussive things going on. I played finger cymbals, tamboura, and tambourine. Our producer Artie Kornfeld also played bongos. More famously he went on to create the Woodstock Festival with Michael Lang. We had two drummers, Anton Carysforth and Gil Fields. There was also a very sweet and good-hearted man named Freddy Ravola, whom we called our "spiritual adviser," because of his positivity. He worked as our roadie. Not that we did many shows.

In the summer of '68 we released our debut album, *Wind in the Willows*. It was my first time on a record. I sang lead on one song, "Djini Judy," but aside from that I was like wallpaper, something pretty to stand in the back in my hippie clothes and with my long brown hair parted in the middle, going "Oooooo." Artie Kornfeld, who produced the album, was working at Capitol Records as their "vice president of rock" and seemed to have boundless company money to spend on us. It was not a quick album to make. Apparently, Capitol was going to give us a big push. All I can recall is playing one big show in Toronto, opening up for a Platters cover band, the Great Pretenders, or something like that. But what I do clearly remember is Paul encouraging all the band members "to get closer to each other" with some helpful doses of acid and free love. Ha! Nice ploy. But I did not drink the Kool-Aid.

I did go to Woodstock with my friend Melanie and her husband, Peter, and that was a massive mud pit. *Torrential* rain. People were covered with mud and jumping into the stream to wash it off. So, we bailed and moved our tent to higher ground. Which was great, until we were forced to move again in the middle of the night, to make room for a helicopter landing place.

I remember there was this group called the Hog Farm from San Francisco who set up a soup kitchen and they were feeding everyone, and I do mean everyone. Hundreds of thousands of people. Amazing. I just walked around on my own, seeing all the people, meeting some of them, watching bands, and waiting for Jimi Hendrix to play.

I quit the Wind in the Willows. I enjoyed performing; I even wrote something for the second album entitled "Buried Treasure." The album was never released and apparently the tapes are lost. I wouldn't bother looking for them. I left because of big musical differences and bigger personal differences and because the band never played. And I wasn't in control, I was just a decorative asset in the band and I outgrew it. And I knew that I wanted to do something that was more rock.

When the Wind in the Willows and I parted company, I moved in with the last drummer that was in the band, Gil Fields. He was a strange-looking guy with a great big Afro and startling blue eyes. He was completely bonkers but an incredible drummer, a prodigy who had been playing drums since he was four years old. I gave up my apartment on St. Mark's Place and decided to get rid of everything and just have one suitcase of belongings and a tamboura and a tiny TV that my mother had given me. I moved into Gil's place at 52 East First Street. I needed a job and it was Gil who suggested I try to get a job at Max's Kansas City. He said, "Well it's this place where everybody hangs out, Max's, have you heard of it?" "No." "Well it's up on Park Avenue South right near Union Square." I had never really worked as a waitress before, except in a diner in New Jersey when I was in high school. But the owner, Mickey Ruskin, gave me a job.

The very first time I did heroin was with Gil. He was nervous and hyperthyroid and excitable—he was a wreck. If ever there was anybody that needed heroin, it was Gil. I remember his tapping out this tiny little line of gray powder. And we snorted it up. And I felt a kind of rush I'd never felt before. And I thought, *Oh, this is so nice, so relaxing,* aah, *I don't have to think about things,* and it was so delicious and delightful. For those times when I wanted to blank out parts of my life or when I was dealing with some depression, there was nothing better than heroin. Nothing.

Max's Kansas City was the place to be seen. That was another fabulous time in New York, no end of creativity and characters, and most of downtown seemed to wind up in Max's. I worked the four-till-midnight shift and other times seven thirty until it closed. James Rado and Gerome Ragni would be in the back room every afternoon, writing the musical *Hair.* Little by little, as the day turned into night, the crowd got wilder and freakier. Andy Warhol would always come in with his people and take over the back room. I saw Gerard Malanga and Ultraviolet, who had been Salvador Dalí's lover and was now a Warhol superstar; Viva, another Warhol superstar; Candy Darling, a stunning transgender actress; the flamboyant Jackie Curtis; Taylor Mead; Eric Emerson; Holly Woodlawn; and so many others. Whatever you were doing, you couldn't help but stop and stare at Candy. Edie Sedgwick was around sometimes, and Jane Forth, another of the Factory's It Girls.

There were Hollywood stars too—James Coburn; Jane Fonda. And rock stars—Steve Winwood; Jimi Hendrix; Janis Joplin, who was lovely and a big tipper. So many of them. I served dinner to Jefferson Airplane two days before they left for Woodstock.

And then there was Mr. Miles Davis. He sat back against the banquette along the outside wall upstairs, like a black king. No way he could have known this little white waitress was a musician too—and maybe she didn't know either at that point . . .

Why did they seat him in my section—not the one at the end of the earth but the one on the other side of the moon? The section that overlooked what often became the stage, late at night. The tables against the wall were slightly raised on a low step-up platform. He came there with a stunning white woman, a blonde as I remember.

I came up to their table in my little black miniskirt, my black apron, and my T-shirt, with my long hippie hair au naturel—limping from a terribly infected foot injury. The blister and my slashed Achilles were so painful I had to wear these clunky backless sandals which were absurd for work, but I was young enough that it didn't matter.

Would they care for drinks? She spoke, he was silent, still as a dead calm, statuesque with his ebony skin shining softly in the dim red light of the upstairs back room. He had his own light, glowing, shimmering, alive with his thoughts. Would they like to eat? He remained silent while she ordered for both of them. I don't know if he ate his dinner. I couldn't bring myself to watch him chew, but I did see him bend forward as if to take a bite of his steak.

At about this time, it started to get busy and I had to keep limping along—and couldn't indulge in watching Miles having dinner on a two-top, upstairs at Max's. Why the hell they sat him up there, I'll never know.

All these people, all doing in their own way what I had dreamed of doing and had come here to do—and I was waiting on them. It was frustrating but helpful in a way, because I was on shaky ground back then, probably hypersensitive to criticism, and I guess it helped toughen me up. It was hard work physically and some days were rougher than others, but I think it was one of the best times of my life, all in all. Very colorful.

But Max's was about more than just bringing people food or cocktails; it was all such a big flirtation, such a scene. Everybody who went there was checking out everybody else. One night, I did Eric Emerson, upstairs at Max's, in the phone booth. My one-hour stand with a master of the game. Eric was one of the Warhol superstars and he was just striking—a musician in a muscular dancer's body. After watching him dance and bound in one leap across the stage at the Electric Circus, Warhol cast him in *Chelsea Girls*. I was one of many who had flings with Eric. He was a piece of human art. He had such intense energy and fearlessness and he had more children than he could keep track of. He was also pretty stoned out.

Everybody on the scene did drugs. That's how it was back then, part of your social life, part of the creative process, chic and fun and really just *there*. No one thought about the consequences; I can't remember if any of us even knew the consequences. It may sound strange when you're talking about drugs, but it was a more innocent time. They weren't doing scientific studies and setting up methadone clinics; if you wanted to do drugs you did drugs and if you got hung up or got sick, you were on your own. Curiosity was a big factor too—drugs were another new experience to check out.

There was this man who came into Max's one time—it was late afternoon—Jerry Dorf. He was an older guy, very handsome, and there were all these pretty girls around him. He was flirting with me like mad. So, we got to talking and I think I was complaining about working at Max's, so he said, "Well, why don't you come with me to California? You can stay at my house in Bel Air." Ha! Another man who wants me to drop everything and go with him to California. "Oh no," I said, "I'm not so sure about that." At that time I had a sitar and I was studying a bit with my teacher, Dr. Singh. But Jerry and I started fooling around. He was loaded. He bought me some clothes from Gucci. "You have to dress well to travel," he said.

I quit my job at Max's abruptly—which Mickey Ruskin never forgave me for; he was very pissed at me because by that point I had become one of his better waitresses—and I went with Jerry. I stayed in his house, but I never felt comfortable. It wasn't even a month, but it seemed like forever. Then Jerry's girlfriend found out that I was living there. She had run away with a rock band, the Flying Burrito Brothers, and was living with them in the desert, but now came running home. So I got moved over into the Hotel Bel-Air. It was nice, but I was lonely. I know a lot of people in Los Angeles today, but I knew no one then. So I said to Jerry, "Put me on a plane, I want to go home." When I was back, I got back with Gil and I went to Max's and asked Mickey for a job. "No way," he said. So that's when I became a Playboy bunny.

Years before, my mom and dad had had a friend, Mr. Whipple, a businessman, really handsome, who traveled a lot and who would regale us with all these wild stories about the places he had been to. He talked about the Playboy Clubs and painted this wonderful picture of the bunnies and how exotic it was. It sounded so showbizzy. That's when it was implanted in my mind. So I decided to try out to be a bunny. It was quite a procedure. First you met with the Bunny Mother—she was a Chinese woman named J. D., very businesslike; she'd been there for a long time. After you were interviewed you came back for another interview with the executives and you did a series of meetings. You didn't ever have to put on the costume; they looked at you and they could see immediately if you were going to make it or not. Then you went into a training period for a couple of weeks—and there was a lot of training involved. You had to learn about all the drinks, all of the cocktails, how to carry the tray, exactly how to do the service. Their whole thing was very involved.

Being a bunny was not at all like what you might think. It was hard work, harder than at Max's, and the clients were mainly businessmen, suits. The club members had to behave themselves and there was always staff to put a stop to anything inappropriate. You got treated well, but really it was just another job and not as much fun as the last one. I didn't meet many famous people except for one. I was working downstairs in the cocktail lounge—I hadn't gotten up into the show rooms, where the entertainment was. Two men came in and sat at a table in my section. I kept looking at this one man thinking, *How do I know him?* Finally I just said to him, "I feel like I know your face." And he said, "Oh, I'm Gorgeous George." The wrestler! As I mentioned earlier on, I was a passionate wrestling fan as a kid and Gorgeous George was one of my favorites. I told him it was wonderful to meet him and that I had watched him on TV many, many times. And that was that; he went back to his conversation. But it really was such a pleasure to meet Gorgeous George.

I lasted eight or nine months at the Playboy Club, about the same as I did at Max's, and then I turned in my corset, collar, ears, and tail. They don't let you keep your costume. And that was that. Gil had been working with a Latin bandleader named Larry Harlow and along with Jerry Weiss, of Blood, Sweat and Tears fame, they started a band called Ambergris.

Paramount Records gave them a budget and put them up in a house in Fleischmanns, New York, outside of Woodstock. They hung out there for months, writing, practicing, and getting ready to record their album. The cover art was cool with its regal-looking, bright red rooster head. In the back of my mind I was thinking, *Oh, maybe I'll get to sing on it*. Secretly, I had been practicing. I would put headphones on and practice how to change my voice and expression. But it wasn't happening. It was all guys. In fact, the singing was handled by Jimmy Maelen, who is best known for his first-call percussion work with everyone from Madonna, to John Lennon, to David Bowie, to Alice Cooper, to Mick Jagger, to Michael Jackson, and the list goes on and on . . .

I'd been in New York almost five years now and it felt like I had come to a dead end. Or something had. The same thing seemed to be happening to a lot of people at that time. Somewhere around that time I found myself out of kilter with everything and with myself, unsettled, losing my temper, crying for no reason. And I was so tired of having to connect. A girlfriend of mine, Virginia Lust (the star of Yoko Ono's movie *Fly*), was now living upstate in Phoenicia, New York. She was then pregnant with her first child and I went to stay with her for four months. Then I went back to my parents' house in New Jersey. They were moving upstate to Cooperstown, New York. I told you my mother was a rabid baseball fan so it wasn't surprising that she would choose to live near the Baseball Hall of Fame, but it did give me a laugh. So, I helped them move and stayed with them a couple of months. After helping them, I headed back down to New Jersey and moved into a rooming house. I got a job working at a health club and I started dating a guy who was a painting contractor. The normal life.

HOUSE LIGHTS

Mick Rock, 1978.

AFTER ROB ROTH HAD SENT ME ALL THE SCANS OF MY FAN ART collection, he drove off back to NYC in his white pickup truck. Rather him than me that day—I'd been tiring of my constant commutes to the city. We had been working on how best to reproduce and organize the drawings and paintings I've accumulated over all the years, while being Blondie or being in Blondie. I didn't have a strong reason to save everything, but I couldn't just abandon them. Mostly, I kept them all because I just like them. The sweet and insightful drawings, paintings, mosaics, dolls, and hand-drawn T-shirts (of which only one remains) have traveled with me on tours around the world, suffering flight delays and bad weather and surviving just like me, a bit frayed at the edges, but still intact.

I've moved about ten or eleven times over the years and am amazed that I've managed to hold on to my fan art collection for all that time. For a while, my files were stored in Chris's basement studio down in Tribeca where they managed to survive a major flood of the Hudson River, followed by the destruction of the Twin Towers, which were only two blocks away. Now that I've written a memoir starting with my childhood, progressing through the years of Blondie almost to the present, I'm even more amazed.

I know some of the artwork is MIA and I'm hoping that more of it will emerge as I go through rediscovered boxes and files and whatever. My methods of preservation were at times pretty much catch-as-catch-can, so things turn up in unexpected places, like a series of surprise parties—which are always good for a little laugh. For many years I didn't travel with a road or wardrobe case, which in later years has been the most useful way to keep these artifacts intact and safe. Sometimes I even wondered why I was doing what I was doing except that I just did it. Now the fan art collection is giving an added meaning to the title of my book, *Face It . . . (cont.)*

June '7?

Captain Crunch: King of the Phone Phreaks

ALBERT GOLDMAN EATS TRASH

MURDER AT FLAMES
Original Mystery Serial

DOPE MANNERS
Were You Raised in a Barn?

Guide to Psychedelic Cacti

Furry Freak Bros. Look-Alike Contest

Swimsuits for the Nude Beach

YIPPIE DANA BEAL
On Not Having Nixon to Kick Around

All About Blondie

By Luca Petrecca

LE BLEU
COMA · ONE

HARRY

MERCURY
From
$5
A DAY
NEW
CARS
From
¢
MILE
PARK
Heather

4

SINGING TO A SILHOUETTE

Coincidence . . . Coincidence came calling for me big-time in the early seventies. Coincidence: it's supposed to mean just these random, disconnected events that concur or collide. But coincidence is not that at all. It's the stuff that's meant to be. Things that are supposed to be drawn together, as if by some extra earthly magnetic force. Things that connect and become woven and then shoot off to form previously unimagined combinations. Small changes that tumble into a fresh dynamic—as coincidence and chaos give birth to a new creation. Coincidence: the "divine intervener" that pushes us to make happen what was always supposed to happen . . .

Nineteen seventy-two. Well, I was still in New Jersey and living with house painter Mr. C, but I'd drive into the city for my social life. I missed the downtown scene that I had dropped out of for a while. Seeing bands was a good way to meet people and make connections. One of my favorite things was to go see the New York Dolls. They were so exciting to watch. They were a real rock band. Their influences were Marc Bolan, Eddie

Cochran, and many others, but they were so New York. They were straight but they dressed in drag, at a time when the cops were still raiding gay bars. They were ragged and raunchy and uninhibited, strutting, swaggering about in their tutus, leatherette, lipstick, and high heels.

The first time I saw them was at the Mercer Arts Center. A labyrinthine place with lots of different rooms, it was built as an annex to the much-neglected, ancient, and very run-down Broadway Central Hotel. It opened near the end of 1971 and closed less than two years later when the hotel actually collapsed, taking the arts center with it. But for that short time, it had its own scene that was fun, cool, and influential. Eric Emerson used to play there with his band the Magic Tramps. They were the first real glitter band in New York, very visually exciting. Their roadie and occasional bass player, who was Eric's roommate for a time, was a young guy from Brooklyn named Chris Stein. But we hadn't met each other yet.

I had a big crush on David Johansen, who I thought was just fantastic. I made it with him once. He shared an apartment with Diane Podlewski, who always came into Max's after midnight. They were the most interesting-looking people and just stood out; they were stunning. These were the night creatures and they fascinated me.

I can't remember how, but I became friends with the Dolls. Since almost nobody in downtown New York had a car, I would sometimes drive them around. I remember one time that the Dolls wanted to meet with Paramount's head of A & R, Marty Thau, who lived upstate, but they said they had no way to get there. My father had a huge turquoise Buick Century, so I borrowed it—this boat on wheels . . . I had the entire band and some of their girlfriends in the car—all so skinny, they were able to squeeze six across the backseat and four across the front.

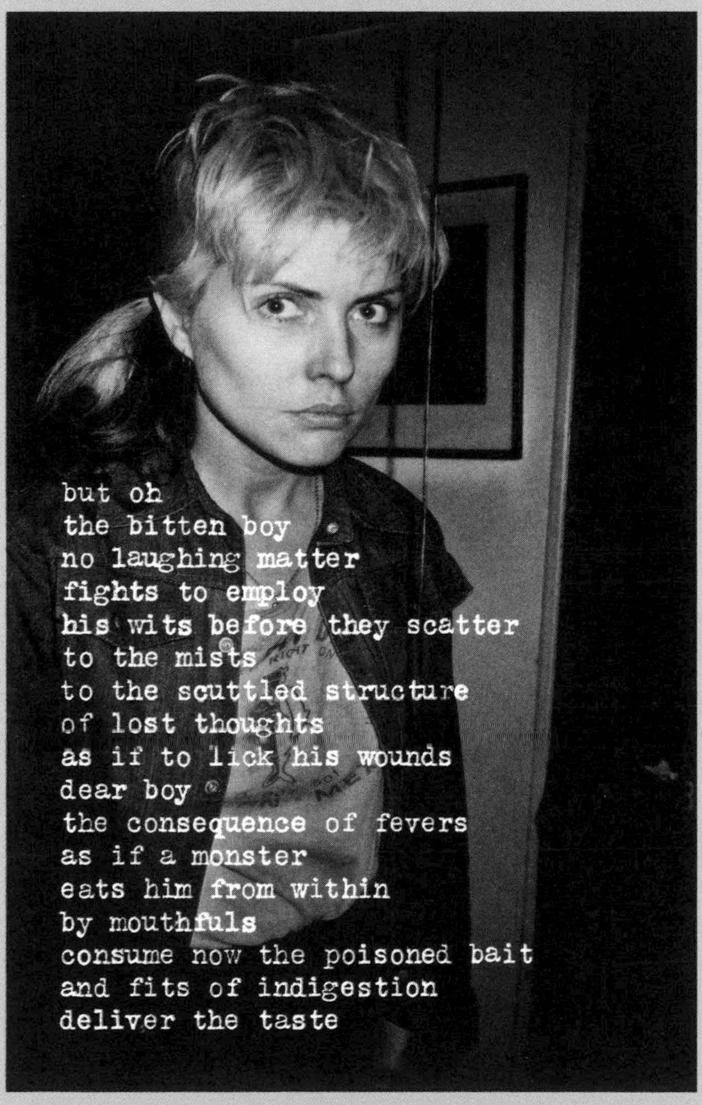
but oh
the bitten boy
no laughing matter
fights to employ
his wits before they scatter
to the mists
to the scuttled structure
of lost thoughts
as if to lick his wounds
dear boy
the consequence of fevers
as if a monster
eats him from within
by mouthfuls
consume now the poisoned bait
and fits of indigestion
deliver the taste

Well, the car broke down. My father had warned me not to use the AC, because the alternator regulator wasn't working. But it was a blazing-hot day. So I used the AC and the car went dead. So there we were, plomped at the side of the road—we didn't have cell phones in those days—when the police pulled up. When they saw all of us with the hair and the clothes and the makeup they didn't say a word. The car had to be towed and repaired. I don't know how I paid for it because I didn't have any money or a credit card. But somehow we got the car going again and I managed to get them to their meeting with Marty.

Turns out that trip was worth all the hassle. Shortly thereafter, Marty quit Paramount to become the Dolls' manager.

Mr. C did not like my disappearing to New York at all. He was one of the many people at that time who were afraid to go to New York City. Their idea of New York was that it was filthy and dangerous, full of no-go areas and rampant crime. There had been a massive white flight to the suburbs. Times Square belonged to the dealers and hookers; a trash-strewn Central Park was plagued by muggers and rats. The city couldn't pay its workers. No one with money would venture below Fourteenth Street. However the upside was all these abandoned buildings, which were a magnet for artists, musicians, and freaks. But I think what really pissed Mr. C off most about my going to the city was that I wasn't under his control.

I don't remember exactly how I met him—maybe at the health club where I was working. I was living in one room in a small rooming house and he said he could help me get a place in the garden apartment complex near where he was working. He had his own business painting buildings and two men working for him. He introduced me to the people in the office and I rented an apartment. It was nice, not fancy, but there were three rooms with a full bathroom. It was on the ground floor and the rooms had French windows that opened onto a small parking lot that was bordered with trees. I am a sucker for French windows. That's sort of how we became friends and then we started seeing each other. Sometimes I stayed at his place, but it got weird pretty quick. I think that he had been treated badly by other girlfriends, so he was extremely possessive and paranoid.

Every Sunday, I would go and see my paternal grandmother in Paterson. She lived alone now that both of her sons, my father and uncle, had moved so far away. My other grandparents had passed so I thought I should see her. One such Sunday, Mr. C followed me. He didn't believe that I was actually at my grandmother's. He barged into the house and there she was, my eighty-nine-year-old grandmother, a very well-mannered lady, saying, "Oh, Debbie, there's someone here for you." He sat there for a while and then he excused himself and left. Afterward he said to me, "You're a good girl, Debbie, you're a good girl." Who was this jerk? That was the end of that. I broke up with him. I tried to do it nicely, but it did no good at all. He called me day and night, at all hours, at home and at work. He came to Ricky and Johnny's, the hair salon where I was working, to curse and threaten me. He followed me home when I left. He was a violent and vitriolic man with a very hot temper. He also had weapons. I was sleepless and jittery and my nerves were shot. So I would drive to the city and see the Dolls because they were sexy and playful and so much fun.

I figure now that what attracted me so much to their shows was that I wanted to be just like them. In fact, I wanted to *be* them. I just didn't know exactly how to get it rolling. Because at that point there really weren't any girls doing what I wanted to do. There *were* girls of course—Ruby Lynn Reyner, Cherry Vanilla, Patti Smith (who was just doing poetry then)—but overall there weren't girls leading rock bands.

One night I went to see the Dolls play upstairs at Max's and there was this girl slouched down at one of the tables. Her name was Elda Gentile. She had a son with Eric Emerson and she lived with Sylvain Sylvain from the Dolls for a time. It really was an incestuous little scene. Elda said that she had a group—it wasn't a "band," she insisted that it was a "group"—called Pure Garbage that she had put together with Holly Woodlawn. Holly was another of Warhol's superstars, a glamorous transgender actress from Puerto Rico. She had starred in the movie *Trash*, along with Diane Podlewski and Joe Dallesandro, and she took over from Candy Darling in the Jackie Curtis play *Vain Victory*. Holly, Candy, and Jackie all had starring roles in Lou Reed's song "Walk on the Wild Side."

They were like living art, which seemed to be the whole concept at that time. Originally outcasts, the Holly Woodlawns, the Jackie Curtises, and the Candy Darlings were starting to claw their way aboveground, as was the whole gay/trans scene. At the core was Andy Warhol, making all those fantastic movies with Paul Morrissey. Plus there was Divine doing her off-Broadway plays; underground theater like the Theater of the Ridiculous; and the Cockettes, with Sylvester and the Angels of Light, showing up from San Francisco. All of these things popping at the same time—all interconnected and producing all kinds of creative combinations.

Well, I was really curious to see this group of Elda's, so I got her number. A week or so later, I called to ask when they were playing next. She said, "Oh, the group broke up." I saw my opportunity, saying, "Oh. Well let's form another group," and she said, "Okay, I'll call you." I waited a bit and called her again and this time she said, "Well I know another girl, Roseanne Ross, she might be available and the three of us can make a trio." "Great," I said.

Amanda, Elda, and me . . . Stillettos.

So, I started going back and forth to rehearsals and the Stilettoes began to take shape: three lead singers, all girls, and an all-male backup band. Musically, it was a real mishmash, a little bit campy show tune, a little bit girl group, a little bit R & B, and a little bit glitter rock; all of us were enamored of the Dolls. We were all very different characters too. Roseanne, who was into blues and R & B, was this Italian girl from Queens, a lesbian and a feminist, very angry at the way women were treated. Elda, who was into cabaret, was this intense, loud, wildly exploding personality. I was into more straight rock songs and I was God knows what at that point, but I was determined to figure it out. And at the very same time as this was going on, I was living in this nightmare because of my stalker and his endless bombardment of calls.

I came home to my apartment one night after working at the salon and I noticed something was off about the fucking French windows. The slider rods and locks were all broken so that the windows couldn't be closed or locked. I thought there had been a break-in but there was nothing missing. Somehow I got those damned windows closed and locked—being on the ground floor I had to—and I made sure all the other windows were locked as well. I was jittery and on edge, but after I settled down a little, I went into the back bedroom to watch TV.

That night Mr. C broke the bedroom window and jumped into the room so fast that I didn't have time to leap off the bed or call 911. When he burst through the window, his face was bright red and he had this twisted, crooked smile. He looked like one of those Japanese demon masks with the bared fangs and bulging eyes. And he had a handgun . . . My heart was hammering triple time—but the rest of time stood still. I felt as if the room was suspended in a thickness—time had congealed. He was waving the revolver at me and screaming, "Where is he, Debbie? Where is he?" I said, "There's no one here." He pulled open the closet door with such force that one of the hinges flew off the door frame. Then he rampaged through the other rooms, searching for the "other man." When he couldn't find anyone, he came back to the bedroom. He slapped me a few times, which scared me good enough, and then he sat on the bed for an hour or so, crouched up and menacing. At one point, he stuck the pistol against my cheek and tried to force himself on me. His threats had come to life.

When he finally left, he muttered that he would repair the windows the next day. I knew I had to get out—fast. I had been rehearsing and playing with the Stillettoes for a month or so by then and Roseanne said there was an apartment that was vacant above hers, on Thompson Street in Little Italy. So I rented it and got the hell out of Jersey, for the second time in my life. I still kept my day job at Ricky and Johnny's salon and I reverse-commuted every day from the city to New Jersey. But Mr. C kept on calling the salon, tying up their phone, or would show up there in person and harass me so much that my boss, Ricky, whom I knew from high school, said, "Look, if you don't get him to stop you're going to have to leave."

One day Mr. C found one of my phone bills with my New York City calls listed. He started calling Elda and the band and all my friends, threatening them to try to get them to tell him where I was. I went to the police in New Jersey and told them that I was being stalked and threatened. I told them that he had stolen my mail, which I thought was a federal offense. The police said that they could do nothing until he assaulted me and charges could be pressed. The nightmare just wouldn't end.

The Bobern Bar and Grill—named for its owners Bob and Bernie—was a dive on West Twenty-Eighth Street between and Sixth and Seventh in the wholesale flower market section of Manhattan. During the day the neighborhood bustled with trucks and vans but after six o'clock it became a ghost town, populated only by the illegals: aspiring painters, actors, and designers who had hunkered down in the "commercial" lofts above the flower-filled refrigerators. A little hotbed of creativity. The only drawback to living there was the four A.M. delivery hour. Those eighteen-wheelers kept their motors running so their cargo would stay refrigerated. Like the garbage trucks, they throbbed noisily and belched diesel fumes all over the surrounding plants.

Elda lived with her son Branch and with Holly Woodlawn, in one of those raw-space lofts. We rehearsed there and sometimes we would just fight; it's not easy being in an ensemble situation. Roseanne left and was replaced by Amanda Jones. Our backing band changed all the time, depending on who was available: Tommy and Jimmy Wynbrandt from the Miamis, Young Blood from the Magic Tramps, Marky Ramone, and Timothy Jackson, who called himself Tot, had blond curly hair, and always wore Egyptian eye makeup, the eye of Horus.

Eventually we got our shit together enough to play down the block at the Bobern. It was really more of a party with a very small ticket price at the door, because everyone who came was invited and knew each other. We played in the back of the bar where the pool table was. Holly Woodlawn did the lighting, standing on the bar, holding up a spotlight with a red gel as high as she could. I don't know how many people they fit into that space, between thirty and fifty maybe, but I was stiff with stage fright. I couldn't look at anyone in the audience. But there was this one guy whose face was in shadow, his head backlit. For some reason, I was totally comfortable delivering all of my songs to this person in semidarkness. I couldn't see him but I could feel him in the room, looking at me. It sounds crazy, singing songs to a silhouette, but I couldn't look anywhere else; I was drawn to him as if by a magnet, a real psychic connection.

After the show the three of us girls went to the "dressing room" in the stairwell, to hang out for a minute, and that's where I met Chris. Elda had invited him and he was there with his girlfriend Elvira, who at one time had been going out with Billy Murcia, the original drummer from the Dolls. Chris had long hair and kohl around his eyes and a sort of ripped-up glamour, a crossover from the glitter days of men in makeup and spandex, smelling of patchouli. His girlfriend looked very much the same but in a long dress. I probably looked like I came from some preppy suburban cocktail party in my long, silver-meshy V-neck sweater, white skirt, and short, pixie-cut brown hair. But it was pretty dark in that stairwell. Mostly I just looked at his incredible eyes.

Pretty soon after that—Chris says it was the next day—we had to replace one of our backup band and Chris came in to play bass. He didn't leave. This was the beginning of our musical relationship and of our friendship. I loved the way he played and moved and looked. He was very laid-back; we laughed at the same things and had fun together. He wasn't macho or possessive. But we were friends first. We took our time. After my last experience, I was determined to be independent. As my father used to say when I lived at home, "You are too goddamned independent." I still was, and now I was determined to remain so.

Mr. C still hadn't given up. He was being very aggressive. Well, I guess that all stalkers are by nature aggressive, but Mr. C was real good at it. He was tireless in his pursuit, calling everybody I knew. I wasn't so much scared as just exhausted by it. Then one night, when I was at Chris's apartment on First Street and First Avenue, his phone rang. It was Mr. C. Chris answered the phone and talked tough—I don't remember what he said, but once Mr. C heard a man's voice, he stopped calling me. At this time, Chris and I hadn't made it, but right after that we did. Then we kept on making it for thirteen years. I didn't think it could be done. But it was so easy.

The Stillettoes had a director, Tony Ingrassia. Bands don't usually have a theatrical director, but we did. Tony was an under- and aboveground theater director, as well as an actor and playwright. He staged Andy Warhol's *Pork* and he wrote and directed the play *Fame* on Broadway. He was connected to MainMan, David Bowie's management company, which had a multigenre approach that was way ahead of its time. Tony did a version of a Jackie Curtis play, *Vain Victory*, in which Elda and I both had parts, and Elda may have been in something else Tony did. Roseanne had gotten me the apartment in her building in Little Italy on Thompson Street and coincidentally, Tony lived on the top floor.

I think Tony got curious about what we were doing as he and Roseanne were friends and he may have invited himself along to a rehearsal. Next thing we knew, he was our musical director, image coordinator, choreographer, and much more. Tony insisted on full attention and dedication from us. He worked us like we were truant little girls from Catholic high school. A real slave driver; the whip was cracking.

Tony believed in and was an advocate of Method acting. The Method—used by some of my favorite actors, like Shelley Winters, Marlon Brando, James Dean, Julie Harris, Robert De Niro, Meryl Streep, Kate Winslet, Johnny Depp, and Daniel Day-Lewis, to name just a few—demanded an emotional and intellectual connection from the actor, not just a technical recitation. Our sessions with Tony were excruciating at times, because he forced us to repeat and repeat a song. This was tough on the vocal cords, but it pushed us to *deliver* the feelings in a lyric, like Brando screaming, "STELLA!!!" That's what he wanted and we worked hard to give it to him.

Now, I'm convinced that being trained as a Method singer was the best thing that could have happened to me—and worth all the sore throat muscles. When you sing someone else's

Joan Jett and me. Original girls of the underworld.

song, the Method gives you the edge over a performance that is strictly technical. Technique, however good, will only take you so far. The Method helps you transcend mere technique. The notorious character that was Tony entertained us endlessly and gave us so much that was important. Tony, a larger-than-life person in every way, died of cardiac arrest at the age of fifty-one. Wherever you are now, Tony, XXX.

We played a bunch of local gigs, downtown bars, all very small-time. We made no money, but it was so much fun. We played a lot of different covers and we had some of our own songs that Elda wrote kitschy lyrics for—"Dracula, What Did You Do to My Mother?" and "Wednesday Panties." We had the most decrepit equipment and the coolest, most fucked-up crowds. Part of the Holly contingency and all the people Eric Emerson knew, which was everybody on the scene. We played at Club 82, the famous drag bar on East Fourth Street, between Second Avenue and the Bowery. It was run by a lesbian couple, Butch and Tommy, but it still had that underworld glamour it had in the fifties, when it was rumored to be run by the Mafia and all the celebrities went there. There was lots of dark wood and booths and mirrored walls and signed eight-by-ten black-and-white photos of Abbott and Costello and others from the showbiz gallery of rogues. I remember David Bowie coming to one of our shows there with his wife Angie.

We opened for Television at CBGB's. Marty Thau, the Dolls' manager, was there one of those nights and told somebody that he was struck by my looks, but that I seemed kind of quiet onstage. My role in the group was to be the relatively reasonable one and to calm things down, which I guess showed up as "quiet" onstage. This was one of the things I learned to grow out of, as time went on. But, as with most bands, there comes that critical flashpoint of disagreement where it just can't be resolved. Chris and I quit the band. I still wanted to do what the

Dolls were doing but I couldn't have if it wasn't for Chris. We formed a respectful, psychic, trusting partnership and a great understanding for each other. We had similar tastes, and where our tastes differed, we usually found a way for those divergencies to mesh in a creative way.

When we left the Stillettoes, Fred Smith and Billy O'Connor, the bass player and drummer, came with us. A few weeks later we played our first show as Angel and the Snake. The name came from a picture Chris saw in a magazine of a girl with a snake that he thought looked vaguely like me. We opened for the Ramones at CBGB's. Three weeks later we were back at CBGB's with the Ramones, playing our second show. It turned out to be Angel and the Snake's last show. After that we became Blondie and the Banzai Babies.

I don't remember which of us came up with "Banzai Babies": Chris and I were both into Japanese pop culture. "Blondie"—well, I had been bleaching my hair again and when I walked down the street the construction guys and truck drivers would yell, "Hey, Blondie!" There was a famous comic strip character from the thirties named Blondie, a flapper—the dumb blonde who turns out to be smarter than the rest of them. Okay, I could play with that role onstage, it was a good start. But really there was no grand scheme behind anything. We just did what we liked to do and everything was just inching forward.

In the beginning we had backup singers, Julie and Jackie, all three of us blondes until Jackie dyed her hair brown. That didn't work out, so we brought in Tish and Snooky Bellomo, a duo I saw perform at the Amato Opera House across from CBGB's. They were one of the acts in this wacky vaudeville show called the Palm Casino Review, with drag queens and theatrical misfits. Gorilla Rose and Tomata du Plenty of the Screamers, who opened for us on occasion, introduced us. I asked the girls if they wanted to come to our rehearsal and sing with us. Because they were sisters their harmonies were terrific and I loved their hair and clothes, so I thought we could join forces.

Tish and Snooky had a storefront on St. Mark's Place between Second and Third that would later be known as Manic Panic. They'd buy old dresses from the forties and fifties that were tied up in enormous rag bundles of clothing, get them delivered, and throw them on the floor, these big piles of clothes, and people would come in and search through. None of us had any money so we only bought clothes secondhand, the sexiest and most outrageous possible. I remember one time Tish and Snooky came in with three pairs of jodhpurs, these riding pants they found in a thrift shop in the Bronx, so we all wore those onstage. Other times we might be very glam with long dresses, stilettos, and fur stoles. There were all sorts of costume changes and props.

We did noisy girl-group rock with three-part harmonies like the Shangri-Las' "Out in the Streets." We covered the Beach Boys' "Fun Fun Fun," with the girls in prom dresses that we tore off at the end of the song, to reveal the vintage bathing suits we were wearing underneath. We did our own kind of rock take on disco songs, like Labelle's "Lady Marmalade." My idea was to bring dancing back to rock. That was important to me, just moving to music, and when it first began, rock 'n' roll was all about dancing. We had great dances in the little town that I grew up in and I really loved going to them. If you grew up on AM radio, they played music to dance to, but then FM came along and it wasn't cool to dance to rock anymore, at least not in New York City. And hardly anyone in the midseventies was doing that kind of retro thing we were doing. We put our own downtown spin on it that made it a kind of crossover between glitter-glam and punk. Chris and I wrote some songs, "Platinum Blonde," "Rip Her to Shreds," "Little Girl Lies," "Giant Bats from Space." Later, the bats turned into giant ants.

We played all over—CBGB's and the Performance Studio, Max's, and White's, where I was working as a barmaid. A lot of straight businessmen would go to White's to drink after work, and one time in the middle of a song we got a conga line going and all the suits joined it. We played a place uptown called Brandi's and got the Ramones to open for us. But the guys who ran the place hated the Ramones. When they started singing "Now I Wanna Sniff Some Glue" they told them to leave and never come back. They liked us because we were cute girls—harmless. Ha!

We just kept on playing and experimenting. After a while, we just called ourselves Blondie.

5

BORN TO BE PUNK

Memory, what did you do to the fun times? Really, the first seven years of Blondie felt insane. Total madness. But I keep thinking there must have been some good times. Feels like I'm always remembering the hard times. I can't for the life of me think of any funny experiences. Have I always been so fucking serious? When we used to go out, I know we laughed a lot. What were we laughing at? What were the funny times? Maybe I'm just demented and the horror stories are more entertaining for me. I have plenty more horror stories to tell—and I will tell them—but I'm going to try real hard to dig out some funny stuff. Early Blondie was such a storm of crossfire emotions that it's hard for me to find the fun. Maybe it's like the King of Comedy said, you just take all the terribly serious and dreadful stories and make *them* funny.

I was happy when we were stepping out around the Lower East Side, so innocent in a way, just trying to put things together. It was always a trip to play at CBGB's. At last call, all the musicians would pack up their instruments and head outside into the sweetness of the city changing from night back into day. That Manhattan breeze would begin to pick up, a breath of fresh air. One night, Chris and I blew into a bodega for milk and cookies. After the bodega, we strolled the two blocks back to the rent-controlled apartment that Chris had on First and First.

As we reached the front door that night, a dude—normally I never use this word, but in this case it fits so perfectly—came up from behind us with a knife. He looked a lot like Jimi Hendrix, very stylish and cool, dressed in a full-length leather coat. His pinned, hard eyes looked very serious. He wanted money; what else? Of course, we were broke after the milk and cookies. Chris did have his guitar, a Fender, which he had carved into a sort of horned demon shape. It was very pretty, honey colored and curvaceous. Fred Smith's guitar, a dark black-red Gibson SG that Chris had borrowed, was inside the apartment also. "Jimi" wanted more than what we had on us and insisted on coming in with us. He asked us for drugs and Chris said there was some acid in the freezer. But this "Jimi" was no acid freak and ignored that particular offer. Chris's friend Walter was passed out in the loft bed and our guest even tried to shake something out of him, but it was useless. Walter just mumbled a few words and rolled over.

"Jimi" used a pair of old pantyhose to tie Chris to the post that held up the loft bed—and used a scarf to tie my wrists behind my back. Told me to lie down on the mattress. He didn't bother with snoring Walter . . . Then he poked around searching for anything worth anything. He piled up the guitars and Chris's camera and then he untied my hands and told me to take off my pants. He fucked me. And then he said, "Go clean yourself," and left. "'Jimi' has left the building."

And we were feeling so good after our show that night. A delicious feeling of satisfaction mixed with flirtation. Then *whack!* An adrenaline rush with a knife at the end of it. I can't say that I felt a lot of fear. I'm very glad this happened pre-AIDS or I might have freaked. In the end, the stolen guitars hurt me more than the rape. I mean, we had *no* equipment. Chris had this tiny little amp that picked up the police radio signal and a bunch of white noise. Then other bands kept stealing our musicians too. Looking back, it seems absurd that we ever made it to be famous.

The scene was starting to change. Patti Smith and the Ramones both had record deals and there was more than one label sniffing around Television. Blondie had become a recognizable name in some small way but nobody in the music business was looking at us. Chris was on welfare, I was a bikini bartender in the financial district, and we occasionally sold some pot to make a few bucks. At this point Blondie was an underdog, way down at the bottom of the heap. There were times I felt, *What's the point, it's just too hopeless*. But we had a patron saint for a while named Mark Pines, a man-about-downtown who had a loft on East Eleventh Street, where our drummer Billy O'Connor rented a room. Mike would let us play in the loft, which had a few amps and other assorted equipment. That made our life a lot easier.

Billy O'Connor had been our drummer since Tot, the drummer with the eye of Horus makeup, quit the Stillettoes. Billy was a nice guy from Pittsburgh, very likeable and easygoing, and he came with his own set of drums. His family wanted him to stay in med school. Like so many teenagers, he wanted to taste freedom, break out, and bang hard for a bigger life. Naturally, he was under a lot of pressure to continue his education. He was conflicted, and the drinking and the pill-popping overcame him. Sometimes he would be semiconscious. He finally passed out backstage right before a gig. That night Jerry Nolan from the Dolls sat in and saved us. And after that Billy left to go back to college. It was too bad really, he was so sweet natured. As with myself, you usually quit drugs—or you don't quit drugs and you burn your last bridge. Years later we reunited and we would see him every time we played Pittsburgh.

But we really had to find a replacement. So, we put an ad in the *Village Voice,* "Freak energy rock drummer wanted." We got a bigger response than we expected: fifty drummers. We auditioned them all one Saturday in the rehearsal space we shared with the Marbles, another band that we sometimes played with. As with many commercial spaces, after the workday, the heat was turned down. It was way up on the fifteenth floor of an industrial building in the Garment District, mostly occupied by furriers and companies that made leather goods. All these drummers were coming in and out of the elevator, a big confusion of players and imposters. Well, finally we got to drummer number fifty: Clem Burke. No shit, he was our last tryout, and he was the one. He looked good and he could play. Our favorite part-time postal worker became Blondie's new drummer and the rest is history.

One strange thing that day was Patti Smith's showing up. She sauntered into the room with one of her band and proceeded to audition Clem. She was very aggressive. After Clem played, she declared that he was too wild, too loud, generally just too *too,* and then she left. What nerve, showing up at our auditions like that. I guess she was just too curious to know what we were up to. You know, the competition. Not that we were very much of a threat at the time—or ever for that matter.

One night, after business hours, when we were allowed to make noise, we went back to our room with Clem to rehearse. But we couldn't get the elevator to work. It was stuck on the ninth floor. We needed to get to the fifteenth. We shouted up the stairwell but there was no answer, so eventually we had to start climbing. Stairs in New York City are not one-floor affairs.

I've been climbing tenement staircases of six or seven stories in downtown lofts and apartment buildings for all the years I've lived here. Old, dried-out, creaking steps worn smooth by generations of immigrants trudging to work in the sweatshops. Inhaling a century's worth of dust-filled sediment in unventilated, mostly windowless shafts. This stairwell was equally airless and dark and thick with dust—but we kept going. Clem is a big guy with lots of energy, but he hates any physical labor other than playing drums. "This blows!" was his usual expletive when he had to set up his own drum kit or move instruments into a club or rehearsal. "This blows!" "This blows!" "This blows!" rang out loudly, floor by floor, in the echo chamber of the giant stairwell. Clem.

At the eighth or ninth floor we started hearing voices and shouted out for them to finish up so that we could use the elevator. There was no response, so we kept climbing, getting madder than ever. By this time, there were a lot more sounds coming from below—like they were moving stuff—and we started yelling into the stairwell, cursing them out for holding the elevator. A mean, tough-guy voice cursed back at us—something out of central casting. He seemed more than serious. Sufficiently intimidated, we went back to pulling ourselves up those stairs on the railings, our lungs and tempers burning. Well, the next day we'd find out that they *were* serious. They were professional fur thieves, filling the elevator with furs and leather coats, doing their job while we were trying to do ours.

Caught in the airless vacuum of a time tunnel, I suddenly remembered that I had also met Chris in a different dusty stairwell. Clem's first show with Blondie was also Fred Smith's last gig with us. We were at CBGB's playing with the Marbles; Tom Verlaine and everybody were in the audience. And then in between sets, Fred announced that he was leaving us to join Television. We were struck dumb. It was so disheartening-

Taking off in Glastonbury, 2014.

ing. I might have thrown it in then if it weren't for Clem. He was so enthusiastic, a real cheerleader. He would keep calling us up and asking when we were going to rehearse. He pushed us really hard and kept us going. One day he brought some friends from New Jersey to the rehearsal. There was a poet called Ronnie Toast, who got his name after he set fire to his dad's suit because he was pissed at him—and the whole house went up in flames. Ronnie had been sent to the nuthouse for a while. Clem also brought along a young, very good-looking kid named Gary Lachman. Gary was one of those people who looked like he ought to be in a rock band. So, we brought him in on bass, though he had never played bass before—although he had played a guitar. His first show with us was another show at CBGB's. "Lachman" became "Valentine."

CBGB's, at 315 Bowery, has become a legend, but in those days it was a dive bar on the ground floor of one of the many flophouses that lined the avenue. The Hells Angels lived on Third Street, so it became a biker bar. In 1973 Hilly Kristal, who ran the place, named it CBGB/OMFUG, which stood for "Country, Bluegrass, Blues and Other Music for Uplifting Gormandizers." Hilly was a big, slow-talking hippie. Apparently, he had grown up on a chicken farm and he thought that country music was going to be huge. He often wore a plaid shirt and had a thick beard and this big mop of untamed hair. Then Hilly decided to give the local "street bands," as he called them, a try. He would say things like, "These kids have something to say and we should listen." CBGB's was still a pit, but it was our pit.

It's amazing to go there now because it's a different planet. The club has become a clothing store owned by John Varvatos and the old CBGB's awning is in the Rock and Roll Hall of Fame. John has kept the style of the original awning, but it's black now rather than white. When we were first there, it was mostly derelict stores and flophouses and a pizza parlor across the road. There was an alley at the back of the club full of rubbish, rats, pissed-on garbage, and shards of broken glass. Inside, the club had its own special reek—a pungent compound of stale beer, cigarette smoke, dog shit, and body odor. Hilly's dog Jonathan had full run of the place and would wander about, relieving itself whenever and wherever. In one corner we jokingly called "the kitchen," a large pot of chili simmered away at all times—adding its own fragrance to the bar's heady mix. The bathroom—well, I read somewhere that Chris and I made out in the bathroom; we may have, but not all the way, for good reason. Chris did manage to capture the "mystique" of the CBGB's bathroom in some great photos.

The club had a bar, a jukebox, a pool table, a phone booth, and a big bookshelf full of books, most of them beat poetry, which Hilly was into. Once you walked past the long bar, there were a few tables and chairs and a small, low stage. The stage was tiered so that the singer was out front at the bottom, the band was in the middle, and the drummer sat perched above on a tiny platform. We played CBGB's every weekend for seven months straight. We didn't make money; we got paid in beers. You were lucky if they were charging two dollars at the door. And Hilly was big hearted, always letting people in for free. Later on, when Roberta Bayley ran the door, things did get a little bit more professional.

The crowd was almost all our friends, all the other bands and all the downtown artists and freaks. Like Tomata du Plenty, Gorilla Rose, and Fayette Hauser, and later Arturo Vega appeared. He would always show up wearing a Mexican wrestler's mask and for months no one knew who he was. Arturo was an artist and his loft was around the corner. Later he became the Ramones' artistic director, logo designer, T-shirt salesman, and lighting man. Dee Dee and Joey Ramone shared his loft. It was an immediate, smaller, tighter, more private world then. It was a time of felt experience—no special effects, just raw, visceral, uncut living. No voyeuristic secondhand selfies being beamed out on the Internet. No cell-phone junkies trading endless texts instead of direct, face-to-face contact. No insistent press trying to video and photo your every move or misstep . . .

One of my favorite people from that scene was Anya Phillips. She was a fascinating woman, part Chinese, part English, beautiful, and always provocatively dressed. Multitalented and multifaceted, Anya could go from a hard-nosed business meeting to a strip job on Times Square. She took me there once and said, "Just sit over here in the audience," and I watched as she did her strip. Anya was very outspoken, as you would expect from a dominatrix, and a creative force. She started going out with James Chance—James White—and she managed his band the Contortions. Anya shared an apartment with Sylvia Morales, who at one time was married to Lou Reed. Since there really weren't many of us girls on the scene, we all knew each other.

Iggy Pop apparently described me once as "Barbarella on speed." Barbarella was a comic-book character from the future, where people didn't fuck anymore, a sexual innocent who gets sent on a mission to save the planet and along the way learns the joys of sex. The director of *Barbarella,* Roger Vadim, was a big fan of comic books, as were we. Our band shared its name with a cartoon character, after all. And I was playing at being a cartoon fantasy onstage. But the mother of that character was really Marilyn Monroe. From the first time I set eyes on Marilyn, I thought she was just wonderful. On the silver screen, her lovely skin and platinum hair were luminescent and fantastic. I loved the fantasy of it. In the fifties, when I grew up, Marilyn was an enormous star, but there was such a double standard. The fact that she was such a hot number meant that many middle-class women looked down on her as a slut. And since the publicity machine behind her sold her as a sex idol, she wasn't valued as a comedic actor or given credit for her talent. I never felt that way about her, obviously. I felt that Marilyn was also playing a character, the proverbial dumb blonde with the little-girl voice and big-girl body, and that there was a lot of smarts behind the act. My character in Blondie was partly a visual homage to Marilyn, and partly a statement about the good old double standard.

The "Blondie" character I created was sort of androgynous. More and more lately, I've been thinking that I was probably portraying some kind of transsexual creature. Even when I was singing songs that were written from a man's point of view—"Maria" for example, a Catholic schoolboy lusting after this unattainable virgin girl—I had to be kind of gender-neutral, so it seemed that *I* wanted Maria. A lot of my drag queen friends have said to me, "Oh, you were definitely a drag queen." They didn't have problems seeing it. It was the same thing with Marilyn really. She was a woman playing a man's idea of a woman.

Rock, like I said, was a very masculine business in the mid-seventies. Patti dressed more masculine. Though deep down I guess we came from a similar place, my approach was different. In many ways, you might say that what I did was more challenging. To be an artistic, assertive woman in girl drag, not boy drag, was then an act of transgression. I was playing up the idea of being a very feminine woman while fronting a male rock band in a highly macho game. I was saying things in the songs that female singers really didn't say back then. I wasn't submissive or begging him to come back, I was kicking his ass, kicking him out, kicking my own ass too. My Blondie character was an inflatable doll but with a dark, provocative, aggressive side. I was playing it up yet I was very serious.

At first, I can't remember there being a lot of competitiveness at CBGB's but there were different camps: the "art/intellectual people" and the "pop/rock people." We definitely

1996. Hi, Joey.

had more of a pop sensibility in that we loved melodies and songs. But the subject matter of our songs was somewhat subversive. We felt that we were bohemians and performance artists, avant-garde. And when you add to the mix this very New York DIY street-rock attitude that we had, you got punk. Nobody was called punk yet. There was no one at CBGB's wearing T-shirts that said "punk." But I was a punk. I still am.

Then came a magazine called *Punk* that began in 1975. John Holmstrom and Legs McNeil. They pulled this brilliant PR stunt, putting up these flyers that just said, "Punk is coming." They papered them all over. Everyone was saying, "What is this? What's punk and what's coming?" Buzz creation, before buzz creation was called that. And then the magazine appeared, which was just fabulous—nasty and irreverent and sick. We loved it. They took the word and branded it and developed the brand around this small scene. There wasn't really a particular sound you could define as punk until much later on—because at first there were many different styles. But I think the universal thread was that we were pointing out the inconsistencies in a hypocritical society and the foibles of human nature and what a joke it all was. A kind of big Dadaist up-yours. Most everybody was writing songs that satirized something.

The New York punk scene didn't have one particular look either. When Blondie started, the guys all had long hair. Chris had very long, black hair and wore black eye makeup. Clem had long, black, wavy locks and he wore a black leather jacket, jeans, and high-tops. When we got to know Clem better, we found out he was a "Deadhead." He was obsessed with rock. His house in Bayonne, New Jersey, had rooms filled right to the ceiling with music magazines like *NME, Crawdaddy, Creem, Teen Beat, Rave, Let It Rock, Rock Scene, Rolling Stone, Jamming, One Two Testing, Dark Star, Bucketfull of Brains,* and *Zigzag*. It's a wonder the place didn't burn down. As for my "punk bombshell" look, old movie stars were the influence, but it developed from buying clothes at secondhand stores or finding things people threw out on the street—then trying it all, mixing it up, and seeing what worked. The famous zebra-striped minidress that Chris took a photo of me wearing and sent to *Creem* magazine? That was a pillowcase that our landlord Benton found in the trash and I made into a dress.

In the early to midseventies, the thrift stores still had all those great pre-hippie sixties clothes. You could walk in, and for almost nothing, you could come out with a mod suit or a spangled minidress and straight-legged pants. No bell-bottoms. I was done with bell-bottoms. We were all fashion conscious, of course. Everyone in Blondie favored the mod look and it was easily available. And we all loved to shop. I think it might have been Gary who was the first in the band to cut his hair, but then they all did. Everything sort of gelled. I really think there was a certain amount of serendipity to the whole business. None of it was thought out other than a synchronistic sense of style and preference. People today who want to make a living at rock 'n' roll seem a lot saner about things. It's a subject taught in school—a totally different frame of reference. We were just in this isolated bubble of economic depression in New York that was artistically so strong. We had to be artistically strong and we didn't think about making long-range plans, only surviving.

There was a garbage strike in the summer of '75. New York City was about to go bankrupt. Tons of trash rotted in the sun and the city stank. Kids would set piles of trash on fire, then open the hydrants so that all the flotsam ran down the streets. Blondie was playing that whole summer, doing shows with Television, the Miamis, the Marbles, and the Ramones. The Ramones were a great band and seriously funny. Sometimes, in the early days, they would stop and have a fight with each other about something in the middle of a song, even though

the songs were so short. Hilly's wife, Karen, would often walk by the stage at CBGB's holding her ears when they played and scream at them to turn it down. We became close friends with the Ramones right up to a terribly sad end.

We left our apartment after we were broken into for the third time. Little Italy really was full-on Italian then, very *Mean Streets,* and one day I saw these big guys beating up a black kid who was running down the street. I made a real scene about it and Chris thought they were going to murder us. That was when the trouble began. We were invited by Benton Quinn to move into his loft, at 266 Bowery, just down the street from CBGB's. It's still there and still pretty beat-up. Benton was a flamboyant character much like the androgynous Turner character played by Mick Jagger in the movie *Performance.* He had an elegant, ethereal, otherworldly feel about him, like someone

Early Blondie, CBGB's.

out of a Pre-Raphaelite painting. Originally from Tennessee, Benton carried himself with an aristocratic Southern grace.

We had use of the first floor. There was a shared bathroom and kitchen on our floor, Benton lived on the second floor, and the top floor was uninsulated and semi-derelict. Stephen Sprouse moved into that space later with a hot plate. Stephen was a designer and a child prodigy. He had been discovered by Norman Norell, who designed for Gloria Swanson, the silent-movie star. After Stephen won a competition for new designers sponsored by Norell, his father had to bring him into New York because Stephen was only fourteen years old. When Stephen moved into the Bowery building, he was working for Halston and was already considered an up-and-comer. At the same time, he was doing his own designs. I was always cutting up clothes and putting things together, and to be honest, I think he only started working with me because he was disgusted with the way I looked! He just said, "Do this, do this, do this," and it was so good.

There was a liquor store on the ground floor of the building. It was *the* liquor store for the Bowery, so there was always a lot of traffic. The customers would use our doorway as a bathroom and the smell of piss wafted up into our loft. One day we found a dead wino on the sidewalk down the street. There was always something dead out there, rats or winos. But on the upside, it was great having all that raw open space where we could play.

Next to the fireplace was a life-sized statue of Mother Cabrini that Chris had bought in a junk store. She had glass eyes that someone had painted over and Chris had scraped off the paint, which made her even creepier. Dee Dee Ramone was spooked by that statue. He stabbed it a couple of times so there were a couple of holes in it. Our building used to be a doll factory employing child labor supposedly. I'm psychic and I definitely felt there were presences there—but we all felt things were a little wonky. There were poltergeists. Pipes kept breaking, things would fall down, shit kept happening all the time. Three of us, me, Chris, and Howie, were trying to light the fire one night. It was full of paper and wood and should have gone right up, but it just wouldn't light. Eventually, we gave up trying. We stood back and then suddenly the fireplace burst into flame. We all were shocked into silence.

One time, Gary, who was staying with us, almost got fried. He said almost doesn't count but I disagree. Chris walked in on Gary as he was clutching this lamp in a kind of electrical spastic paralysis. Chris knocked it out of his hand, just in time. Saved him. And on another night, over the weekend, we all nearly died. Down in the basement of the liquor store there was the oil burner. The water pump was broken, so you had to fill it with water by hand or else the flame would go out and the boiler would just pump fumes and smoke through the system. On this night, the guy in the store forgot to put water in and the boiler's flame did go out. Toxic smoke and fumes flooded our apartment. We were asleep. It was the cats that woke us up, pawing at our faces. We reeled around in a stupor, our noses plugged with black soot. We couldn't talk properly because our throats felt like sandpaper. We threw open the windows to clear out all the gunk. We froze our asses off, but better that than dead. Those cats saved our lives. Service animals didn't exist then, but these three kitties were our heroes and qualified for medals of recognition.

That summer was when we made our first-ever recording, a demo. There was another new magazine on the scene, the *New York Rocker,* whose editor Alan Betrock was an early champion of Blondie. He put us in the magazine and said he wanted to help us out. Somehow or other we wound up in Queens, recording a demo in the basement of a house belonging to the parents of a friend of Alan's. Alan said he was going to give it to Ellie Greenwich, whom he had some kind of connection with. Ellie Greenwich was one of the great Brill Building songwriters. She'd written hits for the Ronettes, the Crystals, and the Shangri-Las. I loved them all, especially the Shangri-Las. It wasn't just us; the Ramones and Johnny Thunders loved them too. They were a real touchstone. One of the songs we'd always done live was the Shangri-Las' "Out in the Streets." Now we were recording it in this humid, steaming basement, on a little four-track. The humidity was so high we couldn't keep the guitars in tune.

We also recorded our own songs, "Thin Line," "Puerto Rico," "The Disco Song" (which was an early version of "Heart of Glass"), and "Platinum Blonde," which was the first song I ever wrote. Alan took the tape around to some record companies and journalists, but nothing came of it. We were always asking Alan for the tape because he wasn't doing anything with it. And as soon as we got some money we said we would buy it from him. He didn't want to part with it though and said he wasn't planning to release it. Four years later he put it out on an independent label and we were surprised he released these early versions without telling us, but it was cool.

In the fall of '75 we had a new band member, Jimmy Destri. We had been talking about maybe getting a keyboard player, and a young photographer/musician friend of ours, Paul Zone, introduced us to Jimmy—who worked at the time in the ER at Maimonides Medical Center in Brooklyn. More important, he knew who we were, he'd seen us play, and he owned a Farfisa organ. He had been playing with the band Milk 'n' Cookies before they had gone to England to make an album and left him behind. After Jimmy joined Blondie, one of the first things we did together was a Jackie Curtis play, *Vain Victory*. Tony Ingrassia was the director. It was the first time we'd worked with Tony since the Stillettoes, so it was a reunion. It was a fun thing to do; it ran for a few weekends and we got some good audiences. I had the role of Juicy Lucy, a chorus girl on a cruise ship, and the band played the music. Playing a part made me feel comfortable and with the band more solid at last, I was realizing that the part I liked most was the one I played with Blondie. Then, over time, little by little, it started to become more personal.

BLONDIE

6

CLOSE CALLS

Driving—and my car—played quite a role for me in the early days of New York. My mom had given me a blue '67 Camaro, a stick shift that she couldn't drive anymore, because she was in very bad pain from osteoporosis. I loved having a car in the city, though to keep it on the street was a nerve-wracking pain in the ass. For a while, we found a construction site down on Greenwich Street in what's now TriBeCa that didn't have No Parking signs and we would just leave the car down there. But that couldn't last forever, so I'd be back up at the crack of dawn on street-cleaning days, to switch sides when the cleaning truck came. But the Camaro was a perfect refuge, a great place to get away from everyone—to have some peace and quiet. On my own in the car, I would think of lyrics as I watched for the street cleaner in the rearview mirror.

That car hauled around a lot of people and gear before it finally died. Sometimes we would pile in and go to Coney Island. I loved the place. It was magical when I was a kid and Coney had begun its decline. There were all those great old rides like the

Steeplechase, which was a crazy simulated horse race—and the 262-foot parachute jump that they'd bought from the 1939 World's Fair. As a thrill seeker, an adrenaline-craving idiot, I loved those rides and had I grown up in a different environment, I imagine I might have become a stunt girl, an astronaut, or a race car driver. I drive fast and I drive well, though these days I have to sometimes talk myself down off the ledge—"What are you trying to prove? Take it easy, drive nicely."

But even when the old rides vanished and Coney became dilapidated, the magic lingered. Perhaps it became even more magical—with the ghosts and remnants of rides, carnies, freaks, and boardwalk oddities. It was also a good place to buy secondhand stuff. There was a strip of garages in a burned-out area sort of across the street at the Wonder Wheel end that had people selling cool things for almost nothing. Which was good because nothing is what we had, aside from youth, desire, love, and music.

One of the thousands of things I love about Chris—and one of my favorite visual memories—is the way he rode shotgun while I drove. He was a quiet passenger, for the most part. He didn't drive yet—like a lot of native New Yorkers who never needed to learn—so he would sit in a trancelike state, absorbed in his thoughts, as he watched the scenery go by. An auto-Zen reverie.

Chris and I would drive to Brooklyn fairly often to visit his mother, Stel. She was a sort of beat painter and lived in one of those great apartments on Ocean Avenue, with large rooms done in a mixture of texture and color in an artistic, lived-in style. Stel always cooked hamburger and kasha for us with loads of garlic and we ate it like greedy pigs. It was usually the best and sometimes the only real meal we'd have the whole week. Gary Valentine came with us one night. He was living with us in our Bowery loft, because he had been run out of Jersey on a paternity rap. After dinner, when we left for the city, it was raining really hard, a blinding rain, a downpour.

My little Camaro wasn't in the best shape. The distributor cap was cracked and moisture would sometimes turn the car off, so I was kind of nervous about all the rain beating down on us. As we headed down a ramp on the BQE, blinded by the storm, I drove directly into a small lake. The water flew up high above us. Momentum carried the car about fifty feet, then it stopped dead, luckily right under an overpass. We knew we were in a terrible position as we climbed out to stand in the road. We pressed ourselves as flat as we could against the wall, expecting at any moment to be crushed by some blinded vehicle. Then I remembered the flares. On one of the family holidays in Denville, New Jersey, with my father's brother Tom, he insisted that I needed some emergency flares for the car. Okay, it couldn't hurt, maybe someday I'd need them. This was that day.

We grabbed the flares and set them up behind the car and waited; sometimes if you waited a bit, the Camaro would dry out and start up again. But we just kept on waiting. Oddly, there were no cars coming down the ramp. No cars at all. We had heard a very loud noise above us up on the ramp. We knew it had to be an accident. As the visibility cleared, we could see a jackknifed eighteen-wheeler on the ramp we'd just come down. The trailer part of the truck was wedged between the guardrails on either side of the road and the cab was bent into an L, forming a complete roadblock. The truck that had been right behind us—and that might have killed us—instead saved our lives. We stood under the overpass waiting for the storm to go by, knowing how unbelievably lucky we were. We got awfully quiet.

Makes me think about some other close calls . . . Other than the one we all share in common, birth. Ha, birth! Squeezed out into harsh bright light, half strangled, dragged down by gravity, deafened by the noise, held upside down by the ankles, slapped on the butt, throat scalded from the first sudden gulps of oxygen . . . A shocking, hazardous, and sometimes terminal event. Death gives us a wakeup call with our very first breath—sort of a reminder of who's the boss. Once I had survived my near-death birth and whatever trauma came from the adoption, my life as a small child was plain sailing. Okay, there was the coma from having pneumonia and there was falling off a trapeze onto my head—but that was really all she wrote. So, other than my obsessive, gun-toting boyfriend in New Jersey, things had seemed pretty safe until I moved into the soon-to-be-bankrupt city of New York in the late sixties and the seventies.

I'm sure I don't have all my experiences on tap, but I remember one from the time when I worked at the Head Shop on East Ninth Street. When I finished work, I walked the half block to Ben's storefront apartment. That famous old TV ad was running through my head: "It's ten P.M. Do you know where your children are?" So, it might have been that time of night . . . I was always cautious and kept an eye on whoever was behind me. In those days we all watched our backs. Ben's door had a tricky lock. Sometimes you had to jiggle it around before it would open, and I was thinking about the lock when I got to the shallow inset of the doorway that night. I had the key ready and this time it opened so easily, I smiled to myself as I slipped inside quickly and shut and locked the door behind me. Just as I did, I heard a man right on the other side of the door, sighing in frustrated anger. It jolted my heart. He had been right behind me, just seconds away from grabbing me.

There was another time on St. Mark's Place and Avenue A when I had a run-in with a couple of street kids. I'd been working uptown for the BBC, so my usual evening trip was to walk back from the Lexington Avenue subway stop at Astor Place. One of the things I wanted back then was a bag from a leather store on West Fourth Street that all the hippie downtowners loved because their bags and shoes were so beautifully designed. I eventually bought myself a shoulder bag—like a smaller version of a mail sack but with large metal rings and made out of thick cowhide. That night, when I got to the last block at St. Mark's Place, the bag hanging on my shoulder, two kids came running and in a flash I was down on the sidewalk, flat on my back, being dragged by the bag strap. I hung on to that fucking bag like I was going for a touchdown. I think the only reason they didn't get the bag was because it was made so well and didn't tear. And fortunately, no knives were pulled or guns drawn, just a snatch-and-run. It's been almost fifty years and I still have that bag.

I got rid of my St. Mark's apartment after the Wind in the Willows broke up and I wanted to change everything in my life. I moved down to 52 East First Street into a second-floor apartment with Gil. It was smaller than my old place but it wasn't too bad. There was a front room on the street end, a kitchen in the middle, and a tiny bedroom in the back with a window just above our heads that opened onto an airshaft. The people in the building were an assortment of musicians, bikers, and the usual Lower East Side types. Loud music day and night was flavored with the scent of pot.

One night as Gil and I were sleeping, something woke me up. There was a strong smell of gasoline coming through the airshaft window. I shook Gil awake and we headed for the door, but he didn't want to open it, because of the running and shouting in the hallway and what sounded like gunshots. Then a guy pounded on our door, yelling, "Get out! The building's on fire!" We opened our door to see flames shooting down the smoke-filled stairs. People were escaping and running outside. Fire trucks, hoses, cop cars, and ambulances jammed the street. Next morning, we got the scoop: a biker gang had been living on our top floor. That night the leader had been tied up, tortured, then set on fire. On the front page of the *Post* and

When everything's gone mad . . .

the *Daily News* the next day were shots of the remains of the blackened chair.

We were homeless. A friend of Gil's, Al Smith, let us crash at his studio on First Street and Avenue A for a while. I think—here's where my sense of chronology gets a little messy—this was when I took off for L.A. with the millionaire I met at Max's, and then decided that I could not live in L.A. in the sixties, for fear of losing my soul. So instead I came back to NYC and became a Playboy bunny and a junkie. Go figure. I also got back with Gil and I found us an apartment up on 107th Street and Manhattan Avenue, which at that time was borderline Harlem. But the only close call on 107th was when Gil—thinking it would be handy to have a connection in the apartment with him—invited some very serious drug dealers to live in our spare room. Old-time junkies, a real mess, with big puffy hands and high all the time. Fortunately, we didn't end up as collateral damage in one of their all-night deals.

Time to move on to the nastiest close call, which went down in the early seventies, back when I was mad for the New York Dolls and went to as many of their shows as possible. One night, I heard there was some kind of party for them on West Houston Street between Sixth Avenue and Varick Street. I was at my friends' apartment on Avenue C, and since they didn't want to come with me I started walking from their place alone—all the way across town—in my very highest platforms from Granny Takes a Trip. It was a hot night, around two in the morning. Walking maybe a mile or more in those shoes was quickly becoming impossible, so I started looking for a cab. But in those days taxis never cruised Alphabet City. It was too dangerous. Eventually I took off my mighty, multicolored shoes and tried walking barefoot. In rough neighborhoods like this, glass doesn't stay in one piece or place very long, and broken bottles, shattered car windows, you name it, covered every inch of the sidewalk and road. Walking on broken glass was even more impossible; even though I tried to pick my way through it, there just weren't enough bare spots to walk without shoes.

While I had been trying to find a cab, there had been a small white car circling me. It would go east on Houston then come back around. Around and around. Finally, it pulled alongside of me and the driver asked quietly, "Do you need a ride?" I was never a hitchhiker, not once in my life, even during the hippie years when it was the thing to do. It never appealed to me to get into a stranger's car. I said, "No, thanks," and kept trying to tiptoe across Houston. The driver didn't give up. He circled a few more times, stopping each time to see if I'd changed my mind about that ride. I finally realized that I wasn't getting anywhere, so on his next circuit, I took him up on his offer and got into the car.

My first impression of the driver was that he was not bad looking. Short, dark hair with a bit of a wave or a curl—in fact, good-looking—and wearing dark pants and a white business shirt open at the neck. After I thanked him for picking me up, there was no conversation, he just kept driving in silence. Right away, though, his stench started to reach me. A fierce body odor that almost burned my eyes. It was very, very hot in the car, but the windows were barely cracked open. So, I reached for the crank to roll down my window. But there was no window crank. And no handle to open the door from the inside. That's when I saw the dashboard was just a metal frame with holes for the radio and glove box and the whole car had been stripped of everything. It was like a scene out of Tarantino's Grindhouse movie *Death Proof*.

A sensation hit me then that I will never forget. The hair on the back of my neck stood up. Like an animal when they are alarmed or ready to attack. Every instinct was on full alert.

Somehow, I squeezed my arm through the crack in the window and sort of jumped up in my seat and managed to open the car door from the outside. When he saw what I was doing, he stepped on it and swung a fast left turn into Thompson Street, which threw me out of the open door and onto Houston, onto my ass in the middle of the road. But I wasn't really hurt and luckily he didn't come back for me. I picked myself up and hurried the last two and a half blocks to the Dolls' party, but it was over when I got there.

I had not thought about that night for maybe fifteen years until one day, on a flight to L.A., I read a story in *Time* or *Newsweek*. It was about Ted Bundy, the serial killer. He had just been executed in Florida in the electric chair. There was a photo of him. He gave the journalist a description of his car and of his modus operandi and how he got his victims, and it matched exactly what had happened to me. My story has been debunked since, because Bundy is said to have been in Florida at that time and not NYC. But it was him. When I saw that article, the hairs on the back of my neck stood up again. These are the only two times in my life I have had this sensation.

Back in the loft, where we had had our close call with death by carbon monoxide, life went on much as normal. We got used to the poltergeists and they got used to us. Poltergeists, I learned years later, almost always manifest through children or adolescents. Chris and I were at a dinner party with William Burroughs, who had a great interest in the paranormal. Burroughs asked us if there were any kids in our building. Chris said no. I said, well, there was one, Gary, our adolescent bass player. Gary was always in some kind of trouble. He was hiding out at our place because the cops in Jersey were after him for statutory rape. Gary was a teenager himself, almost the same age as his girlfriend, but when he got her pregnant her mother reported him, right as he turned eighteen. Gary was a true punk rocker in that he had *attitude* and resisted any form of authority or anyone telling him what to do.

The "Blondie Loft," as it became known, wasn't just where we lived—we rehearsed there, even played a show there. Amos Poe shot some of his documentary about the New York punk scene, *The Blank Generation,* in our loft. Amos at that time was an underground filmmaker whose style was a mix of French new wave and New York punk, very cool and very DIY. He gave me a role in his 1976 movie *Unmade Beds,* where I dressed in silk underwear and sang an a cappella jazz song to the tortured hero. And in his next film, *The Foreigner,* I played a mysterious woman who sang a song in French and German.

Chris shot some great photos of me in and around the loft. The famous baby-doll photos, for example, which were a kind of "garbage art" using props we'd found in the trash. Wandering around the streets—as Chris and I did a lot of the time—you would always find something cool that someone had tossed out. Sometimes the contents of a whole apartment that some landlord had cleared out when the tenants disappeared or didn't pay the rent. Downtown New York was perhaps more transitory back then. One day, Chris and I came across a pile of broken baby dolls discarded on the curb, all messed up and sad looking, waiting for the garbage truck, so of course we took them all home with us. Those mangled dollies hung around with us for quite some time—and they ended up in a centerfold photo of me that ran in *Punk* magazine. I liked the idea of centerfolds. Chris also shot me for the "Creem Dream" centerfold for *Creem* magazine.

Chris had sent some sexy images to *Punk,* but they wanted something that was "more punk." So, I started working on what I would wear for the photo. Benton, our landlord, loaned me his leather bikini bottoms, and Howie, one of our sometimes-extended houseguests, gave me the Vultures T-shirt, which I still have. The sci-fi space glove was one of our junk store finds. The south side of Houston Street between Mott and Bowery had great junk stores, before the neighborhood became safe.

My original oversized, black sunglasses came from one of those places. The stores all had bins and tables and racks out front, piled with anything and everything—really, really cheap. Inside, one low-watt, bare lightbulb would hang from the ceiling, casting a pale, dim view of the proceedings. As soon as you walked in, you were enveloped by the smell of mold and mildew, layers upon layers of dust, old wood, rust, and yellowing paper mixed with hints of exhaust fumes from the street. On a warm day these smells—cool and ancient—would drift out to mix with the truck exhaust as you walked past. Even the Canal Street stores seemed posh compared to these places.

We set up to do the session in the front half of our floor. Chris took his time getting the lights just right. He took his time getting the shots just right too. He wasn't one of those people who shoot fast and use up rolls of film because one shot is bound to be okay. That wasn't because of our financial circumstances. He aimed to get what he planned to get—and he usually got it right. He was a scientific photographer. I knew I looked okay, I had a good face, but I was always unsure about my body. Chris made me look better. He had these voyeuristic leanings, staring at me fixedly for hours in the heat of the lights, as I posed as sexily as I could to get him going. But he didn't need any help in getting going, he was already going. Chris and I would always end up in bed after a shoot.

We had been living in the Blondie loft for a little over a year when Benton threw us out. I don't know why he did it. I guess we must have fallen out over something but really, during those times we never seemed to live anywhere for much longer than a year. The timing was pretty terrible. It was August 1976 and we had just started working on Blondie's debut album. Years later, our crazy ex-landlord would claim it was his pact with the Devil that had made Blondie successful. We were tenacious. We kept working. We didn't give up and disappear—like some people might have liked us to. We kept at it, even when everyone else on the scene except us was getting signed. We sharpened up and we built a following. Now, finally, we had a record deal. But it was complicated. Like most things to do with Blondie and the music business would turn out to be.

Marty Thau, who had managed the Dolls, told Craig Leon that he thought we had potential. Craig used to work with Seymour Stein, who cofounded Sire Records and had signed the Ramones. Marty and Craig had partnered with Richard Gottehrer—who cofounded Sire with Seymour—in a production company called Instant Records, and that's who Blondie signed with. If you think the New York band scene was incestuous, the music business was even more so.

They decided to do a single first to test the waters. We recorded "Sex Offender," a song Gary and I wrote. He was playing the music and as soon I heard it, I wrote the words on the spot. The lyrics were part commentary on how ludicrous Gary's rape situation was, and part commentary on how preposterous it was to criminalize hookers. I had the cop and the hooker fall for each other. The whole song was written and ready to go in fifteen minutes, so to speak; that doesn't happen often. Craig Leon produced the single and they took it around and it wound up at Private Stock Records, a small label run by Larry Uttal—another music business veteran who was part of the clique. They agreed to release "Sex Offender," but we would have to change the title. That was annoying, but then I came up with "X Offender," which was okay.

When it came out in June 1976, "X Offender" wasn't a hit, but I think the single surprised a lot of people who didn't know

With Seymour Stein's wife, Linda, David Bowie, and Danny Fields.

what to expect from us. It really sounded good. One day, we walked into CBGB's and it was playing on the jukebox. That was a big moment for us. There was enough of a buzz for an album, but it seemed we needed Frankie Valli's approval. Frankie Valli was apparently a co-owner of Private Stock or its biggest shareholder. One night a limo pulled up outside CBGB's and Frankie Valli got out. The limo sat waiting for him among the bums and the winos while he watched us play. We didn't get to meet him, so I don't know what he thought of us, but now we were signed to Instant Records and Private Stock.

The recording studio, Plaza Sound, where we made our first album was a fantastic place—enormous compared to the little closet-sized spaces that most studios are—and very grand. It was in the same deco building as Radio City Music Hall, where I went as a kid to see the Easter and Christmas shows featuring the Rockettes. The Rockettes, in fact, could rehearse in another room while we were recording. The studio, on the whole upper floor, had been specially built for the NBC Symphony

Orchestra and its conductor, Toscanini. It was hung from iron girders like a suspension bridge. The dance floors floated on rubber springs, which helped insulate the sound of the orchestra or the dancing girls from the music hall. In the 1930s, when it was built, it must have been a real feat of engineering.

Another remarkable invention was a massive old pipe organ that had sound effects like a synthesizer—but being pre-electronic, it was all mechanical. At the back of the organ, there was an entire room filled with all these amazing little mechanized artifacts that made the effects they used in shows and silent movies: wooden mallets, door knockers and bells, drums and whistles . . . Sometimes we would take the elevator down to the theater and hang out behind the screen when they were showing movies—or ride it up to the roof, where Chris took some more great photos. We were in the studio every day from noon to one or two in the morning and we had the run of the building. Forty years later, when we did the David Bowie tribute there, it was insane getting into the building because of the updated security.

We knew all the songs we were recording inside out by then, since we had played them onstage for so long. One day our producer Richard Gottehrer brought Ellie Greenwich into the studio. They knew each other from when they both worked at the Brill Building. We were all big fans of Ellie because of the songs she'd written for the Shangri-Las, "Leader of the Pack" and another song Blondie always did, "Out in the Streets." Richard asked her if she would sing backup on a couple of songs. Ellie came with the two women who were part of her trio. I sat in the control room, watching as they sang. They were flawless. Their harmonies were just ridiculously tight and good. As it turned out, one of the songs they sang on—"In the Flesh"—became our first international hit. It went to number one in Australia after it was played on their most popular TV music program, Molly Meldrum's *Countdown*. Molly always claimed that he played it by accident, wink, wink; we wondered . . .

To promote the album in the U.S., Private Stock made a poster they plastered all over Times Square. Not a poster of Blondie but of me, on my own, in a see-through blouse, full frontal. We had insisted that the whole band be on the poster—and the record company nodded and said sure, no problem. The way it went down, this very cool Japanese photographer, Shig Ikeda, had done a series of head shots for each of us—along with the customary group shots for the album cover and for general PR. Shig had done this extra one of me in that see-through shirt, which management swore they would crop to just the head. Chris told me later that more than one person he spoke to thought it was an ad for a massage parlor.

I was furious. Not because my little nipples were on display to the world, which didn't bother me that much. There had been photos of me in *Punk* and *Creem* that were more revealing. But those were fun and ironic, playing up the whole idea of a pinup in an underground rock magazine, and quite different from some record company suit exploiting your sexuality. Sex sells, that's what they say, and I'm not stupid, I know that, but on my terms, not some executive's. I stormed into Private Stock and confronted the executive—who shall remain nameless—and said, "Well, how would you like it if it was your balls that were exposed." He said, "That's disgusting!" And I thought, *Now, there's a double standard,* and I wondered about his balls too.

Chris and I now lived in an apartment in a brownstone on Seventeenth Street between Sixth and Seventh Avenues. Gary was no longer living with us—the charges against him had been dropped and he didn't have to hide anymore. Our new place was a cross between a loft and an attic. The ceilings sloped and were lower in the back than in the front, which was a seldom-used living room.

On set with Joan in 2017.

Chris took a lot of photos in that apartment. He set up a darkroom with an enlarger and when the photos were printed he would hang them on a line underneath the skylight in our big kitchen. Maybe one of the best-known photos from that time is the one where I'm holding out a flaming frying pan and wearing a dress that Marilyn Monroe had supposedly worn in *The Seven Year Itch*. Our downstairs neighbor, Maria Duval, an aspiring actor, had bought the dress at an auction and loaned it to me. There is a story to that photo.

About a year after we moved in, while we were out on tour, Chris's mother called us. "Don't be alarmed," Stel said, "but your house just burned down." Although we never found out how the fire started, I had a hunch about it that made me sick to my stomach. Before going on the road, we had arranged for Jimmy's younger sister Donna Destri to stay in our apartment and look after the cats. Trying to make it more comfortable for her, I had put a little TV on a box by her bed. I had plugged it into an electric outlet by the kitchen wall that I had never used before. I had a horrible feeling that it might have shorted out and set fire to the mattress. The only good news was that Donna wasn't hurt. The cats survived too, by hiding in a closet.

Being on tour meant that it would be two or three weeks before we could get back home. When we finally did get back, it was hugely upsetting. The place was strewn with debris from the fire. And because people were able to just walk into our apartment and take things, they did. Although the only items they stole that really mattered to me were some little pieces of jewelry I'd gotten from my mother. Fortunately, Chris had his guitar and camera with him. So he set up a photo session in the burned-out kitchen. The walls were caked in soot and the range was covered in ash. I put on Marilyn's dress, which had been badly singed in the fire, and our latest close call (which wasn't all that close) became a work of art.

CURTAIN UP

Brian Aris, 1979.

NOT ALL THE PIECES OF FAN ART IN THIS BOOK ARE PORTRAITS OF ME. Some are works created by fans that they simply wanted to give me. I like to think that while they were drawing and printing, they were listening to me singing our songs. My old friend Steven Sprouse, who designed many of my famous looks, used to always listen to music while he sketched. Without fail the music was blasting away while he worked—which is how a lot of the artists I know do their work. This may sound like the bragging of an outsized ego, but it's not always my music they listen to. And the influence of any music on artwork is kind of a romantic notion. Still, as I look at all these interpretations of me, my face, my characters through the years, I am touched by it. Many of these images are taken directly from famous photographers' shots of me, like Chris Stein, Mick Rock, Robert Mapplethorpe, Brian Aris, Lynn Goldsmith, and Annie Liebowitz—yet the works have something noticeably their own. Something in the eye of the beholder as they say. The feelings of the artist are present whether from an accomplished illustrator or drawings from the hand of a younger, less experienced scribbler and that's the icing on it for me.

Rob's additions and overview of the fan art concept are exceptional, like all his work, and he's also come up with the idea of starting a website where fan art works like this can be posted; an interactive book. I LOVE IT!

At the Guggenheim the other night I met up with a producer friend of mine, Charlie Nieland, who worked on my solo album *Necessary Evil*. We had come to see the Hilma af Klint collection on loan from the Swedish Museum of Art. Hilma started drawing when she was a young girl, then dedicated her life to drawing and painting and studying art. Who knows if any of my Fan Art artists carried on into the future with their interests in portraiture or other schools of art. Most likely I'll never know. Very likely I'd be glad if they did.

Every musician, actor, artist I've ever met always says, "It's the fans that make it happen for us." So again it's a chain reaction, interaction, and the proof is here in my book. For me it's a way of saying thank you . . . *(cont.)*

A Line Or Two ....

Parallel lines

HAPPY BIRTHDAY
DEBBIE

LOVE
MIYUKI

~ Neste barco
some e color azul
lade e omar e tao c mo.
aea, la la la
aea, la la aea, o calmo
aea, la la ea la la
aea, eae, e tao calmo, solidao. On
this boat navigating sunligh
heat and the blue of
the sea calm
almarie ~ Ah, Calmarie
so still ing pretty
Deep, almarie
~ Ah, Calmarie
la la aea la la
Neste barco
luz, color a
e oma o cal
calmo, e tao
Calma ~ Neste barco
luz, som color

DeaR
BLonDIE
MY
NaMe
IS
AMaNDA
Fusazy

7

LIFTOFF, PAYOFF

I don't like to dwell in the past. You do something, if you're lucky you learn from it, and you move on. What was I learning? How to express myself, how to get better at what I was doing, where I fit into the picture, how to be in control of my own life. How to better express myself? Yes, that happened. How to improve my performance and better position myself? Yes, that too. But the control part? Not so much. Some kind of control you've got, when you've signed your life away on so many dotted lines and they've strapped you to the head of a rocket. The lesson was really the same as it ever was: survive and find a way to create while you're hurtling through space.

Strapped to a rocket and ready to be launched or, as Chris said, "chasing the carrot"? This was that time when we really took off. I mean, *took off*. It was a riotous, breathless, rest-less, crazy period, much of it a blur now, from the speed with which it all unfolded. After the release of our first album, we played a bunch of shows in New York and then in February '77 we hit the road, for the first time. And we stayed on the road. And stayed . . . First we went to L.A., where we were put up at the Bel Air Sands. Our manager had made a deal with the owner: free rooms in return for some free shows. The shows were supposed to take place on a cruise ship. When it came down to it, however, the ship was declared unseaworthy and the permit for a concert was denied. In the meantime, each night we drove in our rented van from the Bel Air to the Whisky a Go Go on Sunset.

But before the shows, we first had to sign a contract. Peter Leeds, the Wind in the Willows' old manager, had come back into our lives, offering to manage Blondie. He wasn't the first to make that offer. Before him, our neophyte managers were these cute little potheads from the Bronx. Oh God, they were so adorable and funny, and crazy about Blondie. They came down to CBGB's, these two munchkin guys dressed like 1970s disco boys with wide-lapeled shirts and long collars and flared pants. But somehow, we were still flattered that they were paying attention to us. Then they said, "We want to manage you." God knows why. There was no contract or anything. They just started preparing different things, posters or buttons or T-shirts, and I think they tried to book us somewhere. Leeds's bolder strategy was to tell us that he'd booked us these gigs in L.A. Unfortunately, his strategy worked.

At that time, the whole L.A. scene was wide open. The Whisky a Go Go had been famous in the sixties as a platform for so many great rock bands but was apparently feeling the competition from the new, fancier clubs that were opening up. The Whisky was looking for something fresh and new to restore it to its former glory. It was the right place at the right time to make an impact and we really wanted to do these shows. Wanted to do them so much that we signed a five-year management contract with Leeds.

Los Angeles was all we could have hoped for. It was a big turnaround for Blondie. Rodney Bingenheimer, a local, influential DJ with an uncanny knack for finding new music who had his own radio show on KROQ, flipped out over us, played us all the time, and had us on his show. In spite of its being "commercial," KROQ was more like a college station and Rodney had complete control of his playlist. He was known for playing music from the hip new kids—and helping those bands to break out. There was even an L.A. Blondie fan club that was presided over by Jeffrey Lee Pierce, a sweet kid who later would have a great band called the Gun Club, which Chris would end up producing. Jeffrey had dyed his hair blond to look like mine. The first time we played in L.A., people were still dressing like hippies—and here we were, dressed in black, or in our little mod outfits. But the audiences really responded to us. When we went back to the Whisky to do more shows later that year, it looked like everyone in the audience had been raiding the secondhand stores—and the girls were wearing cute mod miniskirts instead of those floor-length floral things.

Tom Petty opened for us the first week. The second week we played with the Ramones, which was when things got crazier. There were just a few very small dressing rooms upstairs at the Whisky, which we all shared. Both bands, girlfriends, guests, and various hangers-on all crammed into these little rooms. Joan Jett was a regular visitor, Ray Manzarek of the Doors was there, and so was Malcolm McLaren, who was in town trying to get the Sex Pistols a U.S. deal. One night Malcolm got into some kind of argument with Johnny Ramone and Johnny chased him out of the dressing room, swinging a guitar at his head. Another night, a man came upstairs dressed entirely in black, including his hair, his beard, and his moustache. He wore a cape, aviator shades, a huge cross on a chain, and an "In the

Flesh" button on his lapel. Phil Spector. He was flanked by Dan and David Kessel, two tall, good-looking, impeccably dressed twins who were his entourage that night. They ushered the Ramones and everyone out of the room, except us. While the glamorous twins stood by the door, keeping everyone out—or maybe keeping us in—Phil kept up a long monologue into the early hours of the morning.

Buried somewhere within the endless ramble was an invitation to his mansion. I really didn't want to go because I didn't want to tire myself out. The legend of Phil Spector, of course, always fascinated me, so I was torn about the invite. I'd heard a lot about him, loved his music, and was attracted to his madness, but I was singing every night, two sets a night, with no time off. I didn't want to have to talk, I wanted to rest so I could do the next show. But Peter decided we needed to go. Phil's walled mansion was really quite close to the Strip. I remember the icy AC and how very "Phil Spector" he was. Chris remembers Phil greeting us with a Colt .45 in one hand and a bottle of Manischewitz in the other.

There were a few other guests that night, including Rodney Bingenheimer and Leeds, who might have been hoping we'd work with Phil on a record. Everyone had to sit down; Phil didn't want anyone walking around. He was entertaining everyone with his W. C. Fields imitation. At one point Phil sent out for pizza. Then he sat at his piano and started playing. He wanted me to sit on the bench next to him and sing "Be My Baby" and some Ronettes songs with him. He kept making me sing and sing. I really didn't want to, because I had so many shows, but Phil was in his zone and was not to be denied. Then a little later, when we were sitting together on the couch, Phil took out his gun, stuck it into the top of my thigh-high leather boot, and said, "Bang, bang!"

High tea.
top row: *Siouxsie Sioux, Viv Albertine, me*
bottom row: *Pauline Black, Poly Styrene, Chrissie Hynde*

Phil was working with Leonard Cohen at that time and he took us into the music room, wanting to play us something, but he played it at top volume so it just sounded distorted. All I really wanted to do was go back to the hotel and get some sleep. You never really get enough sleep on tour, and with two shows a night you have to take it where you can. I do think it would have been great to work on a record with Phil and perhaps we could have pursued it. Peter Leeds may have butted heads with Phil, which held us back. He did end up working with the Ramones. Going by what Joey and Johnny said, it wasn't easy. He wanted total control. He was a genius, he had a gun, and his paranoia was enormous—and that doesn't always end well. I do find it sad he's in prison—sadder still for the poor woman that he lured to his mansion and then shot and killed. It's awful: it is madness that such a brilliant mind, such an influential talent, as Phil Spector—the man who created the Wall of Sound, this seminal contribution to rock 'n' roll—now sits behind bars, in poor health, rotting away in a prison hospital.

After our last Whisky show we went to San Francisco and played at the Mabuhay Gardens. It was a small Filipino club that had gone punk with a vengeance. For his promotional efforts, its owner and emcee, Dirk Dirksen, became known as the "Pope of Punk." This was a real city like New York or Chicago, with a diversity of occupations and frustrations. The girls were stylish and pretty, so the boys in the band had some appropriately wild times. I had a few wild times of my own fighting off some very aggressive women; some were after me and some were after Chris. And there was a wild party in an art gallery that the guys broke into—literally broke into, a brick or a cinder block through the front door. We were high on the energy of those few weeks in L.A.; everyone was walking in the footsteps of rock history—and we had a reputation to build!

Next up was Blondie's first real tour. With Iggy Pop and David Bowie.

David had been working with Iggy on his new album *The Idiot* in Berlin. Iggy was about to begin his North American tour with David in his band as the keyboard player. Really, they could have had anyone in the world open for them, but they chose us, basically a local band who'd had a little attention. Of course we were overjoyed. We flew home to pack and to play two headlining shows at Max's. After the second set on the second night, we all piled into a rented RV in the early hours and drove to Montreal, where the tour opened. There was one big bed in the back, so all five of us squeezed in there, trying uselessly to get some sleep because the first show was that same night. When we arrived at Le Plateau theater, we fell into our dressing room and crashed out. And then the door opened and David and Iggy walked in to introduce themselves. We all gasped; we were starstruck and dumb as shit, but they were so congenial and friendly.

We played more than twenty shows with them. Every night we watched them from the wings, and we watched them at sound checks. There were so many opportunities to see them and so much to learn. They watched us too. Chris remembers them saying to me, "Use more of the stage, go back and forth." At first, not being used to such a big stage, I usually stood in one area. Later, I got into the idea of prancing and dancing around. But there was nobody who could use a stage better than Iggy—except maybe David, who was a superstar at that point but still happy to play the role of sideman. Iggy would climb on the speakers and sing and flaunt his amazing, muscular body—and the girls in the audience would take off their underwear and fling it onstage and sit there with their legs open, flashing beaver.

Offstage we would hang around a bit and talk, just day-to-day stuff, but it was a little different for me being the only girl there. I was with Chris, we were a couple, but there still isn't anything to equate to being the only woman on the road with all guys. One time David and Iggy were looking for some blow. Their connection in New York had suddenly died and they were out. A friend had given me a gram, but I had barely touched it. I didn't care for coke too much—it made me jittery and wired and it affected my throat. So I went upstairs with my vast quantity of cocaine and they just sucked it right up in one swoop. After they did the blow, David pulled out his cock—as if I were the official cock checker or something. Since I was in an all-male band, maybe they figured I really *was* the cock-check lady. David's size was notorious, of course, and he loved to pull it out with both men and women. It was so funny, adorable, and sexy. A moment later, Chris walked into the room, but the show was already over. Nothing to see. Which was kind of a relief. Prob-

The set list, a work in progress.

ably the guys said, "Oh, David and Iggy took Debbie upstairs," and he got his testosterone in a tizzy. As Chris and I left the room, I had to wonder why Iggy didn't let me have a closer look at *his* dick . . .

But all the guys were having the time of their life. In Portland, Jimmy kicked in a plate-glass door. He might have been arrested if David hadn't stepped in and paid for it. And after the Seattle show, the local punks invited us to come over and play at their bunker, this cement-walled bomb shelter of a place. The stage was a mattress. Isolated, in the middle of nowhere, you could play music at full volume and jam all night and there were no neighbors to complain. And that's what Chris, Clem, and Jimmy did, playing on borrowed equipment, with Iggy on vocals. Chris always said it was one of his favorite places ever on any tour.

The tour ended in Los Angeles, so after saying goodbye we stuck around to play four more nights at the Whisky, this time with Joan Jett. We got back to New York in time to play both nights of the big benefit show for *Punk* magazine at CBGB's, along with a lot of our friends, like the Dictators, Richard Hell, and David Johansen. Then it was time to leave again—this time for our first UK tour. The day before we flew to London, my Camaro died. It got stuck in reverse, which was nothing new; the linkage was shot. Sometimes I could get it into a forward gear and sometimes I couldn't, so I'd drive down the street in reverse, pulling over when the light changed. But this time it was going nowhere, except back home to die. We couldn't afford to have it towed, but a friend of a friend in New Jersey said he would take care of it. He told us later that he pushed it off a cliff.

We landed at Heathrow in May 1977, just as London was preparing to celebrate the Queen's Silver Jubilee and the Sex Pistols were preparing to release "God Save the Queen." Our first gig, a warm-up show headlining over the British band Squeeze at a university in the quiet seaside town of Bournemouth, was an eye-opener. It was full-on UK punk—which was definitely different from American punk, more tribal and much more physical. People were pogoing, slam-dancing, spitting, and going crazy, spurring us on. The skinheads, in particular, liked to do the full-contact body slam. All these boys with no hair on their head, shaking and shoving and dancing. I was almost dragged off the stage. We didn't like the gobbing so much—"lobbing a loogie," where the audience would hawk up a wad of phlegm and spit it at you. Ironically, our friend Iggy claims to have pioneered that particular gesture of appreciation. Uh, thanks, Iggy. But the pogo thing was fun, everyone bouncing maniacally up and down, heads bobbing, eyes rolling. That was one of the things I always wanted to do in the Stillettoes, to get people up and dancing. I was so tired of people just sitting there being cool or waiting to be entertained. We loved that the audience was a frenzied, crazed mass of feel-good energy. It made us rock that much harder.

But then the real tour began. We were opening for Television.

Sad to say, it was not as much fun as opening for Iggy and Bowie. There were sound problems and equipment problems, and the atmosphere was—shall we say—a bit uncomfortable at times. We weren't experienced enough to know what to do about it and we had no one there to ask. Television wasn't a band we'd played with all that much in New York and our fans didn't always overlap. The first shows were in Glasgow; the Ramones and Talking Heads were also in town and had played the night before, so it felt like CBGB's had relocated to Scotland.

Things started to pick up for us when we got to London to play two shows at the Hammersmith Odeon. The audience was with us and the rock press started paying attention to us. After our ten UK shows, one a night with no days off for travel, we played with Television in Amsterdam, Brussels, Copenhagen, and Paris. None of them were places I'd ever been to before, but there was no time to explore. We flew back home with a stack of great reviews and new fans and got straight to work on our second album, *Plastic Letters*.

Once again, we were in the big room at Plaza Sound in the Radio City Music Hall building and Richard Gottehrer was producing. But there was one big difference: Gary Valentine was no longer in the band. It became clear during the tour that he wanted his own band and we were holding him back—which is understandable, wanting to make a name for yourself. He had talked about quitting after the second album. And then our manager got rid of him. Just like that, very harshly, blunt and loud like a bully boy, as was his way. It was horrible. It was very hard on Clem because he and Gary were close.

But at the same time we were all desperate to continue and carry on, although it was totally, totally uncomfortable. There was a dark mood in the studio. Everyone was a nervous wreck. Chris had to play a lot of the bass as well as guitar and we brought in Frank Infante to help. You can definitely hear some of that anger and attitude on the album.

When we started *Plastic Letters* we were still on Private Stock. By the time it was done we were on Chrysalis Records. It was our manager's idea. It was a British label, we had an audience in the UK and Europe, so he began wheeling and dealing. He got Larry Uttal to agree to release us from our contract with Private Stock for a substantial sum and broke it to us in the studio. Apparently all this was news to Richard Gottehrer, who now wanted to be added to the buyout list. As a result of these machinations we ended up a million dollars in debt.

We had a six-month wait before the album finally came out. We went back to play the West Coast again, taking Frankie with us to play bass. Among the shows we played was a punk rock fashion show with Devo at the Hollywood Palladium. Then came another string of shows at the Whisky. John Cassavetes and Sam Shaw were there to shoot the shows for a little film that Terry Ellis, the head of Chrysalis, was funding. It was an odd sort of thing, about Blondie but also about my fantasy of being Marilyn Monroe's daughter.

Sam had staged and shot that famous photograph of Marilyn in the white dress standing over the subway grating in *The Seven Year Itch*. Since this film was his idea, he was the director, and he brought along his movie director friend Cassavetes. When the shooting was over we had a big show at the Whisky. It looked like every single person from the record company had come. They all climbed upstairs afterward to the room where John and I were posing for a photo. Every time someone from the record company came in, John would wave them over.

"Come in, come in, be in the picture." He kept on directing all these people into the picture and by the time they shot the picture John was standing at the back and you couldn't see him at all. It was so comedic, like a setup from a silent move. It was truly a great Cassavetes moment.

I don't know what happened with that film. It's probably on the Internet somewhere. Zoe Cassavetes acknowledged that there's a copy in her father's archives. But one good thing came from that L.A. trip: our new bass player, Nigel Harrison. Nigel was from England but he lived in L.A. and was playing in Ray Manzarek's band Nite City. I think it was Sable Starr, Johnny Thunders's girlfriend, who suggested we audition him. Apparently Nigel came to a couple of our shows with a cassette recorder and recorded the sets, so that when he came in for the audition he would get the job. Well he did get it. Frankie moved from bass to guitar—which was really his instrument—and we had a band again. The hard part was that we were given no time to rehearse and get to know each other. We had to just get on with it. I remember one time talking to our manager about the insane schedule he'd made for us and he'd say, "See? There's a day off," and I would keep telling him, "No it's not, it's a travel day." We didn't have a personal manager; we had an impersonal manager.

During that entire first leg of Blondie, the pressure was constant. This level of stress and pressure would eventually have dire consequences. I always felt it was particularly hard on Chris. He's a thoughtful, internal, considered person who was thrust into all this rapid decision making and had to shoulder all these competing responsibilities. And he's a manly man—even though he never comes off as macho—so he was always very protective of me. He shielded me from all the incoming nonsense—which added a whole extra level of stress. He was always saying that he wanted more time off, but we were rarely home.

2003 set list.

We were on the road in San Francisco when we got the call saying that our apartment had gone up in flames. We were burned out in every sense. Exhausted, sleep deprived, and living on adrenaline. Chris and I moved into the old Gramercy Park Hotel downtown for a little while when we got home, which was really fun and nice. The other full-time residents were mostly old ladies who wore furs in midsummer. Our manager now decided that I had to go back out, on my own, on a promotional tour, to chat up all the DJs and program directors across the country. So I headed out with Billy Bass, the famous promotion man from Chrysalis.

In November we were back on the road: UK, Europe, then a major tour of Australia. In Brisbane, I was so violently ill from food poisoning, I couldn't even stand. We had to cancel the show. The next day we read in the papers that the audience went berserk and tore up the first two rows of seats. We did two shows in Bangkok where there were lepers in the street, begging. The Ambassador Hotel, where we played, had made a giant flower arrangement that spelled out "BLONDIE," just as it looked on the cover of our first album. Very exotic. We did six shows in Japan, where the fans were lovely and so appreciative. We flew to London to play Dingwalls and ran into some more of the New York crowd, Leee Black Childers, Richard Hell, and Nancy Spungen. The next day it was back to Europe . . . and so on and so on and so on.

Our second album, *Plastic Letters,* was finally released in February 1978. We went to London to appear on *Top of the Pops,* the UK's biggest music TV show, and played our first single, "Denis." It was a song that I'd always loved. Chris and I had discovered it on one of those K-Tel compilations. It was by a group from Queens named Randy and the Rainbows, who'd had a hit with it in the early sixties. Their version was called "Denise." I dropped the "e" to turn her into a Frenchman and sang two verses in French. "Denis" soared to number two in the UK charts and really broke us out in Europe. Our second single, "Presence Dear," a Gary Valentine song, also made the UK top ten. So did our album.

I had made my own dress for the album cover shot: a white pillowcase that I wrapped red gaffer tape around, like a candy cane. Our new record company rejected it; they didn't think it was "nice" enough or something. It just seemed like every step of the way someone was exercising some kind of creative control over the band and taking it away from us. They wanted me to wear something else, so I chose something that Anya Phillips and I put together. Anya was making some great-looking clothes out of spandex for herself and for the backing singers in James Chance's band. We collaborated on the design of my dress and I was supposed to assemble it—but I didn't pay close enough attention to how she did it.

Anya didn't sew, so she would punch holes in the fabric and cut skinny strips of it into laces. It was very cool looking, but I felt a little insecure, knowing that I would be shaking it hard onstage, a whole lot more than the backing singers, so I stitched it. She was a little dismayed at this, but it still had that look, with all of the laces crisscrossing at the front and back. Our new record company's ad for the album didn't put my nipples on display, but it did make this generous offer on my behalf: "Debbie Harry will undo you."

David Bowie once described the music business as a mental hospital: you'd only be let out to promote something or make another record—then back in you'd go. That sounds about right. In the summer of '78, four months after our second album came out, we were finally given a break from the tour—to make our third album. Chris and I were still homeless. I think that was when we moved into a bland, corporate New York apartment hotel right behind Penn Station that gave me a horribly rootless, transient feeling.

For *Parallel Lines* we were in a different studio, the Record Plant, a high-budget place, with a high-budget producer, Mike Chapman. This was the first time we felt that the record company believed in us and thought it was worth spending some money on us. Mike Chapman was the Hit Meister. He'd turned out one glam-rock hit after the other in the seventies for acts like the Sweet and Suzi Quatro. So we were all excited to work with him. Aussie Mike had a real swagger to him. He looked very Hollywood, with his aviator sunglasses and long white cigarette holder, but he had the rock 'n' roll spirit. He saw what was there and locked it down. The ultimate perfectionist, he was quite the slave driver, but at the same time he was extremely patient with us. He was used to working with untrained musicians and knew how to bring out the best in them. That often meant making us do take after take and because it was all analog, not digital; there were things that had to be done, oh, I don't know, thousands or millions of times. Or so it felt like. Mike could be a dictator—he would tell you that himself—but he was a doll, very upbeat. And the album sounded great.

Of course, the record company wasn't satisfied. When Mike played it to them they said they couldn't hear any hits. Oh, really? What do you say to something like that? What Mike said was, "Here it is, we're not redoing a thing." Some of our best-known songs are on that album: "One Way or Another," which was inspired in part by that New Jersey stalker of mine. "Sunday Girl," which Chris wrote. "Pretty Baby," which Chris and I wrote about Brooke Shields. "Picture This" was Chris and Jimmy and me. "Hanging on the Telephone" was a song by the Nerves, a band from L.A. that Jeffrey Lee Pierce had sent us a cassette of. We played it in the back of a cab in Tokyo and the driver, who didn't speak any English, started tapping the steering wheel. Chris and I looked at each other and we thought, *Okay, this guy is going with it and he hasn't got a clue what it's about, he's just responding to the song,* which we took as a sign that we had to do it. We started our version like a Shangri-Las song with a sound effect, a British telephone ringtone.

As for "Heart of Glass," that came later in the sessions, after Mike said, "Do you guys have anything else?" It was an old song of ours that we'd recorded as "The Disco Song" on that demo we made in a hot humid basement with Alan Betrock. The demo version had a funky American sound and thanks to the heat and humidity it had been hard to keep anything in tune. The new version was much more electro and European-sounding. Chris started fooling around with his drum machine—a Roland CompuRhythm—and got that tokk-tikka-tikka-tokk thing. He plugged his little black box into the synthesizer and they laid it down as the foundation track. Everything else in the song was built around that. To Chris and me, it sounded like Kraftwerk, which we both loved. It's disco but at the same time it's not. Rock critics hated disco; *Punk* magazine printed a diatribe against disco and the people who liked it. That song pissed off a lot of critics, but as Chris the Dadaist likes to say, it made us punk in the face of punk.

Stephen Sprouse designed the dress I wore in the "Heart of Glass" video. He had this whole series of scan-line paintings, based on the lines on the TV screen, and he started printing out fabric with the scan lines. For my dress, he had two layers of chiffon, so that the lines would lie over each other and they'd vibrate. He also printed up some cotton T-shirt material and I made the T-shirts that the guys are wearing. Steve also shot a fabulous photo for our album sleeve using scan lines but it ended up not being used—much too artistic.

Parallel Lines was released in September 1978, our second album that same year. As we toured around Europe once again, it made its way up the charts in several European countries and in Australia. Our single "Hanging on the Telephone" was top five in the UK charts but it went absolutely nowhere in the U.S., not even the bottom hundred. Happy as we were to see that all our hard work was paying off, it was definitely disappointing not to have a hit at home. At the beginning of 1979, while we were on the American tour, we saw that "Heart of Glass" had entered the American charts. And slowly but surely it kept on climbing. We were in Milan, where we'd flown mid-tour to do a TV show, staying at one of those old-fashioned Italian places full of dark wood and velvet, when we got a phone call. It was Chapman. "I'm in the bar," he said. "Come on down." So we went downstairs to the lush bar-lounge, wondering what he was doing in Italy, and he greeted us with a bottle of champagne. That's when we found out that "Heart of Glass" was number one.

Mike put it nicely in a *Rolling Stone* interview about *Parallel Lines:* "If you're going to be in the music business, you gotta make hit records. If you can't make hit records, you should fuck off and go chop meat somewhere." Right on, Mike. No meatpacking for us . . .

We were so happy and excited but I'm not sure we had time to let it fully sink in, as we flew straight back to the U.S. to do *The Midnight Special, American Bandstand,* and *The Mike Douglas Show,* and finish our U.S. tour. By the time that tour ended, *Parallel Lines* was in the U.S. top ten and headed for platinum. I can't complain about that, can I? The hard work did pay off after all.

UNION
SQ.
14TH

8

MOTHER CABRINI AND THE ELECTRIC FIRESTORM

Since we were either on the road or in the studio, you might think we didn't need an apartment. But of course we did. I found us one uptown: 200 West Fifty-Eighth Street at Seventh Avenue. Actually, it was Stephen Sprouse who discovered the building. After he moved out of the top floor of the old Bowery place, he found an apartment in one of those prewar buildings with high ceilings and rent control.

Sometimes, I would go visit Stephen and we would talk about ideas for my new look. He was a sweet, generous person. When we were on the Bowery, he gave me my much-photographed pair of thigh-high black leather boots from I. Miller, which at that time I could have never afforded. Stephen probably got them from a show, because he was still working for Halston at the time. I had an old black sateen trench coat that was more like an evening coat. When I wore the coat with those boots and a black beret, I looked like Patty Hearst from the SLA crossed with Faye Dunaway in *Bonnie and Clyde*. Stephen liked that look. He also put me in a Halston black silk, matte jersey dress that I just adored. I wore that dress to death. I wore it to the point where you couldn't be in the same room with me because it smelled so bad. I still have that stinky old rag, even if it might take a few minutes for me to find it right now. I can always just follow my nose . . .

Shortly after that, he gave me a sort of synthetic fabric sheath dress. Yellow stitched with red. Slits up the side. A boatneck, three-quarter-length sleeves, and a little beaded belt made by his mother, Joanne. Then, as our touring became a little bit more organized, he would send me out with drawings of how to put different pieces together in different ways. I still have those too.

From the first time I set foot in this West Side building, I started making friends with the superintendent. I would knock on his door and chat him up and give him a little money and say, "I really want to live here." It took some time, but eventually, in October 1978, he gave me a heads-up on a very special apartment and we moved in. It was on the top floor with terraces on three sides. The paint was peeling, the roof leaked around the skylight, and it was drafty. It had originally been the apartment's old laundry room, I was told. We also had a tar beach over our heads. Lillian Roth, the silent-movie star, had lived there once. I loved it. We had that apartment for a nice long time, three or four years, which was a big change from moving every year. Even when we stopped living there, we held on to it and Chris's mother, Stel, took it over.

Chris moved his life-sized statue of Mother Cabrini—which, of course, being holy, survived the electric firestorm in our apartment—into a corner of the kitchen. We had a big living room with the usual furniture and a smaller room with a wall of closets. It was amazing to have actual closets and the room could be used as our office. The double-wide terrace at the back of the building was where Chris grew his pot. Chris was a pothead. His was an endless quest for the ultimate high. This often included hash as well, and those pungent aromas were soaked into the fabric of our lives—and into the fabric of our couch and bed. For a short while, we even sold pot as a way to pay the rent. It was a good thing that our rent was so low, because most of our hoped-for profits went up in smoke.

We had a couple of interesting connections back then. There was a Greek gentleman whose name was, shall we say, Ulysses; he's still around I think, and I don't want to blow his cover. He was a good-looking middle-aged guy who dealt in some serious weight. We occasionally bought keys from him and sold them in small amounts to an intimate circle of friends. Ulysses was a colorful character and we visited him often. He had a "loft" on Fourteenth Street, which was actually a basement apartment. Since it was an entire floor, he felt entitled to call it a loft, I guess. The place was always full of smiling, cute teenage boys. This made our business efforts, which were pathetic for moneymaking, mostly social.

A more refined source of weed was a sculptor who lived on the fringe of Chinatown. He had a whole building he claimed to have bought from the city for a dollar. He was a good hustler, so I believed him. He was also an artist who understood the layers of dust and debris, the rubble that made up the fabric of our incredible city. "Ray" was very particular about his product and his pot was ultra-strong sensi from Northern California. The pale greenish pollen was sticky and the buds were fat and had very few seeds. It wasn't cheap, but it was worth every penny. You'd think by the way I'm describing this stuff that I was as big a pothead as Chris—but you'd be wrong. I couldn't handle it at all. I'd find myself either floating above my body in a state of blank catatonia or in complete paranoia. I marveled at how anyone could even talk after smoking a joint of "Ray's Famous." But all the boys loved it.

We also had a connection for this gorgeous Hawaiian

Purple. Chris started saving the seeds—a traditional pothead habit—and then he started planting on our terrace, which made for a pretty good garden, with a wall to ensure privacy. We had a friend tend the farm while we were on the road. But when we returned, Chris was crushed to discover that his plants had been pollinated. They were doomed to be less than *chibo chibo*. They'd lost their purity. Somehow that hit me as a biblical reference. You know, the Garden of Eden and the female polluting the male.

One night in our apartment, while Chris and Glenn O'Brien were watching public access programs on cable TV channel C and chain-smoking giant-sized joints, they cooked up the idea of *TV Party*. We knew Glenn from CBGB's. He had a band called Konelrad and he was well-known at Warhol's Factory. When Andy launched *Interview* magazine, Glenn was the first editor and he wrote a regular column called "Glenn O'Brien's Beat." Public access TV was wild. It was open to any lunatic, joker, or proselytizer who had some message or obsession they wanted to share with the community. Just pony up your $40 or $50 and you'd get an hour of studio time. Glenn's idea was to do a weekly talk show—a subversive, art underground version of the classic American late-night shows—and he and Chris would cohost. So, that's what they did. *TV Party* started in 1978 and ran every week for four years on cable TV, channels D and J. At that time cable was only available from Twenty-Third Street up, which meant that if you were downtown you were out of luck. On the other hand, if you were downtown you were much more likely to be on the show.

All those Tuesdays on Twenty-Third Street. First we would meet in the Blarney Stone, the Irish shot bar across the street from ETC/Metro Access Studios, where the show was broadcast. All these talented oddballs gathered together, Glenn and Chris casually figuring out the theme for the *TV Party* show

TV Party!

that night—perhaps a Fellini bacchanal or maybe a Middle Eastern harem nocturne. Like the beginnings of deconstructed fashion, this was a deconstruction of television. As Glenn put it: "We had a good run, fucking up television. Cursing, getting high, advocating subversion, being party desperados . . ."

Amos Poe, the underground filmmaker, was director of photography. Sometimes Amos would get bored and start punching knobs at random, pixelating the screen or inserting sudden jump cuts and shots of people's shoes. A burst of toxic visuals to mimic the "noise" on set. Behind the camera was Fab 5 Freddy, the visual artist and hip-hop pioneer. Jean-Michel Basquiat would sit there playing with the character generator, writing stuff on the screen like he was graffiti-ing on TV instead of on walls. He wanted to write on the studio wall, but they stopped him after he wrote "mock penis envy" on a blank wall. Jean-Michel took his role as street artist and graffiti philosopher seriously. Andy Warhol loved him. We all did. His graffiti tag "SAMO" was everywhere, the writing on the wall.

TV Party, like a mainstream talk show, had a studio band. The bandleader was Walter "Doc" Steding, musician, painter, director, actor, and general wild man. We first met Walter when he was a one-man band playing violin with electronic accompaniment and would open up for people at CBGB's. Each of the programs had special guests—Klaus Nomi, David Bowie, Nile Rodgers, David Byrne, Mick Jones of the Clash, Kraftwerk, George Clinton, and the Brides of Funkenstein. There was a phone-in section, where they took unscreened calls to answer questions or just get nutty comments. Sometimes, it seemed like a sex chat line. Chris would always do the show if Blondie wasn't on the road—and when we were on the road he might send Glenn a video from wherever. I didn't do it every week, but I would be a guest now and then. I did one show right after we returned from the UK, to give a lesson in how to pogo using a pogo stick.

Glenn was the perfect host with his deadpan, anarchic humor. Chris was pretty good too, with his wry smile and funny asides. Everyone on *TV Party* was in a band or in the movies, or was an artist, a writer, a photographer, a fashion designer, or all of the above, or just hanging out. One thing fed off of the next, a very DIY sensibility. It never occurred to you at that time to limit yourself to just one thing. You found a niche and you claimed it and you tried to leave your mark like the graffiti artists did. In 2005, Danny Vinik made a film, *TV Party the Documentary*. I was at the premiere. I sat between Jerry Stiller, the comedian and actor, and Ronnie Cutrone, the artist and one of Andy Warhol's Factory denizens, and we were all quite riveted by the madness on the screen. It was full of old friends, many long gone. All the original footage had been sewn together in film format and seeing it like that, all in one big gulp on a big screen all those years later, made it super-real. The past became more than just my personal memories. I sat there, soaking in those emotional, intellectual experiences from a previous lifetime, as they were stacked together now into the longest Tuesday night in history.

A few weeks before, I had gone to see another documentary, this one about Paris in the twenties and that great era of American authors who changed the face of modern literature. Paris was the city where they could be free of restrictions and storm ahead with new ideas. There were many obvious parallels between that twenties confluence of writers, artists, actors, and musicians and the punk/underground scene in seventies New York. We had, in some smaller way, transformed post-hippie happenings into a creative eruption of new art forms that presaged the advent of computerization and digital communications. It wasn't easy. But at the same time, there was a curious simplicity to the way it unfolded.

It's all about time. Time is what matters. Time had brought me—brought us all—inexorably from the netherworld of the counterculture into the mainstream of today's culture. Such a very different world. I was harshly criticized in 1978 for showing a slash of red panties onstage at the Palladium; today everything is revealed, nothing is hidden. Boundaries have melted away in favor of an often-boring openness. One silver lining, I guess, is that at least the consciousness has changed for the better around our sexuality: it's easier to be open about your gender identity and preferences, with less fear of reprisal. There is the concept of a time being "ripe" but now time has sped up. No sooner ripe than rotten. Today it's all about being famous. But in those days, it was about making something happen. And over time, we did make some things happen.

GLENN DECIDED TO MAKE A MOVIE ABOUT THE DOWNTOWN SCENE. The director was Edo Bertoglio, a Swiss photographer who was part of the *TV Party* gang and who took photos for *Interview* magazine and Italian *Elle*. Edo and his wife, Maripol, a photographer, stylist, and designer, found some financial backers in Italy and work started in late 1980 on *New York Beat Movie*. It was a snapshot of downtown New York before Mayor Giuliani got on his knees with a toothbrush and a bottle of bleach and cleaned it all up. But it was also a fantasy, an urban fairy tale that starred Jean-Michel Basquiat as a penniless artist wandering around the Lower East Side looking for women to take him in, while he tried to sell his paintings. Those last two things were true. Jean-Michel was homeless at the time.

Chris and I bought the first painting Jean-Michel ever sold, *Self Portrait with Suzanne*. Suzanne was his girlfriend. Jean-Michel had said something to Chris about needing some money and asked if we wanted to buy a painting. Chris said, "How much?" Jean-Michel said, "Three hundred dollars." So, we bought a huge Basquiat painting for $300, a ridiculously small amount of money, but Jean-Michel came away saying, "I really took them for a ride!" so we were all happy.

I played the role of a bag lady in *New York Beat Movie* and there's a scene in which I ask Jean-Michel to kiss me. When he does, I turn into a fairy godmother and give him a suitcase full of money. That's the thing I remember most about doing that movie, how much I enjoyed kissing Jean-Michel. He was very soft-spoken and kind of shy and sexy and magnetic, and I had a strong attraction to him. It was a very good kiss.

Just about everybody was in that movie: Blondie; Tish and Snooky; Roberta Bayley; James Chance, a.k.a. James White; Kid Creole; Tav Falco; Vincent Gallo; Amos Poe; Walter Steding; Marty Thau; Fab 5 Freddy; and Lee Quiñones—another member of the Fab 5. The Fab 5 were this graffiti crew from the outer boroughs of New York City that painted subway cars and made the transition from trains to art galleries. These were wonderful undertakings but were belittled by most of the press and the MTA. Some people found it hard to draw a distinction between the kids who would just scrawl away and the real painters who created elaborate moving murals that were genuine works of art. One time, for example, Freddy graffitied cartoons of Campbell's soup cans in tribute to Andy Warhol. These trains would come into the station to spontaneous applause, people on the platform cheering, "Hell yeah!"

Freddy was also a rapper. I remember him showing up at CBGB's when we played and just sort of standing there, but he was very noticeable because very few black kids came in. Then in 1977, he took us to our first rap gig. It was at a Police Athletic League event in the Bronx, just a neighborhood thing. All the guys getting up and shouting about their sexuality and their sense of their own power or protesting about their state of living. It was very tribal. The sound system was really bad, but it was live and it was fresh and it was very punk. It was another punk scene running parallel to ours and we loved it.

Meanwhile, *New York Beat Movie* ran into some kind of money problem and everything stopped. The film sat on a shelf somewhere gathering dust for nearly twenty years. Eventually Glenn and Maripol managed to track it down and get the rights to it, but by that time the audio of the dialogue had vanished. They still had the live music audio, but the dialogue had to be overdubbed and that was kind of complicated. We had to lip-sync what was being said and try to match the mouth movements, and since there was no script nobody really knew what had been said. They had to hire an actor, Saul Williams, to speak Jean-Michel's part, because Jean-Michel was gone by then. We had always stayed in touch with him—and when his drug problem became too serious he went into a methadone program, but it didn't last. Jean-Michel died from a heroin overdose in 1988. He was twenty-seven years old.

I'm never taking this outfit off.

The movie, retitled *Downtown '81*, finally came out in 2000, along with a soundtrack album of the same name. Nineteen eighty-one was the same year Blondie released our rap song, "Rapture." Jean-Michel was in our video playing the role of a DJ. He tried to graffiti the blank wall behind him on the set, but the studio boss said no, just like they did at the cable access studio where we shot *TV Party*. Amazing, isn't it?

THE ALL-SEEING EYE. THESE DAYS IT'S INESCAPABLE. NO ONE NOW thinks twice about being photographed, or they think about it so much that when they're not being photographed, they photograph themselves. Chris was a sharp-eyed chronicler and observer, always there with his camera, always taking photos of me and others. I got used to seeing myself through the way he saw me, which I guess makes me also an observer, or an observer once removed. That is one of the interesting by-products of being a subject—being able to look at yourself through someone else's eyes. On our 1979 album *Eat to the Beat* there was a song that Jimmy wrote called "Living in the Real World." It went:

Hey I'm living in a magazine
Page to page in my teenage dream . . .
I'm not living in the real world

And in a way that's how it was. That year, Blondie was on the cover of *Rolling Stone* and I was on the cover of *Us* magazine and other magazines around the world. I've been photographed so many times by so many people—Chris Stein, Robert Mapplethorpe, Richard Avedon, Mick Rock, Roberta Bayley, Brian Aris, Chalkie Davies, Bob Gruen, Christopher Makos, Francesco Scavullo, Bobby Grossman, the Earl of Lichfield, and more. In the process, I learned what to look for in a photograph. I'm definitely a visual thinker. When I get ideas, I tend to see them as images rather than something my feelings create. My songs are moving pictures. I watch to see where they go; I adjust the character or the lighting and maybe come up with a soundtrack.

For as long as I can remember, I've loved movies and television, been mesmerized by what's on the screen. Feeding into this was a lifelong love of dressing up and experimenting. Of imagining who I wanted to be and by extension who I might become. In the early days of Blondie, I had the security of having a role to stand behind. I was always very interested in the idea of being in movies, and Chris was interested in writing music for film. As Blondie became more popular and my face was in so many magazines, movie scripts came in from all directions. Most were little more than exploitation pieces that read like they had been written on someone's coffee break: "beautiful rock 'n' roll singer in a band plays crummy clubs and takes a bunch of drugs." Nothing at all beguiling, until *Union City*.

Union City was an art house movie. Marcus Reichert, the director, was also a novelist and a painter whose work was in a number of small galleries. Set in small-town fifties New Jersey, it's the story of Lillian, whose paranoid husband, Harlan, played by Dennis Lipscomb, is less interested in her than in catching whoever he believes is stealing bottles of milk from in front of their door. Lillian tries in vain to please him, but as he becomes increasingly psychotic she amuses herself with the building superintendent. Actually, the husband was a victim of PTSD from World War II, although it's not really stated in the movie. Nobody talked about that back then; it wasn't even a "syndrome." If you had problems you had to grin and bear it and be a man, and if you were a woman you had to do the same, by taking one of the roles designated for girls in those days. That's how things were when I was growing up. That was the restrictive milieu I was groomed to perform in—and that I ran away from. Lillian was very much alone in her own private world and I could relate to that.

I had been in movies before, but the Lillian character was my first real lead role. It wasn't a cameo, I wasn't glamorous, and I didn't sing. Chris wrote music for the film and much later Nigel and I wrote a song entitled "Union City Blue," but it was not about the movie. Coincidentally, this was a period when "Heart of Glass" was in the charts, yet Blondie was on suspension for not fulfilling its contractual obligations to the record label, which meant we weren't recording new material and supplying them with the requisite number of albums as per our contract. None of the actors were particularly well-known but they displayed a spectacular array of attitudes and characters—so good to work with. Pat Benatar was in it too, cute as a hot button and not at all camera shy; we were both on the same record label and I think that she had just released her first album. The guy who played her husband, Tony Azito, was a Broadway song-and-dance man who died tragically young. Taylor Mead played a neurotically hilarious neighbor. Everett McGill played Larry Longacre, the janitor who became my lover. C. C. H. Pounder—who was in one of my all-time favorite movies, *Bagdad Café*—made a brief appearance as a woman with nine kids and a husband, looking for an apartment. The makeup man, Richard Dean, was a talented illustrator who made drawings of all the different characters and their looks and makeup. Richard went on to work for NBC for many years. I think I still have his drawings of me, somewhere. Our DP, Edward Lachman, was under the radar, calling himself Eddie Lumiere, at the time.

It was a short shoot because it was very low budget, maybe a few weeks. The first day on set I was quite nervous, worrying about remembering my lines. It was so different in so many ways from singing in a band. A different pace, a different sense of timing, and a different kind of intimacy. There's no audience, no one to feed off; there's a crew and the director but they're all busy doing their job so you do your job and hope you do it well. When it was done, Chris and I watched it together. I think he was more nervous than I was, nervous for me, wanting it to be good for my sake. I think he was pleasantly surprised. I'm the one who always thinks I could be better; you know how that is. But the cinematography and the lighting were so beautiful. The whole movie had a great painterly quality to it. Marcus, the director, now lives exclusively as a painter, in France. At one point he wrote a sequel to the movie but he couldn't get the money to do it.

I remember thinking, *If you don't like it you don't ever have to make another movie.* But I just took to it. I really enjoyed being a character and telling a story in pictures, taking direction, sharing a vision. "Blondie" was a role that I created, and if you think about it, it's one of the longest-running roles in rock. But

On the set of Union City *with director Marcus Reichert*

the *Union City* experience was less like a collaborative creation because Marcus was clear about what he wanted, who the character was, and what he needed from me. So naturally, after that experience I wanted to do more films.

Chris and I were planning to do a remake of Jean-Luc Godard's *Alphaville,* a futuristic French film noir from 1965. We would be the producers and Amos Poe would direct. I was to play the female lead, Natacha von Braun, the part that Anna Karina played in Godard's movie—and Robert Fripp would be the detective antihero, Lemmy Caution, who had been played by Eddie Constantine. Robert, the remarkable guitar player and composer who cofounded the British rock band King Crimson, became a friend after he moved to New York and worked as a solo artist and producer. He sat in with us at one of our CBGB's shows in May 1978 and he made many guest appearances as well as playing on *Parallel Lines,* in "Fade Away and Radiate," the song Chris wrote about my falling asleep in front of the TV screen. Robert and I dressed in character and did some screen tests. You can still find it on the Internet.

Chris and I had met with Godard in person and told him we wanted to do the movie. He said, "Why? You're crazy," but he sold us the film rights anyway for one thousand dollars. We found out later that he didn't own the rights, but that's not why the movie didn't materialize. One element was that we knew nothing about producing a film, but the other was that our record company didn't want us doing it. There was a similar problem when Robert Fripp asked me to sing on a record with him; our record company wouldn't allow it. And later on, when I was sent a script for *Blade Runner,* the record company blocked that too—and I really wanted to do that movie. I'm sure it would have helped us sell records, in any case. But it seemed that the higher we got on the totem pole, the less they wanted us to do anything except for Blondie. Especially me. Chris had an outlet taking photos—he shot the sleeve for Robert Fripp's new album—and for his own company, Animal Records, he produced albums like Iggy Pop's *Zombie Birdhouse* and Gun Club's *Miami*. He also produced Walter Steding for Warhol's label Earhole, and an album by Gilles Riberolles and Eric Weber from the French rock-disco duo Casino Music, and also the soundtrack for the landmark hip-hop film *Wild Style*, plus a whole slew of other ventures.

I loved fooling around and experimenting, but there's no point if it lands in a lawsuit. The music business is a business like every other, but art and commerce make for uneasy bed partners. "Can't live with you, can't live without you." I didn't choose to be an artist to have other people telling me how to create. We felt a deep need for creative freedom, a day-to-day rattling away on the bars of our emotional cages.

So, the bell rang and it was time to deliver another Blondie album. During a short break in a yearlong U.S. tour, we went into the Record Plant studio to start working with Mike Chapman on *Eat to the Beat*. The good news was that our manager Peter Leeds wasn't lurking in the studio putting the pressure on and making us crazy. We had finally cut all ties with him, although we couldn't do so without allowing him to own 20 percent of our future. But now we had to find new people to represent us, which meant endless meetings with businesspeople trying to persuade us how wonderful they were and how good they'd be for us. We interviewed with everyone from Shep Gordon to Sid Bernstein to Bill Graham to Jake Riviera. It's hard to think of anything more distracting when you're supposed to be making a record. So, we canceled the sessions.

But when we started again two months later, it went really, really fast. We finished the album in about three weeks. Maybe it was because after all that time on the road we could record a lot of it live. But what I remember most is sitting in a lounge in the studio, trying to write a lyric, feeling really hard-pressed because the tracks were being put down and I didn't have a clue about what I was going to sing. Maybe that's why some of the songs are so minimal. Take "Atomic." That song sort of happened on the spot. Jimmy had come in with this music that sounded like a Morricone score from one of those fabulous spaghetti westerns by Sergio Leone. I just started basically fooling around with the lyrics and making fun of it. I didn't think it would stick, but it did, and people love that song. And in fact, the song has resonated through the years to the point that most recently there was a movie entitled *Atomic Blonde.* The lead character, who was played by Charlize Theron, was styled in my Blondie image. The album was all original songs this time, no covers, including funk, reggae, disco, even a lullaby, but it was also our most rock album, and the first album we recorded knowing that we really had an audience waiting to hear it. Our first single was "Dreaming." Sometimes Chris would give me a phrase that he'd had in his head while working on the music—in this case, "Dreaming is free"—and I'd write the rest, like I was writing the theme for a film. It was our first single from the album and went to the top of the British charts, our fourth UK number one in two years. The second single, "Union City Blue," wasn't released in the U.S. but made the UK top twenty. The third, "Atomic," put us back at number one.

Blondie went straight back on the road once the album was done. We took some days off in Austin, Texas, to make a cameo in a movie called *Roadie,* whose young director, Alan Rudolph, came from the Robert Altman company. This was the first gig our new manager, Shep Gordon, got us. Shep also managed Alice Cooper, and we signed with him on a handshake, no contract. *Roadie* starred Meat Loaf, who was bigger than life in every sense. At the other end of the size scale, the film also had a number of dwarf actors. There was one scene in a café where a fight broke out with the dwarves and a few of us actually got roughed up, because those little guys were very active and very, very strong. It was chaotic and a lot of fun. Blondie also recorded a rock treatment of the Johnny Cash song "Ring of Fire" for the soundtrack of the movie. Chris's hearing was never the same after he got squirted in the ear during the fight scene.

We took another short break to make a video for each of the songs on the album. I remember our having conversations with the director David Mallet about how all the material on the album seemed to lend itself to cinematic storytelling. The visual side of Blondie was always very important to Chris and me, and since you didn't need to have much money to make videos then, David managed to sell the idea to Chrysalis. Most of the videos were shot around New York except for "Union City," which we shot at the docks along the Hudson on the Jersey side.

It was December 1979, "Dreaming" was at the top of the British charts, and we'd flown to London to rehearse for a major tour that would begin the day after Christmas. Soon after we arrived, we did an in-store appearance in London at a record shop on Kensington High Street. This little shop was mobbed by thousands of fans. The whole street was blocked and the traffic had ground to a halt. The police arrived to close off the street; we'd never had a street closed off for our benefit before. Looking out of the window to see a crowd of people screaming was fantastic. It was like Beatlemania. It was Blondiemania! Coincidentally, we met Paul McCartney on that trip. He was standing in front of our hotel as we were boarding our bus. He knew vaguely who we were and he was very relaxed and friendly, and of course Clem was out of his mind. Clem was and is Beatlemania personified, and was totally infatuated with Paul McCartney. Paul was very nice. He chatted awhile with us until his wife, Linda, showed up and dragged him off.

A crew from *20/20*, an American weekly TV news show on ABC, was following us around London on that trip. They were doing a story on the new wave scene and the rise of Blondie. They filmed the crowds at the record store and they came to the Hammersmith Odeon, where we played eight shows this time, headlining, all sold out. Tony Ingrassia, who was living in Berlin at that time, flew in to choreograph and stage-direct us. Robert Fripp guested on a song with us every night. On our last night, Iggy Pop came onstage for the encore. He sang "Funtime" and it really was a fun time, a big ongoing party. Joan Jett was there; the Runaways were in London to record an album that was never made. We saw her outside the Hammersmith Odeon, arguing with the guy at the ticket office who said she wasn't on the list, so we scooped her into our bus and she came in with us.

Joan was in our hotel room the next day when the *20/20* people interviewed Chris and me. They asked Chris what it was like to live with "the sex symbol of the seventies," and he answered, "I couldn't be happier." When the interviewer pressed for more he said, "As an ego boost to a man, it's fantastic." The questions were starting to drive me crazy. Earlier I'd complained to Joan about having these people up my ass all the time. Joan had been emptying the minibar simultaneously and I think Chris introduced her to the interviewer. Joan went in front of the camera and said, "Fuck you, ABC!" flipping them off with both hands.

It was the end of January 1980 when we left the UK. *Eat to the Beat* was number 1 on the UK charts and a platinum album in the U.S. We flew back to New York on the Concorde. In three hours we were home. Shot through the air like a rocket ship; I felt like an astronaut.

STARLINERS
77

9

BACK TRACK

What's in the woods? Every morning, I let the dogs out for their first piss of the day. Lately, one dog runs toward my neighbor's property, then freezes. She stands at the edge of the wall—something I can relate to—and barks in bursts of three for as long as I let her. It's a very excited kind of barking, almost hysteria, but she doesn't seem to lose her voice. She can bark for thirty minutes or more and I don't hear a single scratchy note. No canine laryngitis for this little lady. What a valuable vocal technique, and what might she have to teach me here? Special, secret doggie vocal skills . . . However as a rock singer I have clearly stood on the edge hysterically bursting into an excited version of "One Way or Another."

Well, I didn't sit down to write about the damn dogs, really, although I do get my entertainment dollars' worth from their antics. What I was trying to do was come up with a name for my book, this hike down memory lane. Today's nominee is *Tempered Glass*. Tempered glass is manufactured to be tougher than its brothers and sisters through exerting heavy compression on its exterior and heavy tension on its interior. It's designed to crumble into pieces rather than explode into jagged shards when subjected to high pressure. And that would be me. Tempered to take the hits without flying into dangerous pieces. I like that. And, of course, there's the reference to "Heart of Glass." Another contender is *Matter-Antimatter;* just a small cog, a tooth on one of the infinite gears that run the universe. One of the earlier titles I came up with was *Perfect Punk*—because I'm punk through and through and have been from my very first breath. The other day, just for fun, I looked up the etymology of "punk" in an older Webster's dictionary. I was surprised to learn that one possible origin was from Unami, an Algonquian language local to New Jersey. Definition: "Wood so decayed as to be useful for tinder to light a fire. A touchwood." I like this meaning. It's cool. I'd heard a number of definitions for "punk," from Shakespeare's "whore," to a lowlife kid, to a jailhouse sex toy. At least the Algonquians had a somewhat higher purpose for "punk." *Face It* became my title choice for three reasons: 1) from all the fan art portraits I have collected over the years, 2) because of all of the photos taken of me, 3) and finally, because I have had to face it in order to do this memoir.

But let's get back on track. The book, remember? Well, "remember" is both the keyword and the bugaboo. Not just trying to remember but reliving all the shit of my life, instead of just moving ahead from day to day into new shit. The sheer living of it back then was already more than enough. It's a chemical challenge to have to experience it all over again. When I was a brat, I would threaten my parents or anyone who treated me badly with, "You'll be sorry when I'm rich and famous!" *And who exactly is sorry now?* I wonder as I clutch my fame in my well-manicured fingers.

Fame was a sensual sort of feeling, initially. It felt like having sex, a wash of electricity coursing through your fingers and

up your legs, sometimes a flushed feeling at the base of your throat. It was exciting, but at the same time strangely anticlimactic. Maybe because it didn't come in one big explosive rush. Fame built itself more gradually, punctuated by moments that would pull you up short and make you think, *It's working, whatever "it" is.* But then you'd just keep moving, like a moth drawn to the flame or a horse straining for the dangled carrot, as Chris liked to put it.

Those times when we came closest to real rock 'n' roll madness: The show we played at Max's before leaving on that first Iggy tour, the room so oversold that someone—probably our manager—called the fire department, and I was onstage watching all these helmets and uniforms trying to wade through the crowd. They shut us down twice but we kept on playing. Then there was the in-store at Our Price Records in London, when there was such a mob that the cops had to block off the street. Or Germany, where we had fans clinging to our bus or throwing themselves in front of it. All these things happened while we were scuttling along from place to place in a state of chaos. There was no time to really take them in. But as the new decade began, for a precious moment the machine stopped. It was late January 1980, we were back in our apartment on West Fifty-Eighth Street with no suitcase to pack or plane to catch, and Chris was able to tend his plants on the terrace. Suddenly there was room to breathe, to shake off the vertigo of being in constant movement and review what we'd achieved.

I think that I had a certain amount of innocence about it all. I would be onstage and there'd be five thousand people pulsing their desire at me. You could feel the heat of it. The raw, animal physicality. Feel them transmitting this strong sexuality. Picking up on it, then working to turn them on even more. And the frenzied feedback cycle would keep building and building . . . This was real. Very real.

But looking back, I think my ego had run amok. Really, it was just business as usual. I was just part of the game, a cog in the machine. I mean, you can pretty much sell *anything* when the corporate structure gets behind it and turns art into commerce. I laid this theory on one of the many labels I've been signed to and they were gagging. For a punk, this confrontation was a revelation.

I was even a punk as a pinup. There was a magazine most of America bought called *TV Guide*. One of the ads in the back was for a company specializing in posters of American pinups like Farrah Fawcett, Suzanne Somers, and "Blondie," as they called the poster they sold of me. I liked that I was on the fans' bedroom walls, helping them to entertain themselves. You can't control other people's fantasies or the illusion they're buying or selling. You could say that I was selling an illusion of myself. But the biggest seller is always sex. Sex is what makes everything happen. Sex is why people dress nice, comb their hair, brush their teeth, and take showers. In the entertainment field, sex appeal, looks, and talent are the primary factors.

There are hazards to that, though. There were many times when people would review how I looked instead of how our music sounded. I didn't do Blondie to become famous for my looks. When I started out, rock music didn't want girls to be anything but window dressing, something to stand there and look pretty and sing "Ooh, ooh, ooh" or "La, la, la." That wasn't me. I tried it for a short time in the Wind in the Willows and knew for sure that it wasn't me. Like most girls of my generation, I'd been programmed since childhood to look for a strong man to carry me off and look after me. I bought into those fantasies as a kid at least to some degree, but by the time I was in my midtwenties I was done with that. I was wanting to have control, and as Dad always said, I was too damn independent for my own good. I looked for adventure and new experiences instead of settling down. I needed to keep learning more and more. I felt like I was a woman with a man's brain and initiative and strength—and being cute does not make you an idiot. One thing I did learn in this crazy world was how desperately important it is for me to keep a sense of humor.

We had finished our UK tour with a number one album and now, just weeks later, we were about to release the biggest-selling single of our career. It all started with a phone call from Giorgio Moroder. Giorgio was the godfather of disco, the producer and songwriter and hit maker behind those great Donna Summer singles. He also wrote electronic music for movies and he was working on the theme song to a new Paul Schrader film, *American Gigolo,* starring Richard Gere as a stud for hire. Giorgio wanted Blondie to perform the song. He'd written the music. For the lyrics, Stevie Nicks's name was mentioned, but he'd ended up writing them himself. He gave us a cassette tape with a demo of the song he'd called "Man Machine."

Giorgio is a real ladies' man, with real Italian machismo, and always had beautiful girlfriends and women around him. I couldn't sing Giorgio's lyrics because they came from the perspective of a man with huge sexual power. So, I took the job of writing new lyrics. We asked to see the film. Paul Schrader invited us up to his room at the Pierre Hotel, where we all watched the rough cut on video. The visuals were what fascinated me about the movie. Such subtle, evocative colors, which I later learned were pulled from the palette of Giorgio Armani, and that stunning image of a beautiful car driving down the coast highway. I walked back to our apartment with the visuals fresh in my mind and the music in my head and the first lines came to me instantly. *"Color me your color baby. Color me your car."* Once I was home I wrote them down right away. The rest of the song, as they say, just wrote itself. It had to be "Call Me," because that's what Richard Gere's character said to all the women. We went into the studio with Giorgio for just one afternoon and recorded. It was released as the first single from the soundtrack album and shot straight to number one in the U.S., UK, and Canada, and number two in the dance charts. It would turn out to be the biggest-selling single in America that year.

I performed that song on *The Muppet Show*. Surprisingly, it was a "moment" for me. I was never a Muppets fan—it was way too goody-goody for me—but after I saw Dizzy Gillespie on the show I thought, *If he did it, I want to do it*. So, I flew to Elstree Studios in England and had such a fabulous time. Jim Henson, the Muppets' creator, was, I think, a big pervert, in the best possible way. He had a cleverly twisted sense of humor and he was giving smart motives and observations to his characters. He and Frank Oz, who performed Miss Piggy and Animal and Fozzie Bear, were like these strange old hippies, sweet but subversive. They dressed me as a Frog Scout and I talked to the scouts about earning their badges. I also taught them how to pogo. I sang "One Way or Another"—I'm not sure if they realized that it was about a stalker—and I did a duet with Kermit on "Rainbow Connection." I sang with the Muppet Band and I became the pinup of the Pond 4 troop. What could be better?

Moving on . . . I've been thinking about Andy Warhol and what an impact he had on my life. Andy was the master of blurring the line between art and commerce. His art played with the conventions of commerce—marketing, mass production, branding, popular culture, advertising, celebrity. He also blurred the line between serious and playful. He was very serious about his work, but he approached it with a sense of humor. His work ethic was incredible. He would wake up early every day and go to his studio and paint, break for lunch, and work all afternoon—often spending hours on the phone—then at night he would always go out and socialize. He went everywhere. In

Andy and the Amiga 2000 in 1985.

fact, I first met him—and his dazzling entourage—when I was waiting tables at Max's. I admired Andy so much. Like Andy, I felt the influence of Marcel Duchamp and a kinship to Dada and Popism, which became foundational to what I was creating.

To my amazement, we actually became acquainted. Chris and I found ourselves on Andy's invitation list. He would ask us to dinner sometimes. He didn't eat much; he'd often cover up his plate with a napkin and take it with him and leave it on a ledge somewhere for a hungry street person. Later on, he invited us to his parties at the Factory on Union Square. Andy would invite all kinds of people from all kinds of backgrounds, uptown, downtown, artists, socialites, eccentrics, you name it. Andy, in his way, was very sociable and hung around with any- and everybody. One of his great skills was that he was a very, very good listener. He would sit there and suck all of it in. His curiosity was endless. He was also extremely supportive of new artists. Chris and I adored Andy—and to find out that he was a fan of ours was heavenly.

Andy put me on the cover of *Interview* magazine and he threw a party for us at Studio 54 when "Heart of Glass" went to number one in America. Now that we weren't on the road, we had gotten to know him a little, and the idea of Andy's doing my portrait came up; somewhere, at some point, Andy had remarked that if he could have anyone else's face, it would be mine.

How it worked was that first Andy took some photos of you. He used one of those unique Big Shot Polaroid cameras that looked like a shoebox with a lens on it. The Big Shot was designed for portrait use only—and the quality of the shots was often striking. Perfect for Andy. After taking the Polaroids, he would show them to us and ask quietly—Andy was very soft-spoken—"Well, which one would you like?" I saw a couple that I thought were good but I said, "That's really up to you." He's the artist; it seemed to be the safest thing to have him choose. I've lived with that Andy Warhol portrait for a long time now, so I'm much more used to it, but seeing all these portraits of yourself for the first time, by an artist who was so important to you, was startling. I guess I was just stunned. And humbled. Over the years, Chris and I came across a lot of those cameras from the early seventies and we would always buy them for Andy. We'd find them in junk stores at around twenty-five cents a pop. He'd always be very grateful. The portrait itself has taken on a life of its own—reproduced countless times and exhibited in numerous galleries worldwide. I still have that original Warhol. I can't imagine parting with it. Well, I will be parting with it briefly next year, when I loan it to the Whitney for a retrospective show of Andy's work.

Later, Andy called and asked me to model for a portrait he was going to create live, at Lincoln Center, as a promotion for the Commodore Amiga computer. It was a pretty amazing event. They had a full orchestra and a large board set up with a bunch of technicians in lab coats. The techs programmed away with all the Warhol colors, as Andy designed and painted my portrait. I hammed it up some for the cameras, turning toward Andy, running my hand through my hair, and asking in a suggestive Marilyn voice, "Are you ready to paint me?" Andy was pretty hilarious in his usual flat-affect way, as he sparred with the Commodore host.

I think there are only two copies of this computer-generated Warhol in existence and I have one of them. Commodore also gave me a free computer, which I passed on to Chris. Chris loves equipment. Our apartment was starting to look like the cockpit of a 747 with all the computers and synthesizers and electronics and wiring. Chris wanted very much at the time to have his own twenty-four-track studio. This way he could set up his own label and work with other bands. But that would cost

Look how cute we are, Freddie!

a bunch of money. Well, it just so happened I'd been offered a whole bunch of money to endorse a line of designer jeans.

Gloria Vanderbilt, the designer for Murjani, and I met just once, very, very briefly, just a hello. She fascinated me. She had led the most extraordinary life: a socialite and an heiress who became an actress, artist, writer, model, and fashion designer. She was what really interested me about doing those ads. That and the Popist idea. I wanted to make the ads as relevant to my life as they were to selling jeans, more like art rock videos. We invited our friends the Lounge Lizards, James Chance, and Anya Phillips to be in the commercial. But what I remember most about this little escapade in art and commerce was how tight those pink jeans were. Ridiculously tight. In fact, I needed several good-looking men to help me get them off.

Memory is subjective. A lot of it depends on the angles you see things from. Having conversations about politics or money—or who's taking what drugs when and how—is like *Rashomon* revisited. Everyone likes to take credit for discovering us, for making me a star, for taming those savage little maniacs running wild in the studio. That last one seems to be Mike Chapman's memory, though that was never my recollection. But we loved Mike and without him would never have made such great records. Loved him enough that we agreed to spend two months in Los Angeles to make our new album with him. We had always made him come to New York, which he did not like. So it was only fair and appropriate to go to the city of cars, where you had to drive to get anywhere, to make the album entitled *Autoamerican*.

They put us up at the Oakwood Apartments, which we hadn't realized were on the other side of the hill in Burbank. They were full of transients and drug dealers; we were often swarmed by unmarked cars that would suddenly appear and surround a cab or truck and arrest some guy, just like the good old days in New York. Except that it wasn't New York, it was Burbank. The thought of spending two months waking up there every morning and driving to United Western Studios in Hollywood wasn't a happy one. Then one day, we heard a huge racket from police choppers over our heads, like something out of Vietnam. Someone had been shot in the parking lot. That gave us an excuse to get out of Dodge and hightail it over the hill. So, we moved into the Chateau Marmont, into one of those great old bungalows they have down below the hotel, near the pool. This little bungalow was much more to our taste. Sadly, the bungalows may have become more famous after John Belushi died in one of them years later.

Autoamerican was a very different album to make than *Eat to the Beat*. We very much wanted to create a work that went beyond the "valley of the dolls" and beyond what Blondie was known for. Popular music had become so compartmentalized. All these little camps for people to join, making them an easier target for the industry to sell things to. We wanted to make

Is there a hairdresser in the house?

music that would cross over these boundaries, bring people together. *Autoamerican*'s theme was diversity—musical, cultural, and racial. There were all sorts of different musical styles: rap, reggae, rock, pop, Broadway, disco, jazz.

When the record company heard it, they were nonplussed. But by this point we were used to their saying, "Where are the hits?" Because we *had* hits, we ignored them. Just like we learned to ignore the critics who turned on Blondie because of our hits and accused us of selling out. Ah, these little armchair heroes, battling on the front lines for the purity of pop and rock. No blurring of the line between art and commerce for them! In a particularly idiotic one-star review, *Rolling Stone* accused us of "proclaiming the death of pop culture" with this album.

By the eighties, new wave had already been co-opted by the mainstream, just as punk had been and the hippies before that. You couldn't move for glossy, major-label new wave bands. It was all too safe for our liking. We wanted to do something radical. We didn't call ourselves new wave—maybe it was the critics who labeled us that—and we were doing what punks do, which is break down walls. I had really had enough of doing what other people wanted or expected me to do.

On *Autoamerican* we did a subversive disco song about Satan, "Do the Dark." We did a score to an imaginary film, "Europa." We did a torch song by Lerner and Loewe from *Camelot*, "Follow Me." We'd gone to see the movie, and afterward Chris couldn't get the song out of his head. I suspect that the rest of the band thought he'd lost his mind. On "T-Birds" we had the Turtles' Mark Volman and Howard Kaylan sing backup. They were these sweet, funny guys who would come to our L.A. gigs and say, "Write us a hit song so we'll be able to work for another ten years." They'd had a couple of big singles in the sixties and really knew how to work it. Then they packed it in, joined Frank Zappa's band, and became Flo and Eddie.

We also recorded "The Tide Is High," a rocksteady/reggae song by the Paragons that we first heard on a compilation album in London. Chris and I fell in love with it. We asked the Specials if they would play on it, but they couldn't or wouldn't, I don't remember which, so we brought in session musicians. Until then, we'd never had so many outside musicians on one of our albums. They included four percussionists, jazz horns, a thirty-piece orchestra, and a mariachi band. "The Tide Is High" was our first single from this "album with no hits." It went to number one in the U.S., the UK, and several other places.

Our second single, "Rapture," was a rap song but with a downtown rock sort of twist. We loved rap. It was still very underground at that point, but "Rapture" went to the top of the charts. I'm told it was the first rap song to make number one and it was the first with its own original music. All the rap songs up to that point were done using rhythm tracks and licks from existing songs. We shot the video for it in New York and asked our hip-hop and street art friends to be in it. There were Lee Quiñones; Jean-Michel Basquiat playing a DJ; and Fab 5 Freddy, who had taken Chris and me to our first rap show in the Bronx. I name-checked Freddy in the song and also Grandmaster Flash, another pioneer. We asked him to be in the video too, but he didn't make it. The voodoo man in the white suit and top hat was played by a break-dancer, William Barnes. He helped us find some genuine voodoo dancers and brought along three Haitian girls. During the shoot, one of the girls started behaving like she really was possessed and fell into a trance. We had to stop while William tried to bring her out of it.

The "Rapture" video was rolling out with its premiere on the TV program *Solid Gold*. It was also the first rap video on MTV. When I hosted the TV show *Saturday Night Live* in 1981 we brought a hip-hop band with us, Funky 4 + 1. I tried to get the TV crew to set up a table with two turntables, so that they

Studio 54.

could do their scratching and dance performance during the show. But the execs were too nervous and only allowed them to perform during the credit roll at the end. Once they saw what it was about, I think they regretted not having them in the show, because it was so great. It's funny how the entertainment industry was so scared of hip-hop. Chris and I were so turned on by it. Chris was so buzzed that he talked to some people in the music industry about all these great bands. Every one of them told him that rap was a fad and it would soon go away.

Autoamerican was released in November 1980. It went into the top ten but didn't reach number one. We had decided not to tour with it. Or Chris and I had decided. Chris thought that being on the road all the time was a waste of time. He felt that his best efforts were better spent being creative than dogging around doing physical labor. Chris is not a road warrior like Clem is. He's Mensa material with an IQ of God knows what and he found it objectionable to be dragged around, more and more exhausted, unable to do all the other things that interested him.

Blondie was a real band in the traditional hippie sense. It was an attempt at democracy; everyone shared in the profits, everyone had a position to take, everyone got to say what they thought, and every viewpoint was heard. But it took a while for us to figure out the division of labor. Chris's job was to make a lot of the decisions, both creative and business. My job was to be the front person and the big mouth, the subject of interviews and the object of photography. The guys had to make their contribution to the music and keep up a strong rock 'n' roll image. No matter how late they'd been up the night before, they still had to get up onstage and play their asses off. But I was being run ragged. I went out on promo tours by myself for three months at a time while everybody was at home, wondering why we weren't out on the road playing. For good or bad, the buck stopped at me. We'd tasted freedom during

2017 "Fun" video shoot. What were those lyrics?

those few months off the road. While the band was often a battle of wills—and we struggled constantly to avoid becoming formulaic—all these different creative possibilities kept arising. So, we decided to explore them. Chris and I wanted to make an album that synthesized black and white music, not just a rock band covering a black song or writing a song that referenced black music but a true collaboration between a black act and a white act. We were serious about it. We thought it would be very interesting socially as well as musically. The racial issue was and still is very heavy in the U.S.

The first artists we thought to work with were Bernard Edwards and Nile Rodgers. We had been Chic fans for years. We'd met them briefly at the Power Station when Blondie was recording *Eat to the Beat* and they were working with Diana Ross. Later we got to know them socially. One time, Chris and I took Nile to a high school in Queens. We walked into the gymnasium where the kids were break-dancing and rapping and the only song they were scratching on was "Good Times."

Chic had had all these commercial hits with songs like "Le Freak" and "Good Times," and we'd had all these commercial hits, like "Heart of Glass," "The Tide Is High," and "Rapture"; they were in a niche and we were in a niche; we were trying to sound like them sometimes and sometimes they were trying to sound like us; so we thought it would be a good idea to see what happened if we met in the middle. Luckily, they were as interested in us as we were in them. This was before they'd worked with David Bowie on *Let's Dance,* and with Madonna on *Like a Virgin,* so we were the first rock artists they'd decided to work with in that way. The collection was later to be entitled *KooKoo.*

It was a full-on collaboration. Nile and Bernard wrote four songs, Chris and I wrote four songs, and we wrote two more songs as a foursome. And it was so much fun to record. They would start the sessions by telling a lot of racial jokes. My face would hurt from laughing sometimes. We had Mark Mothersbaugh and Gerald Casale of Devo on backing vocals for "Jump Jump" and they were credited as Spud Devo and Pud Devo. I loved that album. I feel that we were on the cusp of creating a style of music that exists today without a second thought but was unprecedented then. I guess we were a few years too soon.

10

BLAME IT ON *VOGUE*

If you are a woman and you want to feel inadequate and anxious, then get yourself a copy of *Vogue* and start flipping through it. Works like a charm. It certainly worked that way for me. Not just *Vogue*, of course, but any of the high-fashion magazines: I couldn't help myself, I'd keep on reading looking for some kind of Holy Grail, I guess, but getting more and more depressed. But every now and then, a jewel would fall into my lap and save the day, like an article about *Frischzellentherapie*—fresh cell therapy—which was being offered at this exclusive clinic in Switzerland. I'd gotten to the age where I had abused my body enough to have seen the enemy at the gate. And here was a treatment that claimed to offer an almost miraculous restoration of beauty and health. As the article explained: We are born with trillions of cells that are constantly dying off and being replaced by new ones. However, over time, as we get stressed out or overworked, or don't get enough sleep, or eat terribly, or drink too much, or do a bunch of heavy drugs, the new cells can't keep up with the pace of the destruction. And to my understanding, as the body fails to replenish its dead cells, the aging process starts to pick up the pace. For the last seven years, Chris and I had been poster children for how to speed up that cellular destruction. I took note.

Once Blondie became successful, the pressures of the music industry and the continuing demands for more material, more tours, more press, had taken us to pretty much our limit. Throw in the constant bickering between band members and the lack of understanding from our new management, and we were fried. We were always trying to inject new energy into the band and our music, and now here was something that promised to inject new energy into our bodies. I clipped that article from *Vogue* and carried it around with me for a long time.

We had finished recording *KooKoo*. It was time to start thinking about the album artwork, which is when Chris thought of H. R. Giger, the great master of fantastic realism. Chris was a big fan of his work. We had met him in 1980, at a party at the Hansen Gallery, where they were exhibiting his work. When we arrived, Hans was standing there with an Oscar statuette in his hand, posing for the press. He had just won the Oscar for his work on the Ridley Scott movie *Alien*, for which he created the spaceship, the scenery, and that extraordinary creature, the beautiful, horrible mix of biology and machine, the Alien. I loved how he played with these opposites. Seeing fine art of such high quality in a science fiction movie was unusual and exciting.

Since the gallery wasn't packed out, we went up to say hello to Hans and his wife, Mia, and we invited them back to our apartment. Hans told us that this was only his second time in America. He was from Switzerland and didn't much like leaving Zurich. But, he told us, no city in the world inspired him like New York. New York was a black-magic city, he said. The horizontal line of the subway and the tall, narrow skyscrapers joined together to make a kind of inverted crucifix. Those paintings he did later about New York City may in part have resulted from this visit.

So when it came time to do our album sleeve, Chris and I asked Hans if he would come up with a concept and he agreed immediately. He borrowed a photo that the British photographer Brian Aris had taken of me, with my hair brown and combed back sharply off of my face. Then he painted over it, adding four huge spikes that went in one side of my head and out the other. Giant acupuncture needles, he explained. He had just been for acupuncture treatment, which he called "aku-aku." Hans had a staggeringly thick Swiss-German accent; his English was limited, and he spoke it in a slow and deliberate way. It sounded funny and sweet, and I loved him all the more for it. The contrast between his art, which to most people was subliminally frightening, extreme, and almost intolerable, and this cuddly German teddy bear struggling to say "acu" was endearing.

Aku-Aku was also the name of Thor Heyerdahl's book about his exploration of Easter Island in the 1950s. It was fascinating to watch Hans's mind at work as he combined elements of wizardry and the mystic stone statues, and juxtaposed those gigantic acupuncture needles. A deliberate echo of the punk safety-pin piercings of the day. And somehow Hans's Germanic "aku-aku" became *KooKoo*. Hans elaborated that the spikes going through my head were symbols of the four elements. The source of energy was lightning and the rods would channel the current into my brain. Didn't hurt a bit!

I loved what he did with my face. I had told Hans that I wanted to make this a clear departure from Blondie—not just in the musical style, but in my persona. Hans had never followed Blondie, as he was more of a jazz man apparently. But it worked out perfectly. It was way too goth for my Blondie image but just perfect for my first solo album. Since we were so happy with the album cover, we decided we would make the videos for *KooKoo*'s two singles, "Now I Know You Know" and "Backfired," with Hans. Which meant that we would have to go to his atelier in Zurich. So off we went to Switzerland.

Hans and Mia lived in Oerlikon, a quiet, bucolic neighborhood. From the outside, the Gigers' little house and studio fit right in, except for the garden, where the shrubs were left to grow wild, because Hans liked the random shapes they took. But the interior was definitely in keeping with Hans's fascination with the macabre. The rooms were dark and decorated with goth and fetish art depicting birth, sex, and death. On one table there was a skull; Hans told us that his father had given it to him when he was six years old. Next to his Oscar statuette Hans had placed a shrunken head, the perfect memento mori.

We were there for two or three weeks shooting sixteen-millimeter films that would later be transferred to video. Hans made me an elaborate bodysuit painted with bio-mechanoids—hybrids of humans and machines. They fitted me with a full face mask—which meant two straws stuck up my nose. Ha! I already knew a thing or two about straws up the nose. Then they smeared my face with this fast-setting material used for dental bridges. Yikes! Not so good—I freaked at being closed off like that. So they had to whip the mask off, before it was completely solid. Hans was disappointed with the warped-looking features we were left with, but we topped it with a long black wig and he was able to make it work. Hans was in the video too, wearing a copper, stencil-like mask that was cut out of parts used in making watches. A Swiss-watch stencil mask, so beautiful.

He also made an elaborate Egyptian sarcophagus out of Styrofoam. This time Hans pierced my body with gigantic acupuncture needles, using them like wands to attract the power of the lightning. And *KooKoo* was brought to life like a latter-day Frankenstein. The sarcophagus was incredible but was too fragile for me to lie down in, so he cut a doorway, in the shape of the sarcophagus, for me to come through. I emerged as the reanimated bio-mechanical woman and started to dance around in my painted bodysuit costume airbrushed through the copper watch stencils. While all this witchery was going on, Chris was there with his Hasselblad shooting stills of the wizard Hans and this creature—me—from one of Hans's paintings that he'd brought to life with his art. Those shots Chris took of me are some of my favorite photos ever.

At some point during our stay, I found myself jonesing for smack. Drugs were pretty common in New York at that time and I'd been chipping and dipping for a while now. When I mentioned this to Hans, he handed me a round black ball of opium to eat. Hans was not just a meticulous craftsman, an obsessive artist, and a perfectionist, but he was also a generous and charming man and the perfect host.

I had not forgotten that article from *Vogue*. Since we were already going to be in Switzerland, Chris and I decided to pay a visit to La Prairie, the *Frischzellentherapie* clinic. It was on Lake Geneva in the little town of Clarens Montreux in the French part of Switzerland. Clarens originally became famous as the location for Jean-Jacques Rousseau's wildly popular *La Nouvelle Heloise*. Stravinsky wrote *The Rites of Spring* and *Pulcinella* there, Tchaikovsky composed his violin concerto there, and Nabokov, the author of *Lolita,* died in the town. And now, here *we* were . . . Clarens, with its manicured gardens and its picturesque paths, has historically pulled in a lot of tourists. Chris and I rented boats, drove through the scenic Alps, and visited neighboring Montreux, host city for the famous jazz festival. And then we checked into La Prairie.

The clinic has reimagined itself since then, but back when we were there it was more like a hospital. There were doctors and nurses and a battery of blood tests and X-rays. Then came a series of injections with embryonic cells from a black sheep—why it had to be a *black* sheep I'll never know. At that time, stem cell therapy was a new science and people weren't talking about it like they do today. One of the creators of this therapy and a member of La Prairie's advisory board was Christiaan Barnard, the surgeon who did the first open heart surgery, which led to the development of heart transplants. He was a forward-thinking scientist, so initially that made me sit up and take note. The shots they gave us were huge and the injections were painful, which is something else that's changed over the years. After the treatment, we rested up in the clinic-hospital while they monitored us. Chris felt that little black sheep had definitely reenergized him for a while, and it had a positive effect on me too.

When our record company heard *KooKoo*, they were forced to deal with my potential as a solo artist. And after they weighed their options, it was clear that their hearts weren't really into it. "What do we do with this?" they wondered. And they never did step up to the challenge. They had not been expecting such a departure from cute, hot little Blondie. They were not enthusiastic at all about my dark hair; they thought it would confuse the fans. They wanted Debbie Harry, not Dirty Harry. They didn't much like the artwork with my skewered head either, but to be fair they weren't alone. A number of American record stores refused to stock it, and when our record company in the UK put up posters of the sleeve photo in the London Underground, they were banned—deemed "too disturbing."

What the record company wanted was for me to keep on making Blondie records. They had developed a market for Blondie—they figured—and that's where the money was. At that time, it was uncommon for an artist in the music business to make these kinds of departures. For example, when I was offered a part in the movie *Blade Runner*, which I really wanted to do, the label blocked it. This was ridiculous as far as I was concerned because I was sure it would only have helped sell records. In this day and age, they would figure out how to combine the elements and make the album correspond with the release of the picture, but that wasn't how it worked then. Of course, it might have helped if Shep had gone in and renegotiated our Blondie deal for the better. But as far as I know, he didn't. Basically, communication between us and the label was rotten. Apparently, there were problems within the record company as well, with the partners at loggerheads, although we didn't know that at the time.

KooKoo was never part of a master plan to launch a solo career. It was just Chris and I having the idea of making an album that was equally black and white. Interestingly, just after *KooKoo* came out, Paul McCartney did "Ebony and Ivory" with Stevie Wonder and as huge A-list artists, they got this gigantic push. You can sell anything if you've got enough push. I guess if we were smarter we would have called it *Black and White* or *Oreo* or something . . . But *KooKoo* didn't do too badly. It made the top ten in the UK charts, earning a silver album, and in America it went gold. And in the meantime Chrysalis released an album of old Blondie hits: *The Best of Blondie*.

I've been trying to think what the best of Blondie was for me. I've come to the conclusion that it was the early days of the band when we were struggling artists, scuttling around the Lower East Side just trying to get something going, walking home from work before dawn through the dark, dusty, sweet-dirt smell of the city. Everybody got by on no money. Nobody talked about mainstream success. Who wanted to be mainstream? What we were doing was so much better than that. We felt like pioneers. We were cutting new paths instead of taking the tried and tested roads. Personally, I was also on this desperate mission to discover who I was—and I was obsessed

BA 190382
91
SAFETY
ILFORD FP4

After the flood . . . Blondie, 1981.

with being an artist. To my mind, desperation and obsession are good things. Ultimately for me, it's the overwhelming need to have my entire life be an imaginative out-of-body experience. I fed my obsession by making an album with musicians like Nile Rodgers and Bernard Edwards, or by working with an artist like Hans Giger.

Success, when it finally came, quickly started to feel almost anticlimactic, compared with the exhilarating years leading up to it. The public exposure that came with success had a high cost in lost freedoms. The very same freedoms I had gained while clawing my way up the ladder. Success was a paradox with no easy solution. When your face becomes that well-known, you just have to get away from it somehow. You *need* to get away from it, to stay alive, or at least I needed periods of anonymity. The combination of being famous and being forced and formed into this commercial product makes the whole thing so cookie-cutter.

During my year away from being "Blondie," I don't think I missed her a bit. Chris and I had been so busy, involved in all sorts of new ventures. We wrote the title song for the John Waters movie *Polyester*. We cohosted an episode of *Saturday Night Live*. Chris was busy putting together his own record label, Animal, and producing other artists. The rest of Blondie were doing their own things too. Clem was producing a couple of New York bands and he'd spent some time working in England. Jimmy recorded a solo album. The whole system of the music industry was designed to keep you on the hamster wheel, album-tour-album-tour-album-tour, chasing your tail, never moving forward, or even sideways, or so it felt, but we'd managed to break the rules for a short while. But now they were looking at us to make a new Blondie album.

The Hunter was Blondie's sixth album. I don't remember much about that record other than I just didn't feel comfortable. I always like recording and making albums, but I was in a weird frame of mind, and I think the main reason for that had to do with getting back with the band. Not because things had been so creative and fun during the break. It's just that there was so much tension in the band. When you're in any kind of band, there's always going to be some friction. All these different people with their different ideas and issues, simmering away under pressure, year after year. But now it felt like a major clash of personalities.

Because of our democratic ideals, with everyone sharing equally and having equal say, Chris and I had set ourselves up for problems. What had sounded good in theory proved unworkable. It might have helped some if we'd ever had a manager who knew how to mediate, or who could come up with ideas that everyone could live with. But now there was this divisive dynamic at work in the band that kept us all on edge and competing instead of being a united force. Not the best environment for creativity. I remember one of the record execs saying to Clem, "We hope this isn't going to be another *Autoamerican*." Clem had replied, "You mean, you don't want *The Hunter* to have two big hit singles and go platinum in the U.S. and the UK?" So, we were butting heads within and without the band.

But some good things did come out of *The Hunter*. We did a primitive-sounding remake of "The Hunter Gets Captured by the Game," the Smokey Robinson song that the Marvelettes recorded in 1967. I had no problem relating to lyrics like: "*Secretly I been tailing you like a fox that preys on a rabbit*," although I'd actually been a bunny. "The Beast" was a song we wrote about being famous; it had a rap about the devil going out on the town. We'd originally written one of the songs as the theme for the James Bond movie *For Your Eyes Only*, but apparently Chris and I got it wrong. They already had a song, and they only wanted me to sing it. In the end Sheena Easton did the job. "Is-

On the air . . .

land of Lost Souls" was somewhat similar to "The Tide Is High," with its Caribbean feel, but what I remember most about it is the Isles of Scilly video shoot. Such a wonderful place. The islands themselves are oddly tropical, lying off the southwest coast of Britain and being affected by the Gulf Stream. We had to get there by helicopter instead of the ferry because the seas were so rough. The gliding and the bucking and the swooping over the foaming waves below, a rush all its own.

Then there was "English Boys," a ballad Chris wrote as a tribute to the Beatles after John Lennon was shot. Oh God, that hit us hard. Not long before his assassination, our photographer friend Bob Gruen told Chris and me that John and Yoko wanted to get together with us, because we were a couple just like them. We had taken a copy of *Autoamerican* to the Dakota for them and heard that John played it all the time. Sean, John and Yoko's son, said that "The Tide Is High" was the first song he heard as a little kid. We'd been scheduled to meet with them in their beautiful apartment. And then came the horror of John's being gunned down outside the Dakota while signing an autograph.

The hunter and the prey. People could be so obsessive. They would go to my parents' house and knock on the door and they'd be nice to them. I told them not to talk to anybody. I started getting paranoid. This one time, I saw a guy pick up the garbage bag outside my door and walk off with it. I chased him down the street thinking he was an obsessive fan going through my trash. It turned out he was just a homeless guy looking for something to eat, so I made him a sandwich. I think it was even more difficult for Chris when I became so famous, because Chris was always very protective of me.

The Hunter was released in May 1982. The cover photo was pretty bad; we wanted the makeup artist to do us half human and half animal and it ended up as this weird airbrushed thing. But weirdness of any kind was in keeping with everything else that was going down. The album made the top ten in the UK and number thirty-one in the U.S. If the record company had given it more of a push it might have done better. But there were big changes going on at our American record company. *The Hunter* would be our last album for Chrysalis U.S., although we wouldn't find that out until later. So for the last time, we were going to go back on the road, with Eddie Martinez replacing Frankie on the tour.

That fucking tour. We never should have gone. Chris was sick. Very sick. I have pictures of him where he was emaciated and weighed 110 pounds. I remember Chris talking to Glenn O'Brien beforehand and joking that this was his tour diet. But that tour nearly killed Chris.

I can't say exactly when the problem started, and I think that Chris has succeeded in putting it out of his mind, but he was unable to eat. He was having a terrible time swallowing anything, which is why he was getting so thin. We thought it was strep, we thought it was this, we thought it was that, and he just kept getting worse. Glenn thought that Chris had AIDS. Chris thought so too, or that he had cancer, or he was dying, and none of the doctors could give him an answer. We were doing drugs during that tour because it was the only way we could handle the stress or have enough energy to perform. Our designated gopher, "Bernie," would go out and score the smack for us. There were times on the road, of course, when he couldn't connect, and that would be really rough. Hell. And Chris kept getting sicker and sicker . . .

We were in the U.S. touring with Duran Duran in stadiums at the time, with a UK and Europe tour to follow. I remember there was talk of going to Japan. Our Japanese promoter and our U.S. agent asked me, "Do you want to go?" I said, "Yes, of course I want to go," but I didn't want to say how sick Chris was, because he didn't want people to know. The Japanese promoter ended up suing us: he'd translated my answer into a contractual confirmation and had sold a bunch of tickets. But that was the least of our worries. Chris was wasting away. More than once, he collapsed. We managed to get through the last night of the Duran Duran tour, at JFK Stadium in Philadelphia in August 1982. There was no way we could go to Europe.

And that was it. It was over. Not just the tour, but Blondie. The band officially broke up a few months later. Mike Chapman, our producer, said he could tell things had changed in the band during the recording of *The Hunter*. He could feel something ending, he said, and he was right.

We went back to New York, to our new home on the Upper East Side. It was a huge town house with five floors on East Seventy-Second Street. A symbol of our success. Money had started coming in at last and it was our accountant's idea that we should buy this place. He was the one who set up the deal. The house was so big it had an elevator. Chris had his own studio down on the garden level and on the top two floors there was a separate duplex apartment that we never went up to. In fact we let a couple of people we knew live in it: Patrick, a poet who dealt a little bit of heroin, and Melanie, who was working as a phone operator for call girls and phone sex. Some goons with Doberman pinschers had evicted them from their little apartment on First Avenue downtown. That was happening a lot in the early eighties. Landlords were trying to get everybody out of these places so they could raise the rent. Things were changing in so many ways.

About all Chris and I did at that point was to go from doctor to doctor, all of them testing Chris for AIDS and cancer and everything else and saying, "We don't know what it is." They would check him into the hospital but Chris would get

"Love? What is it? Most natural painkiller that there is."
—Last Words: The Final Journals of William S. Burroughs

fed up and he would check himself back out and return at four o'clock in the morning, saying, "I had to go, I couldn't stand it." I would try to make something he could eat. I would take a whole chicken and pulverize it, making it as much of a puree as I could, but he couldn't even swallow that. The only thing he could swallow, we finally worked out, was Tofutti, an ice cream made from tofu that was cool and soothing and would just slide down his blistered throat. He was living on Tofutti, although there was really no nourishment in it, so he continued to shrink away before my eyes. We felt so desperate and so isolated from hiding his strange illness from the world and imagining the worst. We were terrified.

Then one morning, I woke up and Chris looked horrific; his legs were swollen. "I've had it," I said. "That's it!" and called up a young doctor we'd met, asking him to come over to the house, which he generously did. One look at Chris and he said, "This is real trouble, he can't stay at home like this." So he got us into the emergency room at Lenox Hill Hospital, which was only blocks from our house. Then one of the doctors associated with Lenox Hill got involved in the case. After a couple of weeks, Dr. Hambrick was able to correctly diagnose the disease. During those two weeks, Chris had been put in isolation and no one could go into the room unless they were masked and gowned. All the nurses thought that he had AIDS and many of them refused to even go into his room.

What Chris had was pemphigus vulgaris, a rare and complex disorder of the autoimmune system. Until not so long ago, pemphigus would kill over 90 percent of its victims outright. The throat is the first part of the body to display its characteristic blistering and broken skin. Then it keeps spreading and spreading and spreading externally if left untreated. Western medicine originally thought pemphigus was caused by stress or burnout but later figured out that there was a viral component.

Now that they knew what the disease was, they started Chris on steroids. They gave him a cream used for second-degree burns for external use, because his flesh was raw and open, much as if it had been burned. I'd spread it all over the bedsheet. That Silvadene cream gave him some comfort because without it he couldn't lie down.

Chris stayed in Lenox Hill Hospital for three months. I stayed with him most of the time and some nights slept on a cot in his room. The press were trying to portray me as the second coming of Mother Teresa, but that's ridiculous. Chris and I were a team. We were partners. Of course I would look after him and he would have done the same for me. People would say how difficult it was for me, and it *was* difficult, but it was life-threatening for Chris. For the first month, he was spaced out on heavy steroids, having weird hallucinations, some of them involving me. There was one where he thought that I was running around in a Marrakesh market, or he would wake up thinking he was in Hong Kong. I kept him supplied with heroin. He was on heroin the entire time he was in the hospital. I think that the doctors and nurses knew that he was high all the time but cast a blind eye because it kept him relatively pain-free and mentally less tortured.

The heroin was a great consolation. Desperate times, desperate measures, as the cliché goes. I would head out in the middle of the night and score by myself. Fortunately, at that time in downtown New York City, it was a chic drug, so my connections were more like colleagues rather than some stereotype lurking in a back alley. They were kids, small-timers who dealt to support their own habits. I'm not putting this all on Chris. I was most certainly indulging too, staying as numb as possible. I don't think that I could have coped any other way. Drugs aren't always about feeling good. Many times they're about feeling less.

It took some time but the steroids finally took effect. Chris was released and allowed to come home and return to the clinic as an outpatient for monitoring. He was improving, which was wonderful, but he was still very weak and his body was trying to cope with the side effects of the medication. The steroids made him put on weight, which in the beginning at least was a good thing. They also caused terrible mood swings. The illness had taken a lot of his strength. Chris has a very strong mind and an ingenious brain but he is not the most obviously physical or athletic person. This disease sapped the strength right out of him. He couldn't even walk a block before he was all in. He really was done, and it took him two or three years to fully recover.

I tell myself, "It's not your fault," but part of me blames the rest of me for adding to his stress. He was already under a terrific amount of stress as the leader of the band—and then there was me, the partner. He always took on the role of being my shield and bodyguard—a seriously tough gig for someone with his kind of sensitivities and sensibilities. But now it was my turn to look after him—to be *his* shield and protector—as the world started to crumble around us. We had lost our band. We had lost our record deal. And we were about to lose our home.

We were broke. What else could you be but broke when you've sold more than forty million records, you're at the top of your career, and you've worked nonstop for seven years with no vacation, except for a few days with some black sheep in the *Frischzellen* clinic? Because: well, that's showbiz—or at least, the music biz. Musicians are often notoriously shambolic at taking care of business, which leaves the window wide open for the wolves to come loping in. I guarantee: anything we could have done wrong business- and management-wise, we did it. We had terrible contracts and the people we paid to look after us were naturally more concerned with what was in it for them. We got taken.

Cocaine at the time wasn't considered addictive for the most part and in the industry it was used liberally and frequently. Heroin was considered too dark and dangerous and there was a big divide in many people's minds about using H. Our relationship with Shep came to an abrupt end when he found out that Chris and I were doing heroin as well as coke. He had been to the house and then left and that was it. No calls, no messages, nothing. And it turned out that we had huge tax problems. Because unbeknownst to us, our accountant hadn't paid our taxes for two years—the two years when we were making the most money. I suppose he just kept getting extensions, trying to look for loopholes and tax shelters, which might be one reason for the big town house on East Seventy-Second Street. I was happy in our rented penthouse on West Fifty-Eighth Street, but he insisted the house was a good investment. So Chris's mom had moved into our old place and for the first time Chris and I had a house of our own.

When we first moved into our house, the shock of it was at times intimidating and then exhilarating. I didn't feel comfortable in the neighborhood. The Upper East Side in those days was very conservative and there were none of the colorful people and the street life of the Lower East Side that I loved. But it was good being in such a gigantic space for a while. I remember going up on the roof one night to look at the moon and stars through this high-powered telescope. I had zero experience at looking through any kind of telescope, so finding focus was a whole new deal in itself. I thought that I would be able to just lie there and look into space and drift into whatever ideas came my way. Well I did find focus, and in finding it I found that I had lost my way. In order to keep the moon or a single star in my sights I had to keep resetting the position of the telescope, and it was while making this adjustment that I suddenly felt the spin. For the first time, I could feel the rotation of the Earth and exactly how fast the planet was moving through space. I was stunned. It was an amazing physical sensation, something I'd never felt before. It was an awakening about the size and the power and the weight of this planet that I lived on. It was magnificent. I went back downstairs into the house, my own tiny little space on the planet, thinking, *Wow, I'm an earthling!*

There have been times when I've felt the immensity and weight of the world. One of them was directly connected to this house on the East Seventy-Second Street. When there was blood in the water, you could count on our former manager, Peter Leeds, to swim right up. And sure enough—as I was signing the papers to give up all legal rights to our home—I looked up and lo and behold there he was again and I don't know how he knew, but he was sitting across from me at the table. In my mind he was legitimately involved in protecting his interests, but as far as I could see, he had no other reason to be there except to put me down and gloat over my failure. He always seemed to show up when he could pay witness to any kind of loss or downfall or negative threats that came my way. He certainly hadn't been around to save us from the piss-poor business manager that helped us into tax hell.

Much later, when a few of the tax problems had been set aside and we were about to reunite the band, some former members of Blondie wanted to be paid even though they weren't going to be working with the band. They decided to take us to court and sue us for this potential future income. Well of course, once again, Leeds turned up. The judge asked, "Why are you here?" I sort of remember him saying, "I have a vested interest in their fortunes, Your Honor." Ha! What "fortunes" was he talking about, exactly? He could have mentioned our *mis*fortunes—but then he might have had to plead the Fifth. The judge told Leeds to scram. I felt so vindicated;

the New York court system had declared Leeds to be exactly what he was: a *nothing*.

We didn't just lose our house. The IRS took away everything they could lay their claws on. They took my car. They even took my coats—which was bizarre. I was pissed: what were they possibly going to get for them? They kept looking for things that were valuable, but we really didn't have that much. They couldn't get their greedy little hands on my Warhol because I'd already taken it to a usurer, who had his own claim on it.

The sickest thing of all was that the IRS took away our health insurance while Chris was in the hospital. They weren't legally entitled to do that, as far as I knew, and it shocked me. Here was Chris, in a private room for an extended stay, with no way of paying for it. But Chris's doctor, Dr. Hambrick, saved the day with his generosity. He arranged things with the hospital so that Chris could stay in his room and continue to be treated. Since we had nowhere to live, I went out looking for an apartment to rent. I found one downtown in Chelsea. I borrowed some money for the security deposit. Since they had also taken our bank account, the only way to pay the bills was to buy postal money orders with cash. So I started looking for jobs that paid cash.

PEEKABOO

Robert Mapplethorpe, 1978.

BABIES LOVE TO PLAY PEEKABOO, RIGHT? YOU HIDE BEHIND YOUR hands, then quickly open them and squeal to peekaboo, then laugh like crazy. This infantile little game is probably the earliest recognition of one's own face, another step on the road to consciousness and perhaps even self-consciousness . . . And then come the mirrors and those images gazing back at you, inevitably inducing a change in you as you view your own reflection. Imagine the startle and then the fascination when primeval creatures first caught a glimpse of themselves in a body of water . . . Or remember Narcissus, the original selfie man, frozen by the beauty of his own image in a pool . . . And now we hang mirrors along the halls and the bedrooms and the bathrooms and the living rooms and the dining rooms, so we never quite lose sight of those precious reflections.

So much of what has been written about me has been about how I look. It's sometimes made me wonder if I've ever accomplished anything beyond my image. Never mind, I like doing what I do regardless of appreciation and there really is no accounting for taste. Luckily, the face I was born with has been a huge asset and I have to admit I like being a pretty person.

I had a few art and drawing courses when I was in school with the study of portraiture included. What I noticed in my drawings and paintings was some subtle reference to my own face when I was drawing someone else. I have noticed the same phenomenon with my fan art.

Before anything, when fans started giving me their paintings and drawings, I was flattered. After collecting these sweet tributes for a while I wondered why I was saving these fragile pieces of paper with their often odd-looking interpretations of me drawn on them. But I just couldn't throw them away. Partially because I know how hard it is to sit down and make a portrait and also how brave, loving, or curious one has to be to give a piece of themselves to me. Wanting to be known to me but in ways they perhaps never realized. But when I look at my fan art collection I can see little bits of the artist drawn into their attempts to reproduce my face that they don't even know are there . . . *(cont.)*

© Majewski
ChainsawChuckm
© webtv.net

Ms Harry;
This is a copy of
a portrait I drew 19 years
ago. I would like to give you
the original. I brought it tonight.
Call my cellular phone @ 972/670-10
(I can meet you
at your convenience)

Thank

"Deborah Harry"
NEILSEN 1980

Meet Me at the Clock
The clock on top of the
Information Booth in the
middle of Grand Central Terminal
Out of the crooked timber of
humanity, nothing entirely straight
can be built.
It's Worth It
2-Trip Card
What does
Subway Emergency
IF YOU SEE SOMETHING
SAY NOTHING

ellen mackellar

11

WRESTLING AND PARTS UNKNOWN

After the IRS grabbed our happy home and other valuable possessions, we moved back downtown. Our next place was on West Twenty-First Street in Chelsea. It was remarkable to finally live in a neighborhood that I had discovered accidentally in 1965. The block was so pretty, with big leafy chestnut trees and brownstone houses on one side and the General Theological Seminary and church on the other. I had always wanted to live on this block. Our new rental was a duplex apartment upstairs from the actors Michael O'Keefe and Meg Foster, of the ice-blue eyes.

Chris was still recovering from his ordeal as an outpatient and we were both fighting off our drug demons. We were watching a lot of TV back then, mostly soaps and wrestling. Wrestling is usually booked as a theatrical event with its constant battle between good and evil—it's more like a sporty soap. One of the things Chris and I had in common was that we had both loved to watch wrestling since we were kids. The difference was that when I watched it, in Jersey, I would thrash around on the rug in front of the TV, pounding my fists and straining to beat up my opponent, while Chris, over in Brooklyn, would maintain a relaxed indifference, keeping cool and insouciant while he lounged in bed.

We'd watched it together a lot more in the late seventies when we were living on West Fifty-Eighth Street. Wrestling was making a comeback, with the advent of Vince McMahon and Gorilla Monsoon. A few years before, we had met a man named Shelly Finkel who managed fighters and musicians. It seemed like an odd combo of professions, but Shelly somehow pulled it off. Mr. Finkel had gotten us into a few wrestling events at the Garden, some of them big productions, with good seats too. We missed having Shelly as a friend, but as luck would have it, when we moved to Chelsea we made a new friend.

As I became used to the faces on the block, certain people stood out to me. One of these was a beautiful young woman with very healthy black hair. Being a bleached blonde for so many years has made me acutely aware of what healthy hair looks like. She dressed business-preppy and had a way of walking that signaled confidence, strength, and sexuality. We started to nod to each other as we passed on the street. Then one day she stopped me. She mentioned having seen me and Chris at the Garden, at a wrestling match. I said, "Are you a WWF fan?" and she told me she did PR for the venue. Nancy Moon was her name and she offered to comp us tickets to any event we wanted. We just had to say the word. So we did. This really was a lucky break.

Thanks to Nancy Moon, we went to as many events as we could, every Big Bang, steel cage, tag team, or championship challenge that came along. Nancy even introduced us to Vince McMahon, who took us backstage, where we met many of the greats of wrestling, such as the Grand Wizard, Andre the Giant, Bret Hart, Lou Albano, the Iron Sheik, Sgt. Slaughter, Rowdy

Roddy Piper, Randy Savage, Greg Valentine, Hulk Hogan, and Jesse Ventura, the future governor of Minnesota. I even appeared on the cover of *Wrestling Magazine* with Andre the Giant, who really was a giant. Instinctively, I stood on my toes, but it made no difference.

A little while into our trips to the Garden we found out that Lydia Lunch of Teenage Jesus and the Jerks was a wrestling fan too. Or a fan of one wrestler in particular, Bret "the Hitman" Hart. Bret Hart was from Canada, but he said that he came from "parts unknown," which was meant to make him sound like an escaped criminal or maybe a backwater wild man. Lydia Lunch was hot for Bret big-time. We took her and her gorgeous boyfriend, Jim Foetus of Scraping Foetus Off the Wheel, to see the fights. I had never realized from seeing Lydia perform just how loud her voice was until she started screaming, "Parts unknown! Parts unknown!" Heads turned, eyes stared—and given how much shouting there was at the matches, you can imagine how earth-shatteringly loud she was. She really was a fan. But Chris had it worse than any of us. He would theorize and try to figure out in advance what the next big drama in the story line was going to be. When we were busy recording or touring and didn't get to the big shows, Chris would start getting antsy and frustrated at missing out on the latest histrionics.

In the West End of London there was a musical comedy that had run for a few years that took place entirely in a wrestling ring onstage. It was called *Trafford Tanzi: The Venus Flytrap*. The flytrap being an unbeatable hold, the coup de grâce that would automatically crush any opponent and win the match. This "play in ten rounds," as they billed it, was about a girl who seeks revenge on all the jerks in her life: her parents, her friends, and her chauvinist husband, to whom she finally delivers the winning blow. A kind of coming-of-age story with songs and wrestling moves. The mixture of girl power and the madness of wrestling was really funny. They decided to bring it to New York and sent me the script, asking if I wanted to play Tanzi. You can guess what I said.

This was 1983; I had red hair then and I beefed up for the part, because I didn't think a woman wrestler would be thin. They had already been rehearsing and tossing each other around the ring for a few weeks before I got involved, so I had some catching up to do. I trained hard. Really hard. We had a wrestling coach named Brian Maxine who had a massive, muscular, no-neck upper body and a perfectly busted-up nose. Brian had been a British champion for years and he was very serious about his job as our coach. For weeks he taught us how to do the holds, make the jumps, take the falls, and do all the different wrestling moves that we did in the show. It was all tightly choreographed, and I got beat to shit. Since the show was a musical, we sang as we worked our way from corner to corner in the ring. At certain junctions we would have either a monologue or a dialogue, and then there would be some kind of wrestling move and my character would get thrown, because she was always the victim until suddenly she wasn't the victim anymore. I loved getting my fat ass thumped all over the stage. That's probably how I ruined my back. It turns out pro wrestling is a tough sport and it's not the best thing in the world for your body.

The New York cast was a mix of stage, screen, and television actors. I shared the lead part with Caitlin Clarke, a Broadway, TV, and film actress, because the role was too strenuous for one person to play every night and matinees too. The referee was played by the comic genius Andy Kaufman. Andy was in the TV show *Taxi* and a regular on *Saturday Night Live*. Andy's comedy wasn't boisterous, it was understated. A kind of comedy of the absurd. I think he was asked to be in *Tanzi* around the same time he had begun his own little obsession with the bad boys of professional wrestling. In tribute to the crazy showbiz side of the sport that we both loved, Andy had an act where he would wrestle women. He proclaimed himself the Inter-Gender Wrestling Champion of the World. But in person he struck me as a quiet man, meditative. When we were doing *Tanzi* he was on a macrobiotic diet. Maybe he already knew that he had the cancer that would kill him one year later.

The only problem with the show was the British director, Chris Bond. His wife, Claire Luckham, who wrote the play, was charming and easygoing, while he was a snob and sometimes a giant pain in the ass. On the upside, he created a unique and creative theater experience; however, he made no secret of his disdain for Americans, especially American theater. It was obvious to him that—matched against Britain's theatrical superiority—we were just a bunch of witless, jibbering baboons. As a result, he was a prick to everyone. As a director in my band, I know that if you want to get the best performances from people, belittling them does not work. In the end, his West End snobbery didn't get him too far with the stagehands, because they walked off the job on opening night!

They renamed the show *Teaneck Tanzi* for the U.S. audience and it ran for five or six weeks in previews, in a loft space downtown near Union Square. It was great. The audiences were loving it, watching little Tanzi grow up before their very eyes, crawling at first and being kicked around by the hard knocks of life and eventually learning to stand on her own two feet. They would cheer and boo and behave like they were at a regular wrestling match, though sadly nobody shouted "Parts unknown!" I was overjoyed and very surprised when a favorite actor/singer of mine came to the show one night, Eartha Kitt. After that run of previews, they took *Tanzi* to Broadway, where it opened and closed on the same night.

The critics slaughtered it. More snobbery, perhaps. They knew nothing about wrestling and the audience participation horrified them. The critic from the *New York Times* did say something that I agreed with, though. He said he found the script's feminism "anachronistic" and so did I. I had tried talking to the director, explaining that things were different in the U.S.: we'd had this kind of take on women's rights five years ago, so it wasn't the hot topic anymore. I offered suggestions, but he didn't want to listen. I'm guessing, but I think he felt threatened by the fact that this was a play about women being superior to men.

It was fun while it lasted. Too bad we didn't stay downtown where we did the previews. I was disappointed when it closed. I had literally thrown myself into that part. This reminds me again of the time when I was a Playboy bunny and I served drinks to Gorgeous George. Watching him as a five-year-old, I'd beat the rug to shit, just like I had been beaten to shit in that ring.

That same year, 1983, David Cronenberg's *Videodrome* came out. My biggest movie role up till then. I had been sent the script two years earlier, in that busy, creative time before everything fell apart. David's movies are beyond original—fascinating, disturbing, and thought-provoking at the same time. He would target a deep, subconscious level in the viewer. I was a fan and had seen some of his earlier low-budget movies, like *The Brood, Rabid,* and the psychosexual *Shivers,* his "body horror" movies.

David had a clinical fascination with visceral bodily transformation and infection. There tended to be some mad medical scientist in each movie, whose evil striving for transcendence through bio-experiments would spark mass contagion, mutation, and general havoc. *Videodrome* included the same strong doses of David's patented viscerality, but also broke new ground into a hallucinatory world of techno-horror. It was visionary and often cited as one of the first cyberpunk movies. David took fellow Canadian Marshall McLuhan's famous statement "The

Videodrome.

Hairspray.

My Life Without Me.

medium is the message" to a whole new level of subtlety and complexity.

The part he offered me was a substantial one. But in the script he sent me, my character was not even fully formed and the story didn't yet have an ending. They planned to work on both those things as they went along. It looked like a challenge—and I couldn't wait to work with David Cronenberg. I had confidence in his talent and his vision and I was extremely over-the-moon flattered that he wanted to work with me.

The movie is about a man named Max Renn who owns a small cable TV station in Toronto, David Cronenberg's hometown, where, in the middle of a freezing winter, we shot the film. While looking for some cheap, sensational new content for his sleazy station, Max comes across a videocassette of an underground sex show called *Videodrome* that broadcasts hardcore porn and what looks like real-life torture and murder. Max tries to track down this mysterious program and along the way he meets and becomes obsessed with Nicki Brand, a TV psychiatrist who shares his taste for S & M. She seduces him and then she disappears. Things start to get very complicated, as the movie does a deep dive into the notions of man and machine, what is real, who is real, if we are watching TV or if we *are* TV. And all this was before there were even names or terms for technologies like touchscreens, virtual characters, and interactive TV. My role in the movie was the mysterious, kinky Nicki Brand, and Max was played by James Woods.

Jimmy had already made his name as an actor in movies like *The Onion Field* and *Holocaust,* and he was a big help to me, making a lot of suggestions about how to enhance my performance. He realized that I was working/learning while trying to get a handle on this character that blurred the lines between real and virtual. I believe David got frustrated with my indecisiveness as an actor sometimes. Maybe he had a different vision for Nicki that he somehow couldn't convey to me. One time, David told me that I acted too much with my eyebrows and it was too exaggerated. I've known people who do that when they speak. That was a useful lesson to learn. Later, I read that David thought I'd held up well, given the pressure of the ever-mutating script.

Jimmy not only was generous with his help but was always lightening things up. He was such a nut. At the end of every take, while the camera was still rolling, he would make some kind of quip, an obscene or absurd joke about the scene or the people in the cast, and he cracked me up. The crew loved it. I don't know if David especially liked it, but it was funny. To me it was a relief from the seriousness and threatening atmosphere of the story. I wish more people could know this side of James Woods instead of his more recent persona. There were some intense sex scenes, but the crew were sensitive around it. I think Jimmy might have been more self-conscious than I was, or maybe he was being self-conscious on my behalf. There was one time, I remember, when I was standing on the set naked, with a towel around me, clinging to that towel like it was a life raft and thinking, *I can't do it*. But I did it. I never felt, though, that any of the graphic sex or violence was gratuitous.

At that time, people had started talking about "video nasties," which were movies on video that contained sex or violence that supposedly made viewers leap off their sofas and rush out and commit acts of perversion or violence. The week that I went to London to promote the movie, they were actually debating in Parliament about putting age restrictions on videos, and some of my interviews were canceled as a result. But *Videodrome* was way deeper than that. The line between real and imagined sex and violence in the movie was constantly blurred. It was more of a mind fuck. I am proud of being in that movie and the reviews were good. One critic said that I might have been the first postmodern tough cookie. I liked that. People expected this movie to be Cronenberg's breakout, but in the end the timing wasn't right. However, *Videodrome* was in fact a big step forward in David's evolution as a writer and director.

There's one more *Videodrome* story that I had forgotten until I saw an interview with David. There's a scene in the movie where Max grows a big slit in his stomach that sucks things into itself. At one point even Max's own fist gets ingested. After a long day wearing "the slit," Jimmy cranked out on us. He complained, "I am not an actor anymore. I'm just the bearer of the slit!" To which I replied, "Now you know how it feels."

There were other movie offers, most of them on a scale between lousy and shit. But one script stuck in my mind. Samuel Z. Arkoff, the presenter and often producer of exploitation classics like *I Was a Teenage Werewolf*, *Blacula*, and *The Amityville Horror*, wanted me to star as a girl who is locked up in a nuthouse and forced to take drugs until all sex breaks loose. Now, one of my worst nightmares was that I would get locked up in a mental hospital one day and not be able to get out. So that movie might have been a cool thing to do—face your fears and all that—but it was never made as far as I know. Samuel Arkoff intrigued me.

My mind started turning back toward my music career, except that there really wasn't a music career. I didn't have a record deal. One day I was talking about my problems to Andrew Crispo. Andrew was a roguish art dealer and was well-known in the New York gay club scene. He was also involved in a strange, twisted incident involving a boyfriend, a henchman, and a grisly S & M murder that could have been straight out of the Marquis de Sade, but that's another story. I was crying on his shoulder; Andrew listened and suggested I go see his friend Stanley Arkin. Stanley was a smart white-collar criminal lawyer who loved the ladies. After hearing my story, he decided that he was going to dip his toe into the music business and manage me. Stanley happened to be friends with John Kalodner, the head of A & R at Geffen Records, who was also a big ladies' man, so they shared a hobby. And that's how I made my second solo album, *Rockbird,* for Geffen records. It's all part of the ins and outs and machinations of the small, incestuous world of the music business.

My first day in the studio for *Rockbird* was the same day that NASA launched the space shuttle *Challenger.* Among the crew was Christa McAuliffe, a schoolteacher, who was chosen to be the first civilian in space. I loved the space program and I was so excited about the launch. I had my eyes glued to the TV in the studio lounge. In the early stages of the launch/liftoff the spaceship exploded in flames. Oh no! Oh no! Oh God! We were all beyond shocked. It was horrifying. This was not an auspicious beginning for the album. I felt a keen sense of loss when I walked into the studio that day. It had been five years since my last solo album and a lot had happened since then. I had no band to get back to. And, for the first time in the thirteen years that we had been a couple, Chris wasn't there, although he was involved in *Rockbird* as a writer and as a creative force. It felt odd not having him to talk to and I missed him tremendously. Inevitably, when we were working Chris would come out with the most sarcastic and funny remarks. I loved that about him. So, there were a lot of things I was still trying to figure out. All I knew was that Geffen hadn't paid me to make another experimental album, they wanted something they could sell.

My producer was Seth Justman, the keyboard player from the J. Geils Band. I wanted a producer who was also a musician. My best working relationships have been with people who play an instrument. And he was also a writer, so working with him was a no-brainer. Before we recorded, I would visit him in Boston, where we would write songs together and discuss the

kind of sounds we wanted. A sound that was commercial, was personal to me, and at the same time related to eighties music, with its drum machines and shiny synthesizers. Our concept was to create music that was "loose but tight." There must have been more than twenty people on that album, some great musicians, including six backing singers and a horn section. Most were Seth's guys I think, except for James White, my old friend from the downtown days, who played saxophone. I love what James does because he's always such a unique quantity. He can be completely abstract and off the hook, and he can also play funk. He fit right into that "loose but tight" concept.

Chris and I cowrote three songs for *Rockbird:* the title track, "Secret Life," and "In Love with Love," which is one of my favorite songs. It's beautiful and it works for me, musically and lyrically. I wrote the lyrics for every song on the album with the exception of one, "French Kissin' in the USA." That was a song that somebody had sent to Geffen. As soon as I heard it I thought, *Wow, what a great song, how come nobody has done this?* I found out later that the woman who had sung the original song had submitted it to Geffen to try to get a record deal. Her version was beautiful but she got screwed when I took the song, because I loved it and didn't know her side of the story. She was not happy about the situation. I wouldn't have been happy either. It was *Rockbird*'s biggest hit.

The album came out in November 1986. On the album sleeve there was a big headshot of me, blond this time. I'd been in a color rotation and my hair had been red, brown, and some other colors in between, and now I was back to blond. I was wearing a camouflage dress against a camouflage background. My friend Stephen Sprouse had the idea for the cover and collaborated on it with Andy Warhol. The camouflage pattern was something that Andy had been working with. Steve designed clothes from it in some of the most hysterically anticamouflage colors. At the photo session for the cover, Linda Mason painstakingly did my entire face with a matching camouflage pattern. I was overjoyed when Geffen agreed to release *Rockbird* with the title in four different colors of Day-Glo ink, so you could buy the colors you liked best. What an honor it was to have both Andy Warhol and Steven Sprouse collaborate on this cover with me!

When the reviews came out almost everybody called *Rockbird* a "comeback," a term that I think is thrown around too often. These days, taking three years off between album releases wouldn't seem odd. I've lost count of how many comebacks I've had. This comeback unfortunately did not translate into big sales. Part of the problem was that I was fighting a battle on two fronts. Everybody was always saying, "Can we call it Blondie?" or "Are you Blondie?"

When I started out in Blondie, it was before women in rock became as commercially viable as they are today. I had to fight my way into getting record deals and to be taken seriously. But when the eighties rolled around many of those blocks and conflicts started to evaporate. And that turned out to be a mixed blessing: where once we had had a virtual lock on the attention from labels and the public alike, now the field had become much more crowded . . . And reinventing myself beyond "Blondie" was a challenge. But you must know by now that I do love a challenge.

I didn't tour with *Rockbird*, for mixed reasons: not wanting to tour without Chris, not wanting to leave him when he still wasn't completely well, and not wanting to tour with a stage band. But really, I didn't feel that there was any mad necessity for me to hit the road. Instead I did a few TV and movie things. I was in an episode of George Romero's *Tales from the Darkside*, "The Moth," where I play a sorceress who is dying and convinced that her soul will come back as a moth. I was in a comedy movie too, *Forever, Lulu,* a.k.a. *Crazy Streets,* playing a mysterious woman pursued by a cop played by Alec Baldwin in his movie debut.

I was also on Andy Warhol's show on MTV. *Andy Warhol's Fifteen Minutes,* directed by Don Munroe, was one of MTV's first non–music video programs. It was a show based on Andy's famous quote about everybody being famous for fifteen minutes, and an extension of *Interview* magazine—print gone to video. Andy's guests covered the spectrum: musicians, artists, actors, singers, drag queens, rich, poor, big stars, struggling artists—the same kind of people Andy cultivated off-camera. Andy was really in his element with this show. TV had always been one of his many obsessions, and on this show he was a real star. He asked Chris to write the music and I had a job as an announcer. Jerry Hall was an announcer too.

I was in the first program in 1985 and so were Stephen Sprouse, Ric Ocasek, Moon and Dweezil Zappa, Sally Kirkland, the novelist Tama Janowitz, Bryan Adams, and some flamboyant drag queens from the Pyramid Club. I was also on the last show in 1987. Andy was filming a new episode when he had to go to the hospital. It was for a routine surgery on his gallbladder. But later it came out that Andy was much sicker than he let on. He had never fully recovered from his bullet wounds after Valerie Solanas shot him in 1968. The last episode of *Andy Warhol's Fifteen Minutes* ended with footage from his memorial.

Andy's death hit me hard. A terrible shock. His death was an enormous loss that changed my life as it changed the art world and the social life of New York City. Because Andy had always been a part of everything that went on—going out practically every night to openings, films, concerts. Andy was always curious and open to everything and interested in what everyone was doing. He was a big supporter of me and Chris. After Andy's death I went into mourning. I didn't realize this

until some time later, but I was actually in mourning for Andy for about two years. It was doubly emotional for me for another reason. Earlier, on the same day that Andy died, Chris and I had split up. I came home that afternoon, not having heard the news about Andy. When Chris told me, the bottom fell even further out of my world. Thirteen years of deep intimacy and creativity with Chris was changing to a different dynamic. And now the sudden death of a revered idol. These were losses beyond tears. I felt myself suspended and spun by a force that left me dazed and miserable.

We never really talked about our breakup to the press. Some interviewers made their own assumptions. Not long ago, when Blondie was on our 2017 UK tour, Chris and I went on Johnnie Walker's BBC Radio show. Johnnie Walker started going into the whole thing about Chris's falling ill and he said,

"And then you walked out on him." I was completely taken aback. I looked at Chris and he said nothing, so I let it go. And then he said it again, to Chris this time, 'When Debbie walked out on you." I couldn't believe that he was actually saying that, and he said it twice; I don't know if he was looking for a fight. I think that somebody must have walked out on him. A lot of times with a man, if they're having a problem with a girlfriend or a wife, they transpose everything onto you. This has happened to me many times with managers and record company execs, so I shouldn't have been so shocked. As you well know, though, I have never stopped loving Chris, or working with him, or caring about him, and I never will.

Chris had been saying that he wanted a studio and a loft. I had started exercising with Kerry, who had mentioned in conversation that she owned a loft building in TriBeCa and two floors that were empty, so I said, "Oh, you should let me rent them." Kerry said that they were in disgustingly bad shape and we should see them first. They were in fact worse than bad; they were horrific. Somehow we got some money and cleaned up and renovated the basement and the first floor, and Chris moved in there alone. I found an apartment down the block from where Chris and I had lived on Twenty-First Street. We continued to see each other every day.

12

THE PERFECT TASTE

How do we edit our life into a decent story? That's the rub with an autobiography or memoir. What to reveal, what to keep hidden, what to embellish, what to downplay, and what to ignore? How much of the inner and how much of the outer? What's going to compel and what might bore? What tone, what voice, what edge, what rhythms, what colors to paint when patching together the memories into a sequence that has some magic to it?

Recently, I was reading Gabriel García Márquez's memoir, *Living to Tell the Tale*. I found it so intricate—and had to keep rereading passages so I could keep all the names of the people in his immense family straight. Márquez paints his life story with the same brilliant imagery and beautiful turns of phrase he employs in his novels: the heat, the jungle, the immense physicality. It's almost frightening to experience, as he transports us back into an alien culture and environment. I remember reading a review of *Living to Tell the Tale* that was unenthusiastic at best. Do I even stand a chance? My jungle isn't nearly as exotic as Colombian banana plantations in the 1930s. Well, some might say that the jungle of CBGB's in the 1970s could come close. But I don't have nearly as many relatives as Gabriel García Márquez, though I have a surprise coming up in that department.

Even more daunting, though, is the thought of having another person involved in the "edit" of my memories. Losing control of my own art, of my voice—it's an old fear from a long battle to be who I want to be and create what I want to create. Glenn O'Brien was the editor who took my virginity as a writer. He'd put together a new magazine called *Bald Eagle,* a collection of stories and poems. Glenn asked me to submit a piece for the first issue. The issue's theme was 9/11, and I wrote a poem about souls passing. The very idea of having someone molest my sad little poem with their "clammy" hands made me anxious. I mean, I'd been corrected in school of course, but that was a long time ago. It felt so invasive. Having someone reshape my poem was startling and threw me off a little. Glenn knew exactly how I felt by my reaction on the phone. "Oh yeah, this is your first time being edited, isn't it?" So yes, Glenn O'Brien broke my editing cherry, as it were . . . I'd sometimes imagined having sex with Glenn but not exactly this kind of sex. But now we've reached chapter 12 without a body count, and there is no turning back.

Writing my story still feels like unexplored territory. Since I'm too old, too claustrophobic, and too bad at math to travel into outer space, I've been forced to go into inner space. Not so physically confined a feeling but maybe even more scary. Looking at what we have so far, it's good to see that I've accomplished more in my life than was ever expected of me. Last year in London, a journalist asked me what I had done that I was most proud of. My answer: Even trying to do it, that was a major step. And sticking with it through everything, because there certainly have been some ups and downs.

This reminds me of when I went to the cigar store.

See, I smoke. Took it up in my sixties. It was never an intention as such, but somehow at some point there I was, drawing and puffing away. Go figure. As a teenager and at various times through the years I had tried and failed to be a smoker. Cigarettes mostly. Pot in the sixties too, but I'm such a lightweight I had to give it up. I marvel at potheads who smoke herb every day, all day, year after year. I just wonder how they do it . . . Anyway, back to my nasty habit, which I have finally been able to maintain.

I've admitted my vice, my lack of control, my weakness, but I do try to keep it down to just a few a day. And when I'm working, I definitely cut back to only two or three a day. The one smoke I always enjoy very much is the after-show ritual with a glass of wine—so satisfying, meditative, and calming.

I buy cigarettes in either a small convenience store that sells lottery tickets or a real cigar store. When I spent more time in NYC I used to go to the Sweet Banana Candy Store, mostly because of its name, but that place is gone now, gentrified right out of existence. There is one cigar store I particularly like, with lots of boxes of cigars, all shapes and sizes and prices, with a small lounging area as you enter the store. This is not fancy or exclusive but there are of course "regulars" who hang there.

The cashier, who might also be the owner, is a friendly guy who knows me from around and through music. We always chat a little bit when I purchase my habitual two packs of cigs, which will last me two weeks, sometimes more. So, I'm not in there all that much but enough for us to know each other. There are always men sitting around, waving and puffing their fat cigars, and the air is full of the lingering bluish haze of cigar smoke, with that unmistakable smell. They say that secondhand smoke is just as bad for you as puffing away directly and I'd have to agree that when I step into the cigar store, I may as well have smoked one of those big fat cigars myself.

When making one of my recent biweekly purchases, as usual I took my little dog who always wants a ride in the car. We did a few errands and then ended up at the smoke shop in this little strip mall across from the supermarket. Most often this little strip has a full parking lot and I have to pull in much further down, but that day I found an opening right in front. The doggie climbed up on the center console and watched me carefully as I entered the smoky haze of maleness.

I said hello and walked over to the cashier, bought my two packs, and exchanged a few chatty words with him, then said bye and left the store. When I looked into the car as I was leaving I saw that little big-eyed fur ball staring at me from inside the car. I realized she had never seen the inside of the store but had probably smelled me as I reentered the car after buying cigs. I thought that this was a perfect time to introduce her to the place, so I picked her up and walked right back into the cigar store. Well, all the guys were surprised when I said that she wanted a cigar and fell madly for that furry white cuteness with the big brown eyes and had a little laugh. Then we left and climbed back into the car.

I was just about to pull out when one of the men—a tall, biggish guy—stepped up to my window and told me something so insightful and generous I just had to write about it. He leaned down and told me, "Everyone has talent, but to persevere and to achieve success is what separates the real talent from the wannabes. I want you to know this." And he went on, "You've done what so few have ever carried out. You didn't just think or dream about it, you hung in there and weathered the rough road to success." He didn't look like he was going to say this. I really had no idea he was about to pay me such a compliment. In fact, I had been surprised when I'd watched him walk up.

At the Cafe Carlyle 2015.

What the fuck? I would never have guessed his insight or thinking would be so generous and acute. This moment has stayed with me—imprinted itself—and even if I quit smoking, I might just go into the cigar store to say hello.

So, onward with the tale . . . The second half of the eighties had been pretty awful and sometimes downright diabolical. But then John Waters asked me if I would be in his next movie, *Hairspray*. Working with John was one of my best experiences ever. In fact, *Hairspray* and *Videodrome* are two of the things that I am most proud of, in addition to working with Marcus Reichert in *Union City* and the Catalonian director Isabel Croixet in her movies *Elegy* and *My Life Without Me*.

Before I ever met John Waters, I met Divine. Divine was a larger-than-life actor and drag queen. ("Drag queen" is no longer a PC term, of course, in these days of rapidly shifting gender identifications. But then, in many ways, Divine defied classification.) Brought up in a conservative middle-class Baltimore family, Mr. Harris Milstead's first job—to the horror of his parents—had been as a women's hairdresser. He specialized in beehives, while developing his taste for drag. One day I would like to do a study on how many hairdressers were sent to a psychiatrist by their parents—as Divine had been. John Waters comes from Baltimore, so of course they met. John, like Andy, was drawn to people who were what is considered out of the ordinary. It was John who gave Harris the name "Divine"—inspired by the character from Jean Genet's *Our Lady of the Flowers*. He joined John's experimental acting group and had roles in all of his movies, including the notorious *Pink Flamingoes*, in which he famously scooped fresh dog shit off the sidewalk and ate it. In the seventies, Divine was living in New York and became a notorious local fixture. When Chris and I were on West Fifty-Eighth Street, we lived one street away from him, and we would bump into him all the time, walking down the street in colorful, flowing kaftans—just as colorful as he himself. Seeing Divi was always the highlight of the day.

The downtown scene was very small and we all took it for granted that we all knew each other to a certain degree, even if we didn't actually hang out. Our bass player Gary Valentine had a girlfriend, Lisa Persky, who had a part in the 1976 production at the Truck and Warehouse Theater of *Women Behind Bars*—a parody of all those exploitation movies about women's prisons. Divine played the cruel, evil bitch of the Women's House of Detention. Later that year, the *Women Behind Bars* cast played a show with us, along with Talking Heads, Richard Hell, Jackie

Curtis, and Holly Woodlawn. We were fund-raising for Wayne/Jayne County, who had been arrested after a fight with Handsome Dick Manitoba of the Dictators. Dick had been drinking and was shouting homophobic insults and then jumped onstage. Jayne hit him with a mic stand and assault charges followed. They made up eventually and later recorded together.

Through Divine we met John Waters. He was working on his new movie *Polyester,* and he asked Chris and me if we would write the theme song. When it was done, we went to the studio to watch Tab Hunter sing our title song. Tab, the Hollywood movie star, had been a blond teen idol in the fifties and sixties and was still gorgeous. Chris and I showed up with Bill Murray, the comedian from *Saturday Night Live.* We had been hanging out with Bill at NBC and discovered that he had this preposterous, croonerlike voice. Who knew? He was a comedian with the voice of Tom Jones and Frank Sinatra. His singing voice was beautiful, but he only used it occasionally or comically. Fortunately, when we told him where we were going, he didn't hesitate.

John wrote *Hairspray* as a parody of a pop music TV show he would always watch in Baltimore. They didn't have *American Bandstand* in Baltimore, he said, just this one show, *The Buddy Deane Show,* where the girls' hair was higher and the boys' pants were tighter than on *Bandstand,* and these kids were huge local stars. They took their dance contests seriously. In 1962, the time in which the movie was set, there was still serious segregation. Baltimore was on the border between North and South. It had been Southern in the Civil War and there were and still are lingering effects. *The Buddy Deane Show* would play black music, but they didn't want black kids dancing with the white kids and definitely not out-dancing them in the contests. So for John to tackle this subject in this bizarre but heartfelt comedy was amazing. And he did it in a way that was kitschy and cute and innocent, yet took on this very serious, toxic subject and made it a massive hit. In *Hairspray* John gave the story the happy ending that often didn't happen in real life.

My role was Velma Von Tussle, an aloof, racist, power-mad stage mother. Her daughter, Amber, played by Colleen Fitzpatrick, is entered in the Miss Auto Shop contest by her dad, who sells used cars. But her biggest rival is the bubbly, chubby Tracy Turnblad, played by Ricki Lake. Divine played Tracy's mom. Sonny Bono played my husband. John was having some trouble getting Sonny to confirm in the beginning, so I joked, "Just tell him I'll blow him!" Not a joke you could make today. Sonny said yes, without any promises from me. It was strictly a working relationship. Apparently Sonny had been running for mayor of Palm Springs when John approached him. It was pre-election, but Sonny said yes to *Hairspray* and he won the mayor's race.

Sonny was very easy to work with. True blue, no pretense at all. The only time he got a little prickly was when people would come up and say, "Where's Cher?" That has to get stale after you've been divorced for ten years. In fact, he had his new wife with him, this beautiful young woman, and you could see that he was just so smitten; he was totally attentive to her. Sonny was a bright guy and also a bit of a smart-ass, which I liked. There's nothing like a smart-ass to give you a laugh.

The kids in the movie were GREAT. John was in love with those kids, and they were real kids; a lot of them were not even wannabe actors. But they all took it very seriously. I think some of them went on to have a showbiz career, like Ricki Lake, Colleen Fitzpatrick, and the one that looked like Elvis, Michael St. Gerard. The casting really was genius. John had Ruth Brown, the queen of R & B, play the DJ Motormouth Maybell. The one and only Ruth Brown. In the 1950s, Atlantic Records was called—for good reason—"the house that Ruth built." I was in awe. She was fantastic. She did raise holy hell when John wanted her to wear

I love you, John Waters.

a platinum-blond wig. Then finally she got it—and saw that it was a big send-up. Ric Ocasek of the Cars and Pia Zadora played a couple of beatniks. Pia was like a Broadway baby, sweet, cute, very sociable. Afterward, she would invite us up to her penthouse apartment in the Zeckendorf Towers, which was built by her real estate mogul husband, and we hung out a little bit.

John wanted me to do music in the movie but my record label was against it. So that was that. Rachel Sweet sang the title song and I sang a few lines uncredited. When Rachel sang, *"Hey, girl, what you doing over there?"* I replied, *"Can't you see? I'm spraying my hair."* Those wigs I wore in *Hairspray* deserved Oscars of their own. Nineteen sixty-two was the era of big, teased-up beehive hair. (I actually wore a beehive in my high school yearbook photo.) The wig that I wore most of the time in the movie was sort of a question mark lying on its side, a brilliant idea. The other wig was a monument, two feet tall, three or four wigs attached to a chicken-wire frame that held a bomb inside, which would explode later in the movie. I had to balance this big hairy bomb on my head. It was good for my posture and I felt like a Vegas showgirl.

When the shoot was over, none of us wanted to leave. All of us were broken up. We wanted it to go on forever. How many times can you actually say that about any job? I didn't want to go home, I wanted to keep on living in this movie. John said that making that movie was one of the nicest experiences of his life and I feel the same way. Every accolade and every benefit that he's achieved or received because of *Hairspray,* he categorically earned, because it came out of his soul. So the wrap party was a bittersweet occasion. But I left with a memento that I still have to this day. They held the party down on the piers in the Baltimore harbor, where I was bitten by mosquitoes. Now, Baltimore mosquitoes have a ferocity that is all their own. I've been eaten alive by mosquitoes over the years, but this is the only time I've gotten scarred. I still have the scar from that bite. I should have it tattooed with the *Hairspray* logo.

There is a sad afterword to this story. *Hairspray* turned out to be Divine's last movie. Two weeks after *Hairspray* was released, he died in his sleep, forty-two years old. Everyone was completely shocked. John was crushed. The doctors said he had an enlarged heart. None of us will ever forget that fierce, big Baltimore heart known as Divine.

AS A KID I WAS ALWAYS SEARCHING FOR THE PERFECT TASTE. A flavor that I couldn't describe—but was sure I could identify if I found it. Sometimes I got a hint of it in peanut butter. Other times, a hint when I drank milk. It was maddening because I was driven to have it, whatever it was. I never ate a meal or snack without wondering if I was about to finally experience the perfect taste.

Love you, Steve.

As an adult, I mostly forgot about searching for this elusive taste. The flavor of complete satisfaction—but there was a giveaway: I never felt fully satiated after a meal, although I could eat until I burst. I worried about getting too fat, as most women do, and with terrific willpower I tried to appear normal in my eating habits when I was with other people. It was when I was alone that I could just keep eating, usually until I fell asleep or got a headache and went to bed. Occasionally, my thoughts would roll back into search mode and I would remember sadly the quest I had been on throughout my childhood. And once again "the perfect taste" would become part of my daily vocabulary.

I have a protein and vitamin powder now that I mix with coconut water that has a satisfying familiar flavor to it. I love this mixture and I try to blend one up every day. I know that my birth mother kept me for three months. I reason that during this time she breast-fed me and *this* was the perfect taste. My birth mother kept me and fed me for as long as she could, then she sent me out into the world of choices. The world of flavors. The world. Now, finally, thanks to my maturing, my searching, and my magical shake, I have regained the ability to feel full, to feel hunger, and to enjoy filling up and ending the hunger. True satiation. It seems so simple. Probably as simple as infinity and the universe.

The search for the perfect taste links to a ghostly question that haunted me through my entire life: who were my genetic family and what might they be like? I know I'm not alone in this. We all want to know where we come from and who our ancestors might be. We want to know if there's anyone out there that's a part of the "tribe." A survival thing; after all, we are finally communal creatures, pack animals. Today, adoptees are able to discover almost everything. But back then, the laws in the U.S. gave an adopted child no options to find out anything.

Every time I tried, I hit a brick wall. Was I innocently a part of some witness protection program?

I was adopted at the end of the Second World War, that great world upheaval that took so many lives and made so many people and babies homeless. After the homelessness of the Great Depression, institutions tried to keep more detailed records of the population. But those bureaucracies were most often impossible to access. Before computers made it easy to explore your genealogy or establish contact with old friends and family, agency clerks or private detectives would have to search for people in phone books and newspaper obituaries or other public records, which was a slow, laborious process.

When I first learned, at age four, that I was adopted, I found myself on shaky ground. I had an unreasonably deep-rooted fear of abandonment. I would burst into tears easily if someone got a little bit angry with me. When I was six and a half years old, my sister, Martha, was born, and it was wonderful having this amazing little bundle that was part of my family. I loved looking after her. I even changed her diapers, though that was my least favorite thing. But as I grew more independent, I would always fantasize about who my birth parents were. My curiosity would wax and wane over the years, depending on how busy I was. And I didn't want to upset my parents while they were alive because I felt it might have made them hurt and unhappy.

But around the late eighties, my active curiosity came up again. I decided to try to find out all I could before it was too late. I hired a detective and sent him to find my mother. And he found her. He tracked down her address and drove to her house. He rang the doorbell and my mother came to the door. When the detective started to talk to her and say why he had come, she came outside and closed the door behind her. According to the detective, she said, "Please don't ever bother me again." She wanted no contact. She must have been quite old at that time and maybe she had made a resolution long ago to let the past lie. I found out who my father was too and that he had died at age seventy-four.

Recently, I called up the agency from which I was adopted. The laws had changed, things were more open now, and the woman who worked there tried to be helpful and said she would do a search for me. She was successful. I have found out some things and I do feel a whole lot better, even though the results are not particularly splendid or exotic. Just grounding. It seems that I come from a long line of plumbers on my father's side and amateur musicians on my mother's side. I found out that I have siblings, half brothers and sisters, and even a disturbed, incarcerated nephew. The woman at the agency said that she would see what else she could find out. She finally reached one of my half brothers. And, according to the representative from the agency, he just said that I had ruined his family. I was a homewrecker, heartbreaker. Me, this innocent little baby, a homewrecker, a heartbreaker. What a picture. Then I realized that all I ever wanted or needed was to see what they looked like.

But back to showbiz . . . It was two years since *Rockbird,* my first album for Geffen, which was actually my only album for Geffen and wasn't successful enough to make them want to do another. Stanley Arkin, who got me the deal with Geffen, didn't last long as my manager either. He was extremely clever and well intentioned and had been a big help at that difficult time, but as he said himself, he knew little about promoting an album; it wasn't his world. I remember having a big crush on Gary Gersh at Geffen but this was a very one-sided attraction, sad to say.

Eventually and luckily I found a terrific new manager who had been in the music business his whole career: Gary Kurfirst. Gary had great taste in music and the best artists, like Talking Heads, the Ramones, Big Audio Dynamite, and the Tom Tom Club. Gary went to Seymour Stein and somehow I was shifted over to Sire Records, which, like Geffen, was distributed by Warners. I knew Seymour pretty well from the old days. Sire Records had been cofounded by Seymour and our first producer, Richard Gottehrer. We didn't socialize much, but we were on good terms, and the albums I ended up making for him are terrific.

The first was *Def, Dumb and Blonde*. It was Gary's idea that I should work on some songs with Alannah Currie and Tom Bailey from the Thompson Twins. We didn't know each other at all, but Gary worked his magic and I was on my way to London to stay with them. It was June, I remember, because I was so looking forward to summer and to some hot, sunny weather, and when I got to London it was freezing cold. Oh my God. And I had completely brought the wrong clothes with me. So there I was in their big old apartment with clothes made for a sweltering New York summer, freezing my butt off. Which actually turned out all right because it gave me an excuse to go shopping with Alannah. The apartment was a wonderful place and I got to sleep in a small Gothic tower with a pyramid-shaped roof. In the tradition of grand old Victorian stone buildings, this had once been a school or an orphanage for young girls; Alannah and Tom had transformed it into a warm, welcoming, elegant space. They were a successful songwriting team, Tom focused and serious, while Alannah had no boundaries—and not just in her songwriting. She was a creative, inquisitive person and we had so much fun together.

On another visit, Tom and Alannah gave me a big bedroom upstairs while they camped in the master suite downstairs, as Alannah remembers. Alannah had just become a mother. This was her first baby, and also her first real songwriting project. She was worried sick that the baby might cry and wake me up and I'd think she was unprofessional. So when little Jackson woke up at five the next morning crying to be fed, she climbed into her wardrobe with him and sat there under all the hanging coats and dresses, trying to muffle the sound of his cries. She didn't know that I was an early riser. I heard the whole thing. The next morning, when the baby cried I swooped downstairs and opened the wardrobe and handed her a cup of tea. I grabbed Jackson and went off to play with him. When we worked on songs in their little studio, he slept in a Moses basket, which was used to keep the door ajar. Now that he's grown-up, Alannah tells Jackson that his first job was "Debbie Harry's doorstop."

The house was on Wandsworth Common, opposite the prison. Since Alannah and I both wanted to lose some weight, in the evenings we would go running around the green. Alannah would bring her scissors and when we walked back through the neighborhood, she would sneak into the gardens and snip off roses. She was nuts about roses. She'd have armfuls by the time we got back to the house. Sometimes there would be paparazzi waiting outside, trying to take pictures of me sweating and unmade-up. Alannah would get mad on my behalf, shout at them, and hit them with her stolen roses.

Alannah and I would ride around on those wonderful red double-decker London buses. We did a lot of walking too, which I love. One day, when we were out shopping, she asked me how I could do it without being recognized. Easy, I said. David Bowie had shown me how. I was wearing a hoodie and trainers; I dropped the hood, pulled back my shoulders, lifted my head, and smiled. People started to recognize me and call out my name. Then I put my hood back up and my shoulders went down and I was invisible again. It's nice to be able to step out of the light when you're shopping with a friend. It's only a matter of projection.

There are so many stories with Alannah. I've stayed with her in London on other occasions, back in the tower, where I had such strange dreams. Alannah said that the building had been occupied by MI5 or MI6 during the Second World War and it was rumored that Rudolf Hess, Hitler's deputy führer, had been held prisoner in there. Her son, Jackson, was a toddler by then and such an imp, running around, tearing off his clothes. I got used to seeing his cute naked butt flying by. Alannah also came to stay with me in New York. Once I took her to meet my friend Vali Myers. I loved Vali. She was a fabulous, redheaded wild woman, a visionary, a dancer, and an artist, unfortunately long gone now. At that time she was living in the Chelsea Hotel. There was newspaper all over the floor and a few bits of dog shit, so Alannah and I perched on the kitchen table and talked with Vali about her paintings.

I first found out about Vali in the sixties when I moved to the city. I used to see her walking around the streets with her wild red hair and tattooed face. I didn't really know her at that point but I was blown away by her look. She was way, way ahead of her time. Vali was from Melbourne and used to dance with the Melbourne ballet, but she left Australia in 1949 at the age of nineteen to pursue a dance career in Paris. Her friends there included Salvador Dalí, Jean Cocteau, Django Reinhardt, Jean Genet, and many other creative luminaries. She was an adventurous woman and an interesting artist. She would do fine-line drawings, in pen and ink, with great detail and a lot of patterns, as well as portraits and studies of animals. I have a beautiful drawing of hers of a redheaded wild woman with a large red vagina. It's incredible. Chris actually named his daughter Valentina after Vali. I think Vali loved Chris very much. Of course Chris is lovable, so there you go.

But back to London and *Def, Dumb and Blonde*. Before we had met, Tom and Alannah had written one song for me: "I Want That Man." Alannah said she wrote the lyrics imagining I might be a demanding diva and a predatory femme fatale. She said that she slipped in the line *"I want to dance with*

Harry Dean" because she'd had a long-standing fascination with Harry Dean Stanton. She didn't know that I had one too, ever since seeing him in Wim Wenders's mesmerizing *Paris, Texas* and, of course, the hilarious *Repo Man*. I loved how he made such exceptionally good role choices throughout his career. He always played the most interesting characters, often with no obvious commercial appeal, and it always worked out so well. As he loved to say, "There are no small parts. Only small actors." He was so smart and talented, just a charming person, and a smooth operator. He also had this craggy, weather-beaten look that exuded a sexy soulfulness . . . I didn't know him personally before "I Want That Man" came out, but when it did, Harry Dean became convinced that the song was about him and that he was the man I wanted. When I was back again in London, Alannah and I went to see Harry Dean sit in with Ry Cooder singing "Across the Borderline." Since I love the way Alannah tells the story, I'll hand the mic over to her:

"We were both swooning like teenage girls when he sang and afterwards, backstage, we met him. He politely took both our phone numbers down with a stub of a pencil in a little notebook but then I looked the other way and Debbie just disappeared with him. I think that was the beginning of her dalliance with him, but I'm still waiting for the details on that one! Anyway, he was courteous and the next day there was a message from him on my answer machine inviting me over to his hotel to 'take tea' with him, 'maybe with some milk in it.' Ha ha! I still have the taped recording. So Debbie got to shag him and I got the invite to tea. That's what happens when you play with Dirty Harry: she gets the man and you get the tea!"

Harry Dean and I made out a few times. As I said, he was a charmer. But he was living in L.A. and I lived in New York. But I'm happy he thought that the song was about him. "I Want That Man" was *Def, Dumb and Blonde*'s first single and its one

Red Hot + Blue—*Red, Hot, and Byrne.*

big hit. The song I wrote in London with Alannah and Tom, "Kiss It Better," was the second single. Of the fifteen songs on that album, more than half I wrote with Chris. We weren't a couple anymore, but he was still my closest friend and musical partner and the dearest person in the world to me. One of those songs we wrote, "Brite Side," I sang on *Wiseguy,* a TV series where I played an aging rock star. Ha! Ian Astbury of the Cult came in to sing vocals with me on Chris's song "Lovelight." Gary Valentine was a guest vocalist on the album too. Alannah didn't sing with me, but I was on the Thompson Twins' 1989 album *Big Trash,* singing my part over the phone from New York to London.

Def, Dumb and Blonde was released that same year. The name on the front sleeve was "Deborah Harry." I had started

2006—Starliners tour.

to feel pretty strongly about differentiating between Blondie and the solo projects, and that was one simple way of doing it. Plus, I had come to the point where I thought that Deborah was a prettier-sounding name than Debbie. The album did well in the UK, Europe, and Australia and did nothing in the U.S. I loved that album and I put a band together to go on the road. Chris was the first person I turned to; then our bassist Leigh Foxx, who had played with Yoko Ono and Iggy Pop; and another guitarist, Carla Olla. You might think that it would feel strange, with Chris and I going to different hotel rooms at the end of the night. But it had been a while since we split up and both of us were seeing other people.

The four years between *Def, Dumb and Blonde* and my fourth album, *Debravation,* were very busy. I did a lot of TV and movies: *New York Stories;* the *Tales from the Darkside* movie; *Dead Beat; Intimate Stranger,* about a poor aspiring rock singer who makes her living as a phone-sex girl; *Body Bags,* where I played a nurse; and *Mother Goose Rock 'n' Rhyme,* where I was the Old Woman Who Lived in a Shoe. No one can say I'm typecast. I was on an episode of the TV drama series *Tribeca* with Dizzy Gillespie. I sang Cole Porter's "Well, Did You Evah" with Iggy Pop on *Red Hot + Blue,* an AIDS benefit album. In 1993 I made my debut at the fabulous outdoor drag festival Wigstock, and I played my first show at my friend Michael Schmidt's new club Squeezebox. That place was always jumping and stuffed with people. One night we did a crazy show there with me and Joan Jett headlining, plus the Toilet Boys, Lunachicks, Psychotica, and some drag performers. At one point Joey Ramone got up onstage with us. The whole show went out live on the Internet, which was still rare in those days.

I first met Michael Schmidt in the seventies. Blondie had played a show in Kansas City and we were going up to the hotel room when this gorgeous kid came over. He was just a teenager and his parents had bought him tickets for his birthday. He was so good-looking and well-spoken, with an enigmatic energy, that he made an impression on me. Years later, I saw him again in the oddest circumstances. He was wearing my camouflage dress and blond wig while acting as my stand-in for the photographers as they did their lighting tests for the *Rockbird* album cover. Later, Michael was shocked that I remembered him from all those years ago in Kansas City. Michael designed jewelry and clothes in his loft on West Fourteenth Street. At that time, a lot of artists in New York were being thrown out of their lofts due to gentrification, with landlords raising rent. I heard from my friend Guy, the singer with the Toilet Boys, that Michael had been evicted. My apartment in Chelsea was large and had an empty bedroom, so I invited Michael to move in, and he lived there for a while in the early nineties.

Schmitty made some remarkable clothes for me too. The most famous dress Michael made for me was a floor-length gown made from thousands of double-edged razor blades. It took him months to make. Michael blunted each of those blades himself, but you could still get caught on them; these double-edged blades were made to last through multiple shaves and they weren't easy to dull. It was definitely a dress I had to put on carefully. But once it was on, it felt sensual and snake-like. Dirty Harry meets Slash Harry. That gown was a kind of daredevil, exciting piece. It was showcased at the Metropolitan Museum of Art's Costume Institute. I'm not sure where it is now; maybe it's still there.

For my fourth album, *Debravation,* I'd wanted to try something more avant-garde and experimental. I've never wanted to repeat a hit song by copying it for a new song. I've never had much interest in doing something I did in the past, which is why I would often end up in some catch-22 situations with the labels. We had around thirty people on that album and eight

Bunny . . . you taught me everything I know.

The double-edge razor blade dress.

different producers—Chris of course, and Anne Dudley of Art of Noise, and on "My Last Date with You," R.E.M. We did an instrumental: Nino Rota's theme for the Fellini movie *8½*. I love Rota's music. I had sung "La Dolce Vita" on Hal Willner's Nino Rota tribute album. We also did our own version of Led Zeppelin's "Black Dog." When we presented the finished album to the record label, they rejected it. So we made some changes and they released that version of the album in 1993. A year later, we released the original album ourselves as *Debravation: 8½: The Producer's Cut,* on an indie label. That was the end of my relationship with Sire. But I had always felt that Madonna was the only one that really mattered to Sire. When *Debravation* came out, Madonna went on her Blonde Ambition tour. John Waters said, "Debbie blinked for two minutes while she was looking after Chris and Madonna stole her career."

Debravation made number twenty-four in the UK charts and the first single, "I Can See Clearly," did pretty well in the clubs. The video for the second single, "Strike Me Pink," turned out to be controversial. The theme was the Houdini water tank trick, in which an escape artist has to break from his bindings before he drowns. The video was not supposed to imply any kind of fatality, and it was never really completed. For some reason, we were not allowed to finish it the way we had envisaged it. I should never have let that video be shot, because it had nothing to do with the song. It isn't an angry song, it's a sexy song with a sort of bluesy, positive lyric. *"Strike me pink."* Not "Strike him dead." *"Baby your touch is magic . . . Maybe you'll bring me a lucky streak / Well strike me pink."*

The original plan was that I would come in wearing a fantastic pink dress, looking very feminine and lovely, and then I would wave a magic wand and the guy would escape. There's something powerful about the color pink. It's something that dates from the cradle, a system created to distinguish male and female sexuality, hence there are some adult males who get the instinctive drive to do that "man" thing for a girl in pink. Because the pink one is usually smaller and weaker and needing protection, and there go the testosterone levels. Pink was a smart move for the singer Pink. Just or almost as smart as "Blondie." I have always thought the contrast between innocence and lusty sexuality, like that between good and evil, is irresistible.

The problem was that the woman who was supposed to send this wonderful pink dress didn't send it. At the last minute I tore around looking for another fabulously exotic pink dress, but I couldn't find one. So for some reason the only other costume at the shoot was a man's suit and tie, a completely opposite signal to a feminine pink dress. And there was no magic wand and the man drowned.

I was dating a magician and illusionist at the time, Penn Jillette, so that must have been why the Houdini water tank trick was going through my mind. Penn is a very interesting man, six feet six inches tall, a big man, big personality, big everything. He is well-known as a magician—Penn of Penn & Teller—but he also had a secret rock life that not many people knew about. He played drums and bass and recorded under the name Captain Howdy. I guested on one of his two albums, *Tattoo of Blood*, in 1994.

Penn is also an intellectual, well-spoken, well mannered, and smartly reserved, so I will just tell this one story, because Penn has told it himself. We were in Florida, watching the space shuttle launch, and when it was over I went out to the hotel hot tub. Penn said that I came back to our room complaining loudly that the men who designed Jacuzzis put the jets in a very inconvenient place to get a woman off, which caught me in an embarrassing position when this young, red-faced boy walked by . . . Penn asked where the jets ought to be. In the seat, I said. "So when I was building my house and they were putting in the Jacuzzi," Penn later recalled, "I asked him to do it so that the jet would hit the clitoris. The designer said, 'So you want that halfway back and straight up?' I said, 'No, I was thinking toward the front and at a forty-five-degree angle.' It worked! I kept expecting that man's wife to send me at least flowers." Penn patented the orgasmatron tub and called it the "Jill-Jet"— the first syllable of his last name and the female equivalent of jack-ing off. It's described in the patent as a "hydro therapeutic stimulator."

I've always liked sex toys. Who doesn't . . . They are a lot of fun. The last time I saw Alannah, we went to Sotheby's in London, where they had an exhibition of erotica that was up for auction. It was a good exhibition with all kinds of paintings, furniture, and sculptures. There was a jade dildo that was a thousand years old and I was surprised and delighted to find that Pamela Anderson was there too. I had met Pamela at a MAC's Viva Glam photo session. The cosmetics company held an annual event where they would choose a diva and design a new lipstick, giving all the proceeds from sales to AIDS charities. I was a Viva Glam diva one year and so was Pamela. But that day at Sotheby's she was giving a talk about the importance of sex in a relationship. Alannah went off and looked at furniture, since she was now designing and making furniture herself. I have a couple of her wing chairs in my house and they're wonderful. She made them to personify two Victorian whores. They're tattooed on the legs and dressed in layers of silk, velvet, and leather.

As for Penn and me, we saw each other for a few years in the late eighties, early nineties. Then Penn moved everything to Vegas. And I went on the road with Blondie.

13

ROUTINES

Could my routines reveal some further insight into what makes me tick? After all, what's a memoir for, if not to pull back the curtain and check out the lady who is pushing the buttons? And when you've been on the planet for as long as I have, those routines have made their marks. There have to be some telltale indications of my predilections and preferences, right? "Routines" come in all shapes and sizes, of course, and being a showbiz type, I immediately jump to "song and dance." But I think there's a lot even in the most apparently humdrum of routines. And further, where do we draw the line between routine and ritual?

I guess we could start with anything. Okay, morning coffee. I would prefer to have my morning coffee in hand before letting out the dogs—but piss rules. I know exactly how much that first morning piss means, so I get those dogs out there pretty damn quick. Then the coffee: French press, French roast and espresso combo, half decaf, half regular. Why cut it with decaf? I am not a slammer. I want the buzz—but slow-release, if you don't mind. Nothing too jagged to start the day. Then back to bed with the coffee, the dogs, and a book. The first hour of the day I spend with my nose in a book . . . I've loved reading since I was a little girl. And the love affair continues to this day. So, this first hour is supremely precious to me—it lights me up—and I'll do what it takes to protect that time and make it happen.

The routine for the rest of the day depends on appointments and errands. Gigging or touring sets the clock ahead and I try to sleep till ten thirty. Then I'll follow pretty much the same coffee/piss/reading routine, except minus the dogs, when I'm on the road, with some occasional moments of panic, trying to hunt down a civilized cup of coffee in the middle of nowhere. Oh, and I do miss my doggies when I am on the road.

On tour, after that first hour, my routines become a whole lot less private. I'm meshing with a group schedule that can feel almost factory-like in its regularity, or like military troop movements. Wherever we are, the show usually starts at nine P.M. During the day there may be some promotions to do, interviews or a visit to a radio station, and then it's off to the tour bus: luggage at three o'clock, lobby call three thirty, departure three forty-five, sound check four o'clock; there is an order to sound checking too. Then dinner at five, a break from six until seven thirty, then a meet-and-greet for fans and contest winners or business-related meetings with promoters and media. After that, I get dressed and made up. Then a vocal warm-up. Then thirty-minute, ten-minute, and five-minute calls for the show. And at nine o'clock, walk almost single-file to stage; guitars on, house lights off, show starts. Offstage at eleven o'clock, approximately, and back to the dressing room to change for the after-show meet-and-greet for friends and guests. Then back on the bus around midnight. Drive through the night to the next city on the tour. The length of the drive will determine whether we check into a hotel for some more sleep or just stay on the bus until the next sound check.

Back in the day, gigs and touring were a barely controlled chaos. We didn't have a lot of discernible routine. Now it's mostly a well-oiled machine, which makes for less stress but sometimes also for less opportunity for the unexpected to happen. Punch in, punch out, punch in, punch out . . . Routines can be a double-edged sword that way. And of course, the craziness can be a whole lot more fun in memory than when it was happening for real.

But before we can even hit the road, there is the rehearsal routine. We usually try to block-book a studio. That way we can set up the back line and monitor system for an undisturbed week or more, depending on how much material we have to learn or how long it's been since we've played. We try to start late morning, ten thirty or eleven thirty A.M., and work until six or seven P.M. Sometimes we'll go later, but five or six hours of concentrated playing, and then I'm done.

Rehearsing. It's not my favorite thing. You might say, "Wow, a five-hour workday, that's pretty good," but before we get to play those five hours together there's that time you spend alone, learning and listening to the music you're going to perform in the show. I've never tried to figure these hours out. I just have the music playing at home or in the car, letting it run endlessly through my brain.

I toured for a year with my album *Debravation*. Then I started touring with the Jazz Passengers—a smart, avant-garde New York jazz band. The Jazz Passengers, according to Roy Nathanson, were the punks of the New York jazz scene. They had the same kind of irony as the rock punks did and their roots were in the same downtown scene that we came from. A poet and actor, Roy was also part of a Lower East Side theater group and played in the New York City Big Apple Circus Band with Curtis Fowlkes. Roy and Curtis had first met when they were in John Lurie's Lounge Lizards.

How I came to work with them was through Hal Willner. Hal has an eclectic musical knowledge and is a highly creative music producer; I first met him when he was working for *Saturday Night Live* and I was asked to host the show. After the show, Hal and some of the other *SNL* guys would come over to our apartment and watch public access TV with Chris. When Hal was working on his Nino Rota album, he called me into the studio to sing "La Dolce Vita." Later he was working on a Jazz Passengers album entitled *Jazz Passengers in Love*. Roy had asked him to bring in some singers and Hal brought in Little Jimmy Scott, Mavis Staples, Jeff Buckley, and me. He wanted me to sing a sweet, clever song named "Dog in Sand" that Roy had written about an old man and his dog. Roy was doubtful. He wasn't sure that I could do it. He didn't really know my music. But I went in and nailed it, if I say so myself. After that, Roy asked me to sing with them at the Knitting Factory, and by the summer of 1995 I was playing regularly with them.

Then Roy asked me to go on the road with them. Well, that was a big bite. It meant a lot of songs—and some of them were really obscure, with odd time signatures. All those years in a rock band I had been counting to four, and now I was expected to count to six or seven! I worked hard at trying to figure those songs out, and there were times when I massacred a song, but the band was cool about it—jazz cool. That's one of the things about jazz musicians that you don't always get in rock: they pride themselves on keeping their cool. For instance, at the start of the tour we'd have audiences calling out for "The Tide Is High." So, the Passengers worked out a version of the song, with all those harmonies that were on the original by the Paragons.

So off we went to Europe on a regular working-musician jazz tour. This kind of tour also had its own routine: get on the train, get off in one European city or another, and schlep your instruments and suitcases to tiny little jazz clubs. No roadies, not much equipment; we used the house PA, so less hassle and less stress, and I liked that extra freedom and sense of adventure, and the spontaneity of chance encounters and the up-close-and-personal nature of the shows. It was an intimacy that reminded me of the early club and CBGB's days. Speaking of up-close-and-personal, I remember a gig in Germany where the stage was so low that someone in the audience knocked me over as they got up from their table. I fell back onto Roy's little soprano sax and bent it out of shape. But I guess I must have done okay because on their next album, *Individually Twisted* they had me sing all of the songs.

It was so much fun, that tour, and such a nice experience just being a singer. It was also an exciting musical experience. After a while I noticed how each musician had a capability in a certain style and how they would "go off," as the jazz guys say, into some emotional transformation, and then come back into the basic framework. In rock 'n' roll, that's not such a big part of the stage show, and especially not in my generation, the punk generation, which rebelled against all those boring, gratuitous, ego-trip, awful half-hour solos. The Ramones were the absolute champions of that concept, with their two-minute songs and their strict, stripped-down format. Even today in Blondie we have few solos in the traditional sense, although Clem is always ad-libbing his fills at the beginning or end of a song.

At that time, I was still doing movies. One of them, *Drop Dead Rock,* came out the same year as *Individually Twisted,* 1996. There's a picture of me and Adam Ant on the poster but I honestly don't remember one thing about it. It's the same with most of the parts that I had. Usually they were cameos or mechanical kinds of roles, nothing pivotal, that were shot in one or two days. Parachuting into a picture for a quickie is actually more difficult than you might think. The other actors have been at it together for a while. They understand each other, they have a feel for the cameraman, and they've built a rapport with the director. So breaking into this established dynamic for just a day can feel kind of uncomfortable. But there were some times on those single days when I would feel good about the performance, or something special would happen between me and the camera, which is always very exciting.

I can count on one hand the parts that I think were real parts. There was Jonas Åkerlund's *Spun;* John Waters's *Hairspray;* David Cronenberg's *Videodrome;* two movies that Isabel Croixet directed, *My Life Without Me* and *Elegy;* and James Mangold's 1995 movie *Heavy. Heavy* was a good film and a challenge. It had great actors, like Shelley Winters and Liv Tyler, and a very low budget. My role, as a world-weary, slutty waitress in a small-town café, felt like a real part and a real character that I could develop and understand. We were shooting the film near Lake Mohawk up in High Point, New Jersey. Lake Mohawk was where forty years earlier Shelley Winters had shot the big Hollywood movie *A Place in the Sun.* Shelley played a factory worker in that movie who got pregnant by Montgomery Clift, then demanded he marry her. But Montgomery Clift had fallen in love with a socialite, Elizabeth Taylor, so he drowned Shelley in the lake. And here she was in the same location but in an indie movie this time, playing the owner of a roadside diner. I played the waitress who had worked for her for fifteen years.

Shelley, with her two Academy Awards for best actress and two nominations, was a force to be reckoned with. She had this contained intensity that was immensely powerful. She challenged everyone to step up and deliver. I could see that was how she worked, putting everybody on their toes. When she first arrived, she called me into her trailer and said, "We should get to know each other a little bit, because we're sort of adverse characters." My character supposedly had an affair with her character's husband and there was this simmering tension between us. So I sat listening to her going on and on and at the end of the monologue/conversation, as I was leaving—with one foot down the trailer steps—she said, "I've worked with singers before. I've worked with Frank Sinatra. None of them can act." I knew exactly what she was up to. She's a Method actor, so she was trying to antagonize me just as her character antagonizes my character in the movie. But it wasn't hard for me to play a waitress in a small town. In the late sixties, back when I hit a wall and left the city to stay with a friend upstate in Phoenicia for a few months, I worked at a little coffee shop on the main street, one of maybe five or six stores at best. The owner, Irene, had been running the place forever, and I filled in for her, two days a week. Mostly it was just delivery guys who stopped by, and they would always ask, "Where's Irene?"

A few years after *Heavy* came out, I heard that James Mangold was going to do a new movie set in Jersey, *Cop Land*, and I really wanted to be in it. I begged him, "Please, you've got to put me in your next film." I don't think he was that wild about me. But he put me in one shot as a bartender, no dialogue or anything, just mopping the bar and giving someone a beer. However, when he edited the movie, I ended up on the cutting room floor.

YOU MUST BE MAD." THAT'S WHAT I SAID WHEN CHRIS CALLED TO SAY, "Let's get Blondie back together." I honestly thought that he had lost his mind. We'd had this phenomenal, massive, worldwide success with Blondie, hit after hit and tour after tour, and then went through such a terrible experience with the illness, the drugs, the financial ruin. And neither of us was dead. Yet. I felt for sure that somebody was going to die this time around, especially when so many of the people we had come up with were already gone. On the same morning that Chris called me, I had spent the first hour of the day with my head in a photo book called *Warhol's World* that my friend Romy, one of the "Goody" girls, gave me. I saw a lot of faces that I knew and so many of them were dead. Having survived all of that craziness, to be thinking about doing the whole thing again? God, no. I still had so many bad, bad memories from what had gone on before, with not just the band but the business. Working with the Jazz Passengers had felt like such a relief and a privilege and an education, so the last thing I had on my mind was a Blondie reunion. But as usual, Chris talked me into it.

Chris was almost a million dollars in tax debt, thanks to our former financial adviser, Bert Padell. He'd seen an ad in the *Village Voice* from a collector who was looking to buy rock 'n' roll memorabilia, so he called up and said that he had some gold and platinum discs to sell. The man that posted the ad, Ed Kosinski, turned up at Chris's loft and was pleasantly surprised to see that the seller was actually Chris Stein. So the two of them became friendly. Ed was married to Jackie LeFrak from the famous New York real estate family. LeFrak City is that forty-acre stretch of apartment buildings you see when you're driving through Queens to JFK. He invited Chris and me to their apartment for dinner. We found out that Jackie LeFrak's sister Denise was the subject of the Randy and the Rainbows song "Denise," which we had turned into "Denis." The synchronicity of it was eerie. Ed told us that he had a friend in the music business that he wanted us to meet, Harry Sandler. It was Harry who really pushed Chris to put Blondie back together. He was blunt with Chris: "If you don't do it now, it will never happen." That really sank in for Chris.

Harry at that point was working with a manager named Allen Kovac, who'd had considerable experience in working with older bands that had broken up and were getting back together. He was very persuasive, so we agreed to a meeting. Allen was a smart guy and a good talker. His presentation on how he could help with a Blondie reunion was forthright and compelling. He was also willing to work through the morass of bad business deals and band-member conflicts that made a reunion sound like such a horror show to me. We'd suffered from managers that were either disinterested and uncaring or actively enjoyed our being off balance, because it put them in the catbird seat. Allen had a really clear overview of what happens to people in this situation: the pressures and disappointments and how everyone gets fractured by it. Allen was none of those people and he was an extremely good salesman.

So, Chris set about contacting these people that we hadn't seen in years. He called Jimmy Destri—he and Jimmy always got along—and then he had Clem fly in from L.A. As Clem recalls, "The funny thing was that everyone looked strange and out of sorts, missing teeth, kind of overweight, and disheveled. A bit apprehensive." Hmm. Chris also called Gary Valentine, who lived in London, where he worked as an arts correspondent for the *Guardian*. Chris flew him to NYC and Jimmy met him at the airport and took him to Chris's loft. Here's how Gary remembers it: "Chris's mausoleum, his cavern in TriBeCa, was like Turner's place in the movie *Performance*, only worse. I flew over expecting to hit the ground running, but everything was not as ready to go as Chris had told me. Chris himself did not look well. For a few weeks I was more or less keeping him company, trying to get his spirits up. I liked Chris. He even saved my life once, when I was nearly electrocuted at the Bowery loft. It was only after a while that I realized that Debbie wasn't quite as excited about having me around."

Contrary to his paranoia, I do like Gary. He's a sensitive, multitalented man and his broad-ranging, inquiring intellect has given him a strong worldview. Gary stayed at my apartment for a while and we'd walk my dog together. We talked about his writing, and how the mystery writer Cornell Woolrich used to live in the same apartment building as I did and supposedly wrote *Rear Window* there. It wouldn't surprise me because you really could look into people's windows. In the gardens, the center part of the building, the apartments had a lot of turnover. It was a kind of transient gay ghetto and people didn't seem at all shy about having sex in front of the uncurtained windows.

While Gary was with us we played a handful of shows. One of them was a tribute to William Burroughs held in Lawrence, Kansas, where Bill spent his final years. Being on that show with Philip Glass, Laurie Anderson, and Patti Smith, people I greatly admire, was meaningful for me. Chris and I had come to know Bill Burroughs a little, socially. One time we went to dinner with Bill at the Bunker—that's what they called the place—and I took my little dog Chi Chi with me. That dog was tiny. She only weighed about five pounds. But she would fight like a demon whenever she felt trapped. I gave her the name Chi Chan because it supposedly meant "ferocious blood." Chi Chi was her street name. I thought a creature that small and frail could use a strong name. Bill grabbed my little dog and held her tight all through dinner—and Chi Chi chewed away at Bill's bony hands all night, nonstop. Bill liked to numb himself up with "certain substances," or maybe he liked being bitten, so I guess her incessant chomping didn't bother him too much. Chris and Bill got along like gangbusters. They shared a lot of interests, including weaponry, and they were of equal genius, so I think they understood each other. Hal Willner was working on another of his unique projects, recording Bill reciting the Lord's

Prayer. He had Chris add music to the track and it came out on Bill's album *Dead City Radio*.

The Blondie reunion was moving ahead, but in fits and starts. We were trying to get the best balance of players from the past and kept checking to see if anyone was interested. Christ talked with Gary Valentine and he was willing to come over from London where he was living, to give it a try. Gary has proved himself to be a credible writer and had several books published on his favorite topic, mostly philosophy focused. He hadn't really been playing that much and our vision for the new Blondie was a bit different than the original. I felt that in the nineties a more evolved sound would be expected; that we couldn't get away with our original downtown sound. This was too bad because Gary had that great energy, good looks, and a style that came naturally to him.

I had told Chris and Allen from the start that there was no way I would be in an oldies band—I was adamant about that—so we started writing new songs. At first we worked with Mike Chapman, but the circumstances were not ideal. We were all tentative, having been apart for so long, and not having ended on the best of terms. We needed to mend some fences. We were at the stage of feeling each other out and figuring out if we *could* work together—if there *would* be a future for Blondie and how it would play out.

This was the fragile, dysfunctional, multilayered, complex situation that Mike came into. Mike really loved Blondie, and I have to give him credit for coming to our rescue. It could hardly have been comfortable for him to hang in there as the fifth wheel while this entity from the dark past tried to pull itself back together—but Mike has a formidable inner strength to go along with his exceptional creativity. He had been responsible in many ways for creating the sound of Blondie as a radio band,

and though Mike did not end up producing our reunion album, unfortunately, that was more to do with management and the record label.

We also tried working with Duran Duran. Allen was managing them and thought we might be a good fit. So we went into the studio. But Duran Duran had this crazy, crazy guy in the band who seemed to be whacked out of his head. It was almost funny. We would be trying to record and he'd be ripping off his clothes, complaining that he was getting overheated, which was amusing. He had a good body and he knew it, but he also reeked of this acrid drug sweat and he seemed to be speeding his tits off. Quite a distraction. But we did record two or three songs with them, including Gary's song "Amor Fati." However, things were still not quite right. We were still playing with the combinations, waiting for everything to click into place. And then Clem suggested that we try working with Craig Leon. Craig had produced Blondie's first album. He was forward-thinking when it came to new technology, and Chris was nuts for this new digital system called Radar that Craig was using. So they spent hours in Chris's basement, which morphed eventually into the seventh Blondie album, *No Exit*.

Clem came up with the title, so over to Clem to explain: "Jean-Paul Sartre's play *No Exit* had the famous line 'Hell is other people,' which pretty well nails the many stereotypical rock band scenarios. But there is also the sign you see everywhere that says No Exit, meaning that there is no escape from Blondie. Because whatever you do, you are always going to be 'so-and-so from Blondie.' And Debbie is always going to be 'Blondie.'"

Well, it's true that when Gary Kurfirst was managing me as a solo artist, he was very frustrated by the fact that he couldn't call me "Blondie" despite the extent to which I was identified that way publicly. But it was written in our contract that "Blondie" is certain members and I wasn't entitled to use that name without those other people's being involved. One of them was Chris. I would never, ever have done anything called "Blondie" without Chris's being involved, because Chris was the other half of the origin of Blondie. He and I were partners and had built the whole thing up together from zero. But some of the people along the way who played in the band also felt they had earned entitlement to the name.

After we decided not to ask Frank Infante and Nigel Harrison to join the reunion, they took a lawsuit out against us. Even though they weren't going to be working with the band, they took us to court to sue us for potential future income. But the state of New York found in our favor. And the reconstituted Blondie got back to work with Leigh Foxx and Paul Carbonara joining myself, Chris, Clem, and Jimmy.

We made the decision that we would go to the UK and Europe to play some shows before releasing the album. Tommy Hilfiger designed all the clothes for the band to wear on tour. He did a great job. The boys looked very sharp and my leather skirts were gorgeous. We were going to England to test the waters. Seventeen years had gone by since the last Blondie album, so we weren't sure how we would be received. But we were met by a wave of affection and approval. It was a wonderful feeling, seeing that Blondie had actually meant something to people. I think our fans appreciated the fact that we were alive, but also that we were making new music that was relevant to our lives in the present, not just the past.

The tour routine followed the same old pattern, though it felt a lot saner this time. There was contention, of course, but we had a good manager at last who had an understanding of human nature and would step in and take care of any arguments. And we were older. Perhaps we weren't all that much wiser, but

I think we realized that we had something that was important to us, in our special chemistry and unique sound. It was time to stop acting like babies and start working our butts off to become the best band we could be. A month before the album came out we released our first single, "Maria." It shot straight to number one in the UK and topped the charts in thirteen other countries. All this meant that people would be looking forward to the album. We released *No Exit* on our manager's independent record label, Beyond Records, in February 1999 and it went to number three in the UK. It even went top twenty in the U.S. Chart ratings aren't everything but it was exciting!

At the end of the tour there was a wedding. Chris married his actress girlfriend Barbara Sicuranza. We were in Las Vegas and they snuck off to one of those wedding chapels. I guess they didn't want to make it into a big deal. They wanted to keep it private and quietly romantic. I was pretty disappointed, I admit. I thought at least one of us, me in particular, would be invited. But maybe it was a little bit awkward for Barbara, having me as the omnipresent ex. Had I been in her position, I might have done the same thing. They have been married almost twenty years now, but in the beginning it must have been difficult for her, knowing how close Chris and I were. We never sat down and talked about it in terms of, "He's my husband," "He's my ex." I think we did it in a sweeter, more natural way, by learning about each other and growing to like each other as people, in spite of possible fears and anxieties. Chris is a loving person. I don't think he would do anything to make Barbara feel uncomfortable, or me for that matter. He's a sweet-natured, generous guy. I can't say enough good things about him, obviously.

Since the Blondie tour began, I'd found myself back in the old routine of doing interviews. It's the nature of the game. I can't count how many times I was asked about my relationship with Chris and I always said the same thing. Chris is one of the

most important people in my life, if not *the* most important. I love Chris deeply and I always will. He's a great friend. And I am godmother to their two girls, Akira and Valentina. It was unfortunate that we were put through the wringer so much. Marriages and partnerships break up under financial pressures alone and with us there was so much more going on than that. And we will have moments of doubt when we think the whole thing is impossible and we can't go on.

I STARTED THE NEW MILLENNIUM WITH A STUPID ACCIDENT. WE WERE in London, the tour bus was leaving any minute, and it would be a long drive, so I decided at the last second to grab a sandwich for the trip. We were on Kensington High Street and there was a place—it's burned down now—where I had bought some good sandwiches a few times before. So I ran across the road and into the shop. Only this time, the plate-glass door was closed and I slammed headfirst into my reflection. Smack! The sound of the impact echoed through the shop. I barely saw the startled customers, with their mouths full of sandwich, gaping at me before I passed out. I lay on the ground at the entrance in a semiconscious state, our tour manager Matthew Murphy hovering over me, asking if I was all right. I was surprised that I *was* all right. I don't remember if I got a sandwich, but I do remember getting onto the bus, feeling very stupid, with a bloody nose and a bright red bump on my forehead. The black eyes came later. So did the whiplash. I couldn't believe that I gave myself whiplash just by running into a door.

Do you remember those segmented bamboo wiggle snakes? You know, those cheap little toys sold in Chinatown? How those snakes could move horizontally but not vertically, and they made that clickety-clackety bamboo sound? Well, it was after I ran into the plate glass that my spine started clacking and creaking like a wiggle snake. I tried massage and chiropractic adjustments. Sometimes they helped, sometimes they hurt. I preferred acupuncture, partly because it's got "punc" in it (having a punk attitude—holding stubbornly to an underground sensibility—has served me well). Instead of having my back adjusted, what I do is crouch, much like a peasant woman selling things in a street market, and then simply throw myself on the floor. I thrust myself backward with some force and I flop and hear that satisfying pop in one movement. Then I roll around a bit and stretch. It's a fine thing, that feeling of being well-adjusted/self-adjusted. Ha!

But things did not feel so well adjusted working on the next new Blondie album. Here was the problem. I was in a boys' club. I wasn't trying to be in a boys' club, but the boys' club had been a constant in my career. There were few women in the New York scene—in fact, in the whole music industry in the 1970s—and being a female lead singer in an otherwise all-male rock band was rare. But I wanted to do music and I didn't give a shit if that meant being in a boys' club. My intimate relationship with Chris undoubtedly helped me navigate all the testosterone. Chris is all man, but he's not a bully, not someone who's always trying to control things. He's flexible and he's smart. Jimmy though was a tough customer, a real macho Brooklyn guy, who had more than a little attitude when it came to women.

Our manager Allen came to a rehearsal when Jimmy was being typically abusive, and he was infuriated by this lack of respect. Jimmy would frequently speak to me with his eyes locked onto my breasts. Hello! Exasperating, irritating, demeaning of course, although sometimes the sick punk in me felt flattered. *Hey, I know what you're doing, I see you staring at my tits and you can't look me in the eye.* Sure, maybe it's backward, but as a woman, to know that I have that kind of magnetism gives me a rush. So, generally, I've been able to turn that sexual disrespect around and make it work *for* me, rather than against me. Gender play is seldom simple; it's a complicated, shifting dance. We're primal one minute, civilized the next, and everything in between. I did have some frustration getting some of my ideas carried out in the band and I would often be voted down. Sexism? Sometimes, undoubtedly, but I think more often it was a natural outcome of the band's democratic structure. The majority ruled. So sometimes I won and sometimes I lost and I had to bite the bullet. Fair enough. And maybe, just maybe, some of my ideas sucked.

I was the one who came up with the title for the new album, *The Curse of Blondie*, as a tongue-in-cheek homage to the great old black and white B-movies and an ironic comment on all that we had gone through. The plan was to release it in 2001, but it ran into all sorts of snags and it would take us two more years. Two thousand one was a lousy year. In April, Joey Ramone died of cancer, a terrible shock. I was devastated. I loved Joey. Not in a sexual way but as a singer and as a friend. He was the sweetest and friendliest person. I remember the early days when *Punk* magazine ran a comic-book story of Joey and me as star-crossed lovers. Our parents disapproved of our relationship, then Joey was kidnapped by aliens or something. Roberta Bayley, the door girl and self-appointed house photographer at CBGB's, took photos of the two of us in bed for the story. It was so much fun.

Then came 9/11. I was in my bedroom in NYC and I got a phone call from my friend Kerry. She said, "Are you watching TV?" I said no. I was actually looking out the window. I had a very clear view of the Twin Towers from my window and there was smoke coming out of one of the buildings. Kerry said, "Turn on the news." I turned it on and I started watching the TV and the live coverage while at the same time looking out of my win-

2001—Click+Drag 2.0 . . . New York was about to change.

dow. I saw the plane fly into the second tower. I was watching it live and watching it on TV, and watching them both was so trippy. A surreal feeling of not knowing exactly what I was seeing. Was it film footage or live reporting or reality? After 9/11, some of the people I knew became very afraid and wanted to leave New York right away. They were talking about things like storing cans of food and moving into the basement because we were under attack. I didn't feel that way, not that kind of fear, but I was definitely in a state of shock. Really, I was in mourning. I was grieving. Within a two-week period after the attack on the Twin Towers, I went through a whole series of emotions: shocked, then very sad, then very angry, and very nostalgic about the old days. Around that time, I wrote this poem.

RUSH OF SOULS

The slated sky hung over the Hudson
Reached across the wide waters
And continued, a gray lurking potential above New Jersey.
Landing lights flashed their warnings onto the tarmac
At Newark.
All this doubled in the glassy gliding river.
I wait, weighted by ambitions, by desires,
. . . . . oh what do I do.
Many voices for many melodies confound me.
A problem to speak my mind
So many voices, so many times.
But then there are indelibly clear moments scored plainly
Shaping all time to come.
Recently unsought
My worldly view has stretched
Emotions and instincts long left untouched but still intact
Now roar to the surface surging into my vocabulary
My voice breaks out
I call for survival. Powerless, out of control, saddened
Wakened where sleep kept comfort animal reactions
Racing to live to keep life, the ordinary skills I use every day
fall to
A new proportion.
How insignificant these talents will be in a roughened world.
Walking, roaming, pacing the cage was some temporary relief.
Distraction for a heart turned to a different tempo
. . . . . my heart, my heart, my heart. . . . .
Pounding me out of sleep into some static dimension
Between my bed, the sky, the room, earth, the then, the now,
And this space is filled with fluttering—but no birds
And alive with tiny blinking lights—but no bulbs
And it is crowded with new voices
Large and little, near and far,
Those voices the sound of a boiling
Thousands of them in confusion, bubbling, touching me.
I feel the flutter, an electric tingle, not unpleasant
And I know I have felt the rush of souls.

When I was going through that mourning period I said to myself, *Oh God, I wish it was the seventies again.* I kept on wishing myself back to those early days, eventually coming to the inevitable conclusion that things would never be the same again.

Chris and Barbara moved out of the loft on Greenwich Street and moved upstate. Their place had been only twelve blocks up from the towers and for months afterward you could still smell the smoke there. It was understandable, but it did come as a shock to me that they were even contemplating the move. Barbara was intent on getting out of downtown and raising her kids in a softer, safer environment. So, it made sense—and Woodstock was the perfect choice. I was heartbroken when they left. The thought of that kind of distance between us, of that separation . . . But in a way it was an enlightenment for me. Because their departure gave me a profound insight into something deeply rooted in me that I had never completely understood before. I was riding my bike along the Hudson when this sense of overpowering sadness washed over me. However, this time the sadness was infused with insight. I "saw" my sadness and it spoke to me: my heartbreak was the heartbreak of the abandoned child. Abandonment, the most enduring pain that always lay within me, waiting for its moment to consume me again. With that insight, something shifted in me finally. A new clarity, an acceptance, an acknowledgment, and a kind of release. That moment will live with me forever.

EVIDENCE OF LOVE

Chris Stein, 1976.

AS I WAS LOOKING THROUGH EVERYTHING I CAME ACROSS A CUTOUT of a bee, signed by Jane. I think this must have been given to me recently because of the Pollinator connection which helps save honey bees. But if it wasn't recent, it is so synchronistic, so totally appropriate, I was overjoyed by how perfect it is, I put it on a new T-shirt, orb-shirt, called BEE CONSCIOUS.

So here are some, lovingly saved since the 1970s, a gallery of drawings and paintings done for me, likenesses of me by my fans. You must know by now how precious you are to me and totally amazed by what you've given me I am, because the act of making art is the important part. The art itself is just souvenirs . . . and beauty in the eye of the beholder.

So for better or for worse, I have saved face. My collection of Fan Art is not only portraiture. The works include other things, other subject matter and figures, i.e., dolls and different ephemera with my likeness on them. It touched me, touches me still that another person would go to the trouble and time to create a piece of art and then give it to me. Many of these things aren't even signed except for the evidence of love.

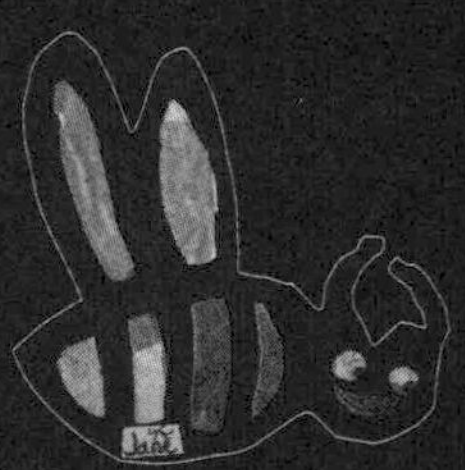

Lizzie

...
We stood in the cold light, though we should be warm - at the back of the lot with me in your arms - the grey rain was pouring the cars were all dirty and slow. We both had our kiss and out of the depth & darkness - with my eyes closed I still see ya fine...
18.10.01
by
VANITY FAIR 'NOV. 2001

HAPPY BIRTHDAY.

Luca 2014

14

OBSESSION/COMPULSION

Coal fueled the furnaces that heated our houses for most of my childhood. I loved to watch the coal delivery: The massive dump truck grinding to a halt beside the house; the dust-covered driver hooking together the metal chutes, with the final one placed into the open cellar window, the gleaming of those chutes—polished bright as silver from the years of rough coal sliding down their throats. Then the best part of all—the mesmerizing, satisfying climax—the electrifying sound a ton of coal made as it rushed down the chute and splashed into the bottom of the basement bin.

Left to my own devices, as kids were in those days, I would sneak into the cool dark dampness of the basement to play in the coal bin. My father would toss those shiny black stones into the open furnace before he left for work and again when he came back home. No final glory as a glittering diamond for these bits of carbon, who were doomed instead to a death by fire. My mother wasn't exactly thrilled by my coal obsession and especially the dirty little Debbie who would keep popping up in her spotless kitchen. What was the big deal? Hey, it was just coal dust all over my clothes. It brushed off just fine onto the floor . . . This was no doubt the same dust that had wrecked the lungs of and killed thousands of miners worldwide.

The coal-fired furnace generated steam heat. Later, when we moved, we graduated to an oil heater and a forced-air system. There's a story here about the origin of obsession and compulsion, if you'll take the leap with me. The fuel delivery for our oil heater lacked the visual and auditory excitement of the coal delivery and it had a strong, unpleasant odor. However, what *did* grab me was the process. How it worked. Clearly, I had an instinct, or as I know now, some kind of genetic feeling, maybe even a calling, for plumbing and heating. But the concept of forced air also led me to another talent, or maybe another genetic predisposition. Singing. And over time, as I learned to create compression in my body as a singer, I could see myself as a kind of combustion engine or bellows. I now know that I am part of a forced-air legacy. Singing for me at first was a way to keep myself company and a way to say things without words. It was a release of air, often inspired by emotion. The difference between heating and singing is the moisture content in that forced air. Singing is hot and wet, and you can take that any way you want. Singing was a compulsion for me, something I was irresistibly drawn to. The need to create was an obsession, something that always preoccupied me.

I'm trying to think if I have any other compulsions. I can certainly cop to some additional obsessive behaviors. At one time I'd gather all my nail clippings and flush them down the toilet—the same for every strand of hair I could pick off my brush. These traces of Debbie have disappeared into the sewers of city after city, in country after country, as I have toured the world. Eliminate all evidence. No trail to track me by . . . If I could, I would vacuum up every discarded skin cell and flush them away too, but even I have my obsessive limits. (Although if you'd seen me scouring my hotel bathroom for any drop of saliva left lying around, you might question that claim.) In fact, I get anxious at the mere thought of my secret identity being found out.

Oh, and let's not forget my campaign against the sprang-a-langs. These devilish, coiled deviants have threatened to betray me in the most embarrassing places. Not on my watch, you little bastards! You can't be too careful, after all, my friend the rogue NYC art dealer got nabbed on a murder charge thanks to his sprang-a-langs . . . Those creatures, they are all so different from one another—and each tiny curl speaks volumes about its owner. When I find them, I flush them. But I worry about the one that got away.

Speaking of obsessive creation, *No Exit* turned out to be pivotal for all of us. That surge of approval and recognition had a big effect on Blondie. On me too. It gave us new life. It fed the beast. Who knew we'd have stayed in the public consciousness after so many years away? But in an odd way, perhaps that long period off was a fortunate bump in the road. We had been forced to stop and when we came back we had to seriously rethink who we were and what direction we should take. I never wanted to make another "Heart of Glass" or "Hanging on the Telephone" and my one main condition for our getting back together was my demand to create new music. In the commerce-dominated pop world, artists are generally pushed to maintain the status quo. Artists who buck the pressure and evolve—like David Bowie or Lou Reed—are often applauded for it in the long run, but not without years of struggle, fighting to convince the moneymen that their new direction is valid and worth it. Getting such a good response to the new songs inspired us to write more. *The Curse of Blondie* was released in October 2003 and we went back on the road, bouncing back and forth across the globe just like the old days, except that it felt much easier than the old days.

In 2006 we got news that Blondie would be inducted into the Rock and Roll Hall of Fame. I couldn't believe it. There were so many famous names I thought would have gotten in before us and Blondie was initially never taken that seriously by the music industry. I had never taken the Rock and Roll Hall of Fame that seriously either, but to be honest it felt great to get that validation. We had flown the flag for NYC rock and helped bring our then-underground culture into the mainstream. So we showed up at the Waldorf Astoria Hotel in New York for the big gala ceremony. Shirley Manson of Garbage gave a beautiful induction speech and we went out on the stage to get our statuettes. Each of us had a minute and a half to say something. I sent my heartfelt thanks to the girls who had been part of our musical journey, Tish and Snooky and Julie and Jackie. And then another part of Blondie's past turned up and all hell broke loose.

Frankie, Nigel, and Gary had been invited to the ceremony. They were sitting in the audience and decided to come up onstage. Frankie was in the mood for a fight. He grabbed the microphone and thanked the Hall of Fame for not writing him, Nigel, and Gary "out of rock 'n' roll history." We had left the awards platform and were onstage about to perform our song, but Frankie wasn't finished: "One thing that could make it better is if we could perform for you tonight," he said, "but for some reason some of us are not allowed to do that." He called out to me, "Debbie. Is that allowed? No? We'd like to play with you guys! Me and Nigel. Not tonight? Pretty please?" Why did he think this was my decision, mine alone? Blondie always operated on a consensus basis.

"Oh, you guys, it's too late, please don't beg!" Chris was furious. "They sued us," he said, "and they wrote themselves out of the band's history. You shouldn't be forced to play with somebody because they did a couple of albums with you back in the past. I worked with Nigel Harrison for maybe four and a half years. Our bass player Leigh Foxx has been working with me and Debbie for twenty years." The Hall of Fame had promised our manager that they weren't going to let those guys go up. But maybe someone in the Hall of Fame didn't think we deserved to be inducted and got back at us in some small way. There's always politics. Or maybe they just decided that a fight would make good TV. When *Billboard* magazine did an article on the "ten most controversial Rock and Roll Hall of Fame moments," Blondie made the cut. So did another band that was being inducted the same year as us. The Sex Pistols had turned down their invitation and Johnny Rotten sent Jann Wenner, the founder of *Rolling Stone* magazine, a letter that called the Rock and Roll Hall of Fame "a piss stain."

Clem, in his Hall of Fame speech, thanked CBGB's and Hilly Kristal, saying that they deserved to be inducted. It

An infamous Hall of Fame induction.

turned out that the awning over CBGB's front door and the phone box inside would soon be in the Hall of Fame museum. CBGB's closed in October 2006. The writing was on the wall for a long time. Hilly's lease had expired. The landlords, like all the other landlords in NYC, hiked up the rent and Hilly started to run into money problems. To make matters worse, Hilly was very sick at the time. There were benefit shows and all sorts of efforts to raise money for the rent and to raise awareness of the club as a cultural landmark, the epicenter and incubator of an underground scene that had become a worldwide influence. But the final eviction notice came. CBGB's made its farewell with a last weekend of shows.

Patti Smith played the Sunday show. Blondie and the Dictators played the final Saturday night. The place was sinuously writhing and grinding like some giant wild animal. CBGB's held around three hundred people, but there must have been five hundred of us packed into the space, with a whole shitload of emotion. I was overwhelmed myself; after all, it was the end of an era and a final goodbye to another massive piece of my past. Like a death in the family. We were time travelers who'd flicked the switch and landed back where it had all begun. Here is where we had worked on our image, developed our style, and grown as a band. So many memories poured through me: the rivalries, the love affairs, the fights, the manic shows, the wild energy, the experimentation, the sense that anything could happen and did. The raw punkness, the intensity of it all . . . Ha! Yeah!!

The year after his club closed, Hilly died from lung cancer. He had been talking about resurrecting CBGB's in Las Vegas. I was sad he was gone. And so grateful that we were lucky enough to have had that haven when NYC was broke, we were broke, and DIY culture was a necessity, not a style that would be copied by the worlds of fashion, music, design, movies, and art. Punk has gone on to become a commodity. CBGB's is a

The closing of CBGB's.

different commodity now, a high-end men's clothing store, and walking past 315 Bowery is like walking on a different planet.

That same year I was on a promotional trip in Las Vegas and I saw Cirque du Soleil's new show *Love*. It was based on Beatles songs, and Paul and Ringo were there, along with Yoko Ono, and they all seemed to have gotten over their differences. Time really does heal, or it can if you let it. Blondie may not have lost anyone permanently—you know, death—just mentally. I saw Sheila E while I was there and she told me she was going to be playing with Ringo at the Garden State Arts Center. I had seen her play with Prince and she is a great, terrific drummer and singer, so I got tickets and went with my sister, Martha, to see Ringo Starr & His All-Starr Band.

Ringo had a lot of different artists play with him and I especially enjoyed Edgar Winter. He was eccentric, but not trying too hard to be so, and a great musician. I hadn't paid much attention to his music back in the early seventies because it was too good-ol'-boy sounding for me. The only way I knew anything about Edgar was by hanging out with one of his ex-wives, maybe his only ex-wife for all I know, Barbara Winter. As I sat there listening to Edgar and the All-Starrs, stories from the past came rushing through my mind. Those days had a physicality that made it seem as if the molecular structure of my senses had more space. I flashed back to when I worked at Max's Kansas City in the late sixties and had that brief fling with Eric Emerson one night in the phone booth upstairs.

Eric ended up living at Chris's apartment for a while. Eric had so many girlfriends and some children, but finally he met Barbara Winter, whom I remember as being very sexy, with large breasts and lush black hair, a real rock 'n' roll babe. I remembered Elda telling us a story about Barbara standing in the front window of Eric's old apartment on Park Avenue and Twenty-Seventh Street, while she swung this giant black dildo around. It was early in the morning and all the office workers from the New York Life building and other businesses were dragging themselves to work, and there stood big-boobed Barbara waving her dildo. I almost wish I had been on my way to work that morning. That vision would have made my day and possibly much more.

When Eric and Barbara moved into an apartment in a brand-new high-rise way down on Greenwich Street, just north of Chambers Street, Chris and I would go visit them. It had a spectacular view across the Hudson and out into the harbor, including the Verrazano Bridge. Wild. Truth be told, living in NYC is all about having one of those views. These were some of the first of the new wave of ultramodern high-rises to be erected in the city. A whole section of the city, long held by the import-export spice merchants, was having an extreme makeover and the heady, rich aroma of all those spices and coffees was disappearing. That smell was heavenly. If I could, I would have made it into incense or something.

One time when we walked over to Eric and Barbara's, I was in a foul mood. I mean, foul. "Unreasonable" would be the most diplomatic description of my temperament. I was being a shit. The building complex wasn't finished. The empty lot next door, wrapped partially by a chain-link fence, housed the construction company's trailer office and equipment and a roving bitch guard dog . . . Well, this bitch wasn't about to roll with my shit, and she bared her fangs and lunged and bit me in the ass. Calmed me right down. Frankly, I don't understand how Chris managed to tolerate my awful mood swings, but he was so sweet and funny about my ravings and he could joke me out of almost anything. And sometimes he too would lunge and bite me in the ass.

So these were the reveries running through my mind.

Thanks, Edgar. I had no idea I would love seeing you perform as much as I did. And thank you for transporting me back to those special times with Chris, when we had no money and walked everywhere, be it hot and steaming or red-nose freezing.

When the Blondie tour was over, and all of a sudden I had time on my hands, I felt the urge to write some songs on my own. Often, when I was working on band material, I'd be mindful that the lyrics could end up being sung by either a man or a woman. It was always important to me that Blondie songs be androgynous. But these songs I was writing were much more personal. My work with the Jazz Passengers was a major influence. Roy Nathanson wrote a beautiful song on the gruesome subject of a suicide bomber for me, entitled "Paradise." Chris and I wrote two songs together and I collaborated with Barb Morrison and Charles Nieland, who were working as Super

Buddha. That's how my first solo album in fourteen years came to be. *Necessary Evil* was released in September 2007 and I went back out on the road.

I never had a Barbie doll when I was a little girl. She didn't exist then. I think the Barbie doll came into existence long after I'd stopped playing with dolls. So when the Barbie people asked to meet with me, I was kind of curious and I said, "Sure." What intrigued me most about this meeting was that they never talked about Barbie as a doll. Every one of them had this unshakeable and complete understanding of Barbie as a real person. When they talked about Barbie they would say, "Oh, Barbie isn't like that," or "Barbie would never do that!" In their minds, Barbie was a real being with a real presence and her own sense of style. I found this fascinating. It reminded me of the puppeteers when I did *The Muppet Show*, in particular Frank Oz. Frank warned me that Miss Piggy would never do the show with me because it would be too much of a conflict to have me around, flirting with Kermit.

When they asked how I felt about a Debbie Harry Barbie, at first I thought, *Why in the world would I want that?* Except that at that point it was kind of like a fetish, and I have no problem with fetishes. Also there were people I thought highly of who had Barbies, like Cher and Marilyn Monroe. And much of Barbie's success can be tied to whom the company had chosen to fetishize. So I said, "Let's do it." And now I have a Barbie doll. Several actually, somewhere in the closet, all of them wearing the pink dress with the laces that I made back in the seventies. The Barbie people liked that pink dress. I think I would have almost preferred the zebra dress. But maybe animal print is one of the things that Barbie doesn't do.

When we started on a new Blondie album in 2009, many of the great seventies and eighties recording studios in NYC had closed down, victims of the shift to digital. The studios that were left charged heaven and earth and then some. So we looked around for a cheaper option and found a great place in Woodstock, near where Chris, Barbara, and the girls lived. Chris came up with the album title: *Panic of Girls,* a collective noun he made up—like "murder" of crows—for girls running wild. Since we were once again without a record company, Blondie's ninth studio album came out on an independent label and made the top twenty in the UK indie charts.

My favorite song on that album was "Mother." I think it has some of my best lyrics. Many people have thought it's about my mother, or even my birth mother, although I'm not sure either of them was into patent leather thigh-high boots! It's actually about the club in the Meatpacking District called Mother that I loved to go to in the mid to late nineties. It was an underground club, literally below street level, very dark, very naughty, and a lot of fun. Mother was a big part of my social life. It was where my friends were. Every week on a Tuesday night they would have a different theme and everybody would come dressed in different drag, such as Pablo Picasso night, or robot night, or Klingon women night—everything you can think of. I love dressing up, and I have since I was a child, and that was one of the reasons that I enjoyed going there so much. Wearing a costume is liberating. It's why people love Halloween, because they get to play a part for a few hours. One night at Mother I dressed up as an Edvard Munch painting. I had a bowler hat so I took advantage of it, and I dressed in a painted-up sandwich board. The costume was absurd and impossible to maneuver in a crowded nightclub, but there was no better place for a good time.

Johnny Dynell and Chi Chi Valenti gave life to the performance club Jackie 60, which later became Mother, and both clubs were exceptional for having a good time. My friend Rob Roth, artistic director for us on many projects, was one of the in-house artists. He'd make short video loops related

Jackie 60—Tuesdays would never be the same.

to the theme of the party and they'd play on multiple screens throughout the club all night long. Some of the regulars were queens who were also professional stylists and they would show up in the most incredible outfits and creations. Like works of art. Really, walking, talking works of art. I am a voyeur; I love to watch. You would get an eyeful and be an eyeful and you could drink and dance all night. Mother was such an important part of my life that when it closed, I felt such a sense of loss that I wondered, *What am I going to do on Tuesday nights without Mother?*

After the *Panic of Girls* tour we made *Ghosts of Download*. On *Ghosts*, we jumped in full with programming. Chris and I had always been drawn to new developments in science and technology, curious about the "new thing," whatever it might be. The new was mysterious and fascinating and we were eager to experiment. Like Chris, I have never been afraid of change.

I wrote a song on *Ghosts* with my friend Miss Guy called "Rave," and I did a song written by Matt Katz-Bohen that included a duet with Beth Ditto entitled "A Rose by Any Other Name": *"If you're a boy or if you're a girl I'll love you just the same."* We had been part of a community that valued androgyny and wasn't burdened by anxieties about sexuality. Outside of that world, though, it took significant courage to be transsexual or have a sexuality that was not the "norm" . . . Modern science is finally recognizing that we are all complex, individual balances of male and female, because every single person is some kind of gender combination, whether you want to accept it or not. For me, it's always been this way. Half man, half woman. Not a transsexual; not a cross-dresser; not bi; not the expression of a frustrated or repressed sexual self. Just both sexes. A double identity.

In the end we released a double album, *Blondie 4(0)Ever*. One disc was *Ghosts of Download* and the other was an album of new recordings we had made of Blondie's greatest hits. Regaining control of our material was complicated and contentious. When contracts run out, there's a clause in the record deal that says your ownership of the material will revert to you after a certain number of years. The labels fight this tooth and nail. It can be a nightmare winning back those rights. So, one work-around is to rerecord the originals. In addition, we wanted to showcase our classic songs in a modern idiom, with the new band. And this was an important time for us. It was Blondie's fortieth anniversary. We released *Blondie 4(0)Ever* in May 2014 with Andy Warhol's portrait of me on the cover.

Chris marked our anniversary with his book *Negative: Me, Blondie, and the Advent of Punk*. It was a mix of text and his photography, with photos of me and the band, plus other artists, filmmakers, musicians, and friends. He manages to document a special time in New York, with the wild beauty of the decayed and dirty city in the seventies. The garbage strewn everywhere, where you found fabulous things that people threw out and you deconstructed them and you put the pieces together with creativity and irony as the glue. The punk aesthetic.

Chris shot his pictures in clubs and studios, in our apartment, in the street, and—as Blondie started to take off—on the road, which gave his work a worldwide perspective. Besides many that had never been published previously, *Negative* includes some of his famous photos of me, like the one where I'm standing in our burned-out kitchen, wearing Marilyn Monroe's dress, holding a flaming frying pan. I didn't keep a journal. I sort of regret that now because this book would have been much easier and maybe better if I had. But Chris documented those times with his camera. His mother, when we first met, told me that Chris had always been an observer, even as a baby. And I became so used to being observed by him that I learned to be comfortable with having my photo taken, which was something I used to hate. I am convinced that this was how I got the

In Marilyn's dress.

confidence to get in front of all those other cameras. But I still think that Chris's photos of me are the most real and the most revealing.

IN MARCH 2015 I WAS OFFERED A SOLO GIG AT AN UPPER EAST SIDE cabaret supper club, Café Carlyle. I'm not a chanteuse or a torch singer so I was surprised. But the idea of performing in an intimate venue was okay. I'd never done anything exactly like this before, though I had sort of touched on it with the Jazz Passengers, except this time I wouldn't have a band at the Carlyle, just one accompanist, Matt Katz-Bohen from Blondie. I was curious also about what it would be like to talk to the audience, commenting on the songs. Roy Nathanson had done all the talking in the Jazz Passengers shows and with Blondie the audiences were too big to connect with on an intimate level. I've been in audiences at festivals myself and I know how speech without music becomes muddied if you say more than three words.

As I was picking material, I started discovering things about the songs that I could share with the audience. "I Cover the Waterfront," for example, is a beautiful, moody, evocative song that I always associated with NYC, but when I looked into it, I discovered it's about San Diego and Chinese laborers and smuggling. The songs I chose covered a lot of territory, as I did a different show every night. My guest artists were people whom I had worked or written with, including Chris, Roy, Barb Morrison, Tommy Kessler, and Guy Furrow, and they all chose the songs they wanted to do, which added even more flavors to the pot. It felt luxurious to do material like "Imitation of a Kiss," "Strike Me Pink," and "In Love with Love," the songs I didn't do with Blondie but that worked perfectly with just me and Matt. And from there, I could switch to something like "Rainbow Connection" from *The Muppet Show*. Playing two shows a night for ten nights was hard work. I hadn't done that since the early days. But it was a treat to tie all of these different pieces together into a coherent, compelling package. I've said yes so many times when I should have said no, so it's special when the yes has such a gratifying outcome.

Meanwhile Chris had come up with a curation concept for the next Blondie album. We would write our own songs but also solicit outside songwriters, preferably contemporary artists, who would send us their favorite pieces. Around thirty songs came in and Chris, John Congleton, and myself made some difficult decisions on what to keep. But we would never have done a song without everyone in the band in agreement on what to include. There were songs by people like Charli XCX, Dev Hynes, Dave Sitek, Johnny Marr, and Sia. We specifically asked for Sia to submit something because we were all such big fans. By chance she had been working with Nick Valensi from the Strokes, and that made it even better, even more New York.

Since our last album had been heavily computer based, with everyone doing their parts separately, we all agreed that this time we would do it as a band album, all of us in a room recording together like the early days. We wanted to record it in New York, so we booked the Magic Shop on Crosby Street in Soho, one of the oldest studios in the city and one of the most historic. Behind the graffiti-covered, gray metal front door were walls that were plastered ceiling to floor with album sleeves from the artists who had recorded there, like Lou Reed and the Ramones. They even had my favorite soundtrack album, *O Brother, Where Art Thou?*, which has nothing to do with rock but it's just wonderful. The Magic Shop was where David Bowie made his last two albums, *The Next Day* and *Blackstar*.

We started recording a few weeks before Christmas 2015, then we broke for the holidays. And that's when David died. January 2016. Going back into that studio having just lost David was more than emotional. David had such a profound effect on us in our early days, giving us our start, taking us out into the real world when he asked us to tour with him and Iggy in 1977. We loved David. He was a visionary and a Renaissance man. He was beautiful and he was fearless. To choose to go out the way he did, by making such a powerful, courageous artistic declaration, is something so rare and so smart, but that's how he always was. We were all conscious of being in the environment where David had concluded his career with *Blackstar*. I believe a bit of David's spirit was there in the room when we made our album.

Steve Rosenthal, who owned the studio, had told us that we would be the last band to do a full record there. Gentrification and rising prices were forcing him out and the studio would close that March. So there was a kind of an end-of-an-era feeling, but at the same time a real excitement—making this album with all these great musicians and all this fresh new music. Joan Jett flew in to sing backing vocals on a song that Chris and I wrote, "Doom or Destiny," the most punk rock song on the album. Joan has been a friend since the seventies, when we first went to L.A. and she was with the Runaways. Joan is a true rock 'n' roll spirit and I love her dearly.

And our longtime friend Laurie Anderson came in with her violin and contributed all those layers of music on "Tonight," in a kind of tripped-out homage to the Velvet Underground.

LATER, WHEN I WAS THINKING OF ALBUM TITLES, A WORD POPPED INTO my head: "Terminator." Then I thought, *No. "Pollinator."* The word had such a nice sound. And several Blondie albums had begun with the letter "P." But what resonated on a deeper level was the cross-pollination of all these different songwriters and musicians sharing their music and passing it around. So, *Pollinator* it was. And then the bees swarmed in . . . My name, Deborah, in Hebrew means "bee." And I had known for a while about the desperate plight of the honeybees and pollinators struggling to live with pollutants and pesticides that were killing them en masse. A guy who has tended hives since he was a kid has been teaching me about the challenges, in addition to conversations I've had with two Blondie superfans, Barry and Michelle. Then I started my new pollinator hives. One of the hives died and we had to go out and find a new queen. But one hive lasted throughout the whole winter and still seems to be thriving. Not to sound pompous, but pollination is essential to our planet's health. I have contributed to many environmental charities over the years, especially Riverkeeper, which is dedicated to cleaning up the Hudson, as well as charities for AIDS, cancer, and kids' music schools, and I'm very happy to be able to do that. But for such an important cause to be so directly related to what we were doing in music was just fantastic. With the *Pollinator* album and tour we had a talking point, saving the bees, and we could make money for organizations that were trying to do that.

I got inspired myself. I had a couple of different bee headpieces made, with designs by Geoffrey Mac, Neon, and Michael Schmidt. I would come out at the start of the show in a cape that said in big letters "STOP FUCKING THE PLANET," which was made by eco-fashion designers Vin and Omi, who make clothes from fabrics woven from the plastic bags that are fucking up the planet for real. When we were in the UK we played a show at the Eden Project in Cornwall. I was speaking with one of the research scientists there and she told me that they were developing a strain of black honeybee that would be more resistant to these little varroa mites that, once they get into the hive, suck everything out of it and destroy it.

The bee sitting on the lotus flower on the album cover was designed by Shepard Fairey, a smart, driven, wonderful artist who is just tireless, doing giant murals all over the world, many of them protesting environmental issues. Shepard is pro-ecology and anti-Trump, and I am too. Shepard's murals are as readable as *Guernica*, telling stories of political and environmental genocide. They scream at you silently. I had bought some of his work a few years ago and we became friends. Then we decided to work together on a line of clothing. It was just for a short run, a little pop-up thing. From my side, I wanted to do simple, affordable clothing, hoodies, parkas, and leggings, using urban camouflage designs with patterns taken from a variety of surfaces in the city, such as ironworks, gratings, barbed wire, chain link, and walls with shredded posters that had been torn or worn off. Shepard, on his side, was working with some people who were more into doing T-shirts and Debbie Harry imagery. So somehow we combined both of these ideas, a little bit of my thing, a little bit of his. There was one T-shirt we came up with that said, "Obey Debbie," Obey being the name of Shepard's company. Excellent slogan.

When our *Pollinator* album was released in May 2017, it debuted at number four in the UK charts and made number one in the UK indie charts, and in the U.S. independent charts it was number four. And *Rolling Stone* magazine, in their annual roundup, named it one of the ten best pop albums of the year.

I GUESS WE'VE REACHED THE PART WHERE YOU ALL GET ON YOUR FEET in a standing ovation as I take my bow and leave the stage, victorious. Ha! I'm still here. I have had one fuck of an interesting life and I plan to go on having one. We live in a disposable, transient-feeling world and usually after five years you go on to the next thing, maybe now even less than five years. I remember how in the seventies we all admired the old R & B and jazz artists, these old-timers who come to think of it weren't that old. Our generation was told that pop and rock were for kids. "It won't last," was what they told us, and then everyone grew up with it and decided that they wanted to keep that music as their music, and it's become its own art form.

Getting older *is* hard on your looks. Like everybody else I have good days, bad days, and those "Shit, I hope nobody sees me today" days, where you look exactly the same from the outside but you see yourself through different eyes. One thing I have learned is that we are often our own worst enemy. I have never hidden the fact that I've had plastic surgery. I think it's the same as having a flu shot basically, another way of looking after yourself. If it makes you feel better and look better and work better, that's what it's all about, so you take advantage of the new possibilities that come into your life. I think I have finally figured out a way of understanding myself. Some days I'm happy with the way I look and sometimes I'm not, and it's always been that way. But I'm not blind and I'm not stupid: I take advantage of my looks and I use them.

I just had a visit with my manager Allen, and he told me, "I hope that you say something about how you broke ground as a female artist in a business that was a man's world, and how difficult it was as a woman to do what you've done." It surprised me that he would say that. I know that it has been difficult but I don't know if it's been difficult *because* I'm a woman. I mean, I know intellectually that being a woman in this business at the time when I started out was not helpful, but in my head I've never used it as an excuse. I know there is misogyny and I know there is bias, but I'm more concerned with being good at what I do. It *is* a man's world, and unfortunately I don't think they are going to lose that title just yet even though the number of women in the music business now is enormous compared to the seventies. But for me, in order to survive, I could never put myself in the position of whining about being a woman. I just got on with it. As much as it was possible, I found a way to do what I wanted to do.

Sometimes I think that I did things backward. In the grand tradition of rock 'n' roll, when you join a band you are supposed to go crazy and act wild, but I did all that stuff *before* I met Chris and we formed a band. I was so very happy in my relationship with Chris and really in love, so in a sense I settled down to do music. Another thing: people say that you're happiest when you are young, but I'm happier now. I know who I am even if I am not more in control. But I'll never forget those early days in New York. As a rock artist, to be coming out of New York City was the best thing in the world that could have happened to me. The only other place I can conceive of our coming out of is London, a place with the same kind of sensibility, but I'm an American and I'm an East Coast girl, so it's simple: it's New York City for me. Wherever I go I'm always comparing it to New York. It's not the way it was (none of us are), but it's still thriving and vibrant. My friends are in New York, my social life is in New York, and everything that I'm attracted to and have ever wanted to be like is in New York. New York is my pulse. New York is my heart. I'm still a New York punk.

NYC

15

OPPOSABLE THUMBS

I think first of that game where you try to trap the other guy's thumb under yours while the rest of your fingers are gripping their fingers. Then there is the old saying "I'm all thumbs," which is a peculiar mental image and is a feeble excuse for clumsiness. At first blush, compared to the fingers, the thumb may seem like the ugly stepsister, but it's actually the most important digit. What else helped us become masters of the universe, or at least of planet Earth? Okay, so many of the images of sci-fi aliens depict a sort of cloven hand with only two large digits like a lobster claw, yet they seem to have mastered interstellar space travel and have developed mental and physical abilities far beyond anything we humans have evolved. But I still love and cling to my thumbs.

During the 1960s, for the road warriors, hitchhiking by thumb was a favored form of travel. Douglas Adams had an epiphany one night while gazing up at the starry sky and he stretched it into a glorious, extended metaphor with his *Hitchhiker's Guide to the Galaxy*. And Tom Robbins turned the thumb into the ultimate totem in his *Even Cowgirls Get the Blues*. His protagonist, Sissy Hankshaw, is a young woman with two massive thumbs—thumbs with mystical powers, special digits, the thumbs of a lifetime. The girl always gets a ride when she puts her thumb out in the road, with a delicacy that belies the enormity of her appendage. Our heroine crosses the country, searching for her place in the universe and possibly true love, but it is the thumb that leads the way.

We love our opposables from the pages of history too. Rebels with or without a cause touch hearts as long as they are not mass murderers. "Thumbs-up," "thumbs-down," "thumb your nose," and "rule of thumb" are all creditable phrases that have stood the test of time and are still used today, though maybe not as much as they once were and often with shifted meanings. Thumbs-up originally meant "Yes, kill that losing gladiator." Thumbs-down meant "Swords down and spare him," so be careful to whom you give a thumbs-up. Folklore has it that "rule of thumb" referred to the width of the rod you could beat your wife with, but let's not go there . . . My mother, Catherine, who liked to go by Caggie, was a big advocate of nose thumbing, which she often did instead of saying "Bullshit" or "No way" or "Ha!" Maybe she meant something else entirely but in most cases she accompanied her finger action with a raspberry or fart noise like the cartoon characters in *Family Guy*, with her tongue sticking out, and this obviously meant "phooey." Thumbing your nose at someone or something is a bit more playful than giving someone the finger, but it doesn't seem to have made the cut in our modern world. We may love our middle fingers and there may be nothing more satisfying than flipping a bird, but come on, they don't quite measure up to the glorious thumb.

Speaking of history, I have to mention Tom Thumb, who rose to fame as Tom Thumb the Great and also Tom Thumb the

Little sometime in the early 1500s. In England's first published fairy tale, Tom hangs out with King Arthur, after being eaten and then excreted by a series of cows, giants, and fish. Little people were often looked on with great fondness by royalty all across Europe, and the next time I'm in the UK, I'm determined to visit Tattershall in Lincolnshire to see Tom's grave, where his tombstone reads: "T. Thumb, Aged 101, died 1620." The grave is sixteen inches long! What a very tiny man he was . . . After this, as far as I know, the next mention of a little person in connection with the thumb is Thumbelina in 1835, in a story by Hans Christian Andersen—whose stories were sometimes condemned as abnormal and immoral. Poor Thumbelina—cast to the dogs for an indiscriminate sex life, I assume—has nevertheless stood the test of time and become a bit of a movie star. So much for misogyny. Then finally, we have P. T. Barnum's famous performer General Tom Thumb, who was a talented singer, actor, dancer, and comedian, whose marriage to another little person had ten thousand guests and whose funeral was attended by twenty thousand. In other words, General Tom Thumb, all two and a half feet of him from head to toe, was as big as a rock star.

There is also the "thumbnail sketch," which means an abbreviation or an outline reduced to thumbnail size. And now we have the online thumbnails—those compressed versions of pictures and videos and memes—which haven't eliminated the finger reference completely. Enter the androids and bots, who can probably dispense entirely with the thumb. Me? I would miss my thumbs horribly if they were gone. I am a voracious book reader, always have been, always will be. Can't imagine trying to thumb my way through a book with no thumbs! Yikes. Plus, my side job as a professional knitter would go out the window.

"Murderer's thumb" or "strangler's thumb" connotes a certain size and shape of thumb. The first joint is rounded and wider than usual, so was considered more effective for closing down the poor victim's windpipe. I don't know of any other digit that is credited with being able to weigh in so powerfully on the struggle of life and death . . . The index and middle fingers are pretty good also-rans with their "Got my eye on you" or "Poke your eye out" threats, à la the Three Stooges; however, murderer's thumbs are clearly in a class of their own!

In line with the grimmer aspects of life and death, I have to mention a medieval method for extracting the supposed truth from prisoners: thumb screws. How dastardly and crude these little devices appear, usually made of iron that has moldered in the dark regions of dungeons deep below castle and prison walls. I know I'd talk, talk, and talk about whatever they asked me even if I didn't know what the fuck they wanted to hear. All those poor wretched chicken thieves with crushed thumbs . . . But there are other thumb screws that aren't used for torture. This kind of screw is simply a regular piece of hardware still available today at Home Depot and Lowe's and Ace Hardware and many other home improvement stores. Those little screws that have a top section that can be turned by using your thumb and index finger. They aren't made of iron anymore and don't look at all scary.

Recently in Mexico I was reminded of another thumb reference by my friend and keyboard player Matt Katz-Bohen. His suggestion was a surprise and I appreciate his contribution to this train of thought: thumbtacks. The tacks designed specifically for application using the thumbs. Which gives us "getting down to brass tacks"—and I'm a big believer in getting down to brass tacks. Are there any other products created for a thumb that have stood the test of time in spite of being replaced in part by the staple gun, but not eliminated from use in today's world? There might be, but I'm passing the thought on to you for consideration. Hit me up through my publisher. Perhaps I'll award a prize to the best entry. Or not.

Once upon a time, when we were wasting time or waiting on something to happen, we would "twiddle our thumbs." "Twiddle" and "twitter", are close cousins, and depending on your accent you might mix them up, but in any case, they both involve the use of or passage of time. We live in the age now of joined-at-the-hip devices—taking a piss or walking blindly across the road while stabbing away on our cell phones. What do we call this frenetic thumb action? Typing away at a furious pace using only our thumbs on this tiny keyboard? The popular new term is "thumbling." But I vote for "twiddling." This seems appropriate and accurate to me, but also suggests efficiency in the world of communication devices. I've seen some of the fastest thumbs in the world and I remember from my typing course days how critical speed was as a benchmark for success. I therefore suggest that "thumbling" speed tests become one measure of a person's aptitude and further, a part of their résumé. "I thumble at 105 tpm. And you, my friend?"

Recently, I've started to drive my car with my thumbs. I use the cruise control on the steering wheel, which lets me thumb my way down the road with just the occasional touch. Truthfully, this only works on freeways, highways, turnpikes, and long stretches of road when there isn't a whole lot of traffic, but I am kind of excited by this and can envision a time when just thinking alone will operate my vehicle.

I thought a little bit of levity might be a good way to end my somewhat morose memoir, hence all this thumb business. I wouldn't want you writing me off as a total sourpuss. Chris and I and many of the musicians I've worked with had a lot of laughs through it all, although some of the humor was a bit dark for the general public. After all, it's what made us the punks that we were then and still are today. We were philosophers more than real musicians at the start. Even while learning how to play and perform, we still managed to entertain thousands of people and create a genre of music. As Mike Chapman said after he first saw us at the Whisky in L.A., he never laughed so much in his life. True to rock history, we follow in the footsteps of the upstarts and rule breakers who stepped away from the niceties of swing and the sadness of the blues into a backlash against the folkies, good ol' boys, and tripped-out hippies of the more recent past. Even though "punk" has several different meanings and the record labels moved the category over to new wave, we all still know what the fuck it means.

I still have so much more to tell but being such a private person, I might not tell everything. At first, it was against my better judgment to do a memoir/autobiography, but it seems appropriate at this time in my life to get it over with and remember. My natural survivor's mentality drives me forward for more and newer experiences and tales to tell, and let's FACE IT, as I've learned in doing shows, it's always best to leave the audience wanting more . . .

Thank you and goodnight. Argentina, 2018.

Havana, Cuba, 2019.

PHOTO AND ART CREDITS

A special thank-you to the following photographers for their contributions:
Robert Mapplethorpe (Deborah Harry, 1978 © Robert Mapplethorpe Foundation. Used by permission.)

Mick Rock

Brian Aris

Chris Stein

These photographers have graciously granted the usage of their images for this work: Jonas Åkerlund (345); Brian Aris (i, iii, 133, 214-215, 260); Amos Chan (180); Pola Esther (204); Guy Furrow (265); Bobby Grossman (79, 120, 171, 197, 199, 221, 258, 288); Bob Gruen (iv-v, 114, 127, 254, 279, 280, 284, 329); Veronica Ibarra (130); Jeff Kravitz/FilmMagic, Inc via Getty Images (327); Dennis McGuire (40, 151, 155, 176, 218, 303, 357-359); George Napolitano (242); Tina Paul (106, 271, 283, 307, 334); Allan Tannenbaum (45, 189, 194, 202); Rob Roth (166, 322, 353); Chris Stein (83, 89, 100-101, 152, 166, 186, 206, 311, 337); Nick Wiesner (354)

Childhood and family photos, courtesy of the Harry family:
(6, 9, 18, 23, 27, 34, 39, 76, 94)

Courtesy of Debbie Harry's personal collection: (vi, viii, 5, 109, 110, 146, 346)

Courtesy of John Waters' personal collection: (269)

Film stills (249: *Videodrome* [1983], licensed by Universal Pictures; *Hairspray* [1988], licensed by Warner Bros. Entertainment Inc.; *My Life Without Me* [2003])

The following artists' contributions have added immensely to *Face It*:

Jody Morlock (illustrations on iii, 83, 94, 115, 171, 186, 214-215, 260-261, 265, 269, 322, 334)

Sean Pryor (illustrations on 6, 23, 27, 39, 89, 100-101, 109, 113, 130, 146-147, 283, 345, 357-359)

Robert Williams (painting on 52-53)

And the fans, who have lovingly sent their own artwork to the author over the years. Some of that artwork is included herein.

There are many more thank-yous and acknowledgments I could include, but I have to start my list with my friend and co-conspirator Chris Stein, without whom Blondie would not exist.

Next, to all the musicians who have played with us, past and present, including Clem Burke, who stuck with it through everything. The present-day lineup of the band includes Tommy Kessler, Matt Katz-Bohen and Leigh Foxx—so thank you to all three.

It takes a lot of people to make a band happen, like managers, agents, promoters, record labels, publicists and merchandisers such as Cathy Cleghorn. Thank you, Allen Kovac, for helping us put the pieces back together so Blondie could get back into business in the midnineties. Without Tommy Manzi's' energy and attention to detail we might not have made it this far.

From the past I'd like to add Shep Gordon for his brief encounter and Gary Kurfirst and Stanley Arkin for keeping me going through the end of the eighties and early nineties. Our early publicists Carol Ross, Beth Landsman and Harriet Vidal, who all fought for us, as did Press Here Productions' Linda Carbone and Sarah Usher.

Carrie Thornton, Andrea Molitor, Renata De Oliveira, Ploy Siripant and everyone at Dey Street Books and HarperCollins Publishers worldwide. Gratitude and appreciation to Sylvie Simmons for her thoughtful and insightful interviews . . .
and John Du Cane for his support and continued interest. For the wonderful illustration contributions, Jody Morlock and Sean Pryor. Special thanks to Rob Roth for his sensitive creativity.

Thank you to all the photographers I've worked with through the years whose visions have made this book possible and also shared with me their affection and talent.

Genuine thanks for the precious time given to me by the fans.

In my song "End of the Run," there's a line that mentions "a family of choice, not an accident," but my little accidental family deserves a loving thank-you for giving me a protected best-intentioned upbringing, a cute little sister, Martha, and some stray dogs, aunts, uncles, cousins and the lovely crazy people I call my friends. Thank you.

FACE IT · · BLONDIE · · MEMOIR

ACKNOWLEDGMENTS

NUMBER 1

50¢

OH S#!T,
I HAVE TO WRITE MY
ACKNOWLEDGMENTS!!!

THANKS,
JOHN HOLSTROM!

DEBBIE HARRY

DEBBIE'S DILEMMA

LATER THAT DAY...

HOW THE FU#K
CAN I GET OUT
OF DOING THIS?

I WOULD AVOID
IT ALL BY PUTTING
ON A **DISGUISE**.

WHAT A GREAT
IDEA. THANKS,
GROUCHO!

DEBBIE DECIDES ON A WRESTLING
MASK TO HIDE HER IDENTITY.

HEY! IT'S ME!
I'M TRYING TO HIDE
SO I DON'T HAVE
TO WRITE MY
ACKNOWLEDGMENTS
PAGE..
DEBBIE, WHY DON'T
YOU JUST SAY "THANK
YOU EVERYONE"?

OH! GOOD
IDEA!
**THANK
YOU
EVERYONE!**
DEBBIE
HARRY

This is a work of nonfiction. The events and experiences detailed herein are all true and have been faithfully rendered as remembered by the author, to the best of her abilities. Some names have been changed to protect the privacy of the individuals involved.

For information, address HarperCollins Publishers, 195 Broadway, New York, NY 10007.

HarperCollins books may be purchased for educational, business, or sales promotional use. For information, please email the Special Markets Department at SPsales@harpercollins.com.

FIRST EDITION

CREATIVE DIRECTION BY ROB ROTH

DESIGN BY RENATA DE OLIVEIRA

Library of Congress Cataloging-in-Publication Data has been applied for.

ISBN 978-0-06-074958-3

19 20 21 22 23 LSC 10 9 8 7 6 5 4 3 2 1